SURE, I'LL BE YOUR

BLACK FRIEND

ALSO BY BEN PHILIPPE

The Field Guide to the North American Teenager
Charming as a Verb

SURE, I'LL BE YOUR
BLACK FRIEND

Notes from the Other Side of the Fist Bump

BEN PHILIPPE

HARPER ● PERENNIAL

NEW YORK ● LONDON ● TORONTO ● SYDNEY ● NEW DELHI ● AUCKLAND

HARPER ● PERENNIAL

SURE, I'LL BE YOUR BLACK FRIEND. Copyright © 2021 by Ben Philippe. All rights reserved. Printed in the United States of America. No part of this book may be used or reproduced in any manner whatsoever without written permission except in the case of brief quotations embodied in critical articles and reviews. For information, address HarperCollins Publishers, 195 Broadway, New York, NY 10007.

HarperCollins books may be purchased for educational, business, or sales promotional use. For information, please email the Special Markets Department at SPsales@harpercollins.com.

FIRST EDITION

Designed by Jamie Lynn Kerner

Hand art on page ix © Arcady/stock.adobe.com

Library of Congress Cataloging-in-Publication Data has been applied for.

ISBN 978-0-06-302644-5 (pbk.)
ISBN 978-0-06-306506-2 (library edition)

21 22 23 24 25   LSC   10 9 8 7 6 5 4 3 2 1

To my father, Robert,
for "Dream bigger and elsewhere."

CONTENTS

INTRODUCTION

It is a truth universally acknowledged that a good white person of liberal leanings must be in want of a Black friend—especially when said good white person is in good fortune. (Rich people love a Black friend, but we will get to that later.)

Hi! 👋

My name is Ben: I'm your new Black friend. Like any good friend, I aim to always be here for you and your concerns, as problematic as they may occasionally be. Let's talk about our hopes and dreams, and feel free to ask me if I can swim. When you're slightly inebriated, you can go on to tell me how white privilege isn't a thing because your ex once cheated on you with one of your coworkers so how could your life ever be considered "privileged"? We will work through it all as buds, don't you worry.

Unless you're someone who has no interest in mixing with "a colored"—and let's face it, that tends to come with an aversion to books in the first place—a Black friend provides a flattering filter to your life. Group photos, parties, social media. Having one is a point of pride you're not supposed to make too big a deal of but that others will notice around you. My quickstepping over to your table at the restaurant apologizing for running late will catch the eye and emphasize your ability to embrace someone who is different from you and truly celebrate diversity. I understand my societal power and will happily share it with you. I'm the person you glance toward at a comedy show when a comedian says something racial and vaguely problematic. The air will fill with awkward tension until I give—decree—the first guffaw. Only then will the rest of the room feel confident enough to laugh. Now that's institutional power.

This will not be a superficial friendship, mind you! I would never do that to you. Trust me: this is so much deeper than a BLM sticker on the Volvo. You will come to learn a truly uncomfortable amount about me by reading this book. This will be the equivalent of making prolonged eye contact sitting pretzel-style across from one another and holding hands. Nude. This book is the stand-in for a dozen grabbed beers at our regular hole-in-the-wall and thousands of non sequitur text messages. What you're getting here is a Black friend with whom you can broach, pardon my *français*, the good stuff. Politics. Religion. Sexuality. Race. The heavy topics.

After all, there's an intimacy to discussing these things with your friends, isn't there? These are the matters that fuel those late-night conversations after which two friends will either end up closer than ever or staring at each other from across a great divide, reconsidering everything that came before, no matter how many drinks they've downed together. And if you are taking a chance here, as you don't normally "think about race that much," don't worry: you're not the first person I've come across who does not typically burden themselves with this topic. You're here for the friendship first, and race second. I've got you. What follows is more or less the written version of a few dozen beers grabbed at our local hangs, walks around the park, or subway rides heading in the same direction after an afternoon movie. Here lies an accumulation of stories, rants, tangents, arguments, and maybe even a few fights. If you are white, don't worry: you're not my first white friend. I've socialized with enough white people to have developed a sixth sense for the looming threat of a game of Cards Against Humanity and Whole Foods wine after dinner. I low-key enjoy those these days.

Another reason why this might all be new, scary, dare I say titillating for you could be the old classic excuse that there just aren't a lot of Black folks in your neck of the woods. This book might be your very first attempt at a Black friend, and that's fine! Friendships, like a good cruise ship murder, are defined by means, motive, and opportunity. Despite good intentions, you might simply not have had access to Black people to befriend until now.

For instance, a quick Wikipedia survey reveals that there are 1,216 African Americans in the town of Morgantown, West Virginia, which works out to about 4.1 percent of the town's population. And I completely buy that all of these people might happen to suck. Black people aren't unicorns; some of us profoundly suck, just like any ethnic grouping under the sun. They might make for bad friends who bring toxicity into your life and whose social media presence infuriates you. Or, they might all live on the same side of town that you simply never venture into—race and class are incestuously linked in America . . . So, yes: it might not be your fault.

But, my new and maybe melanin-lacking friend, we have to be real with each other here, that's the deal. So, I also have to inform you not having many (or any) Friends of Color could also be the result of assumptions, prejudices, and internalized thought patterns. I'm not talking down to you here—a good friend should never do that. I'm just saying that it's important to admit our own biases when scoping the world for kinships, partners in crime, and emergency contacts.

I myself have a true xenophobic loathing for the French tourists who swarm New York City every year only to loudly complain about everything the city has to offer while riding the subway, thinking they are speaking secret, bitchy Dothraki no one around them could possibly decode.

"Non, mais sérieusement, les gars: allez chier. Les Québécois sont généralement corrects mais ciboire que vous êtes agaçants des fois les français de souche. Rentrez donc chez-vous si vous allez chier sur l'entièreté de la culture Américaine." [spit]

> Quick sidebar: "African American" is kind of a misnomer in my case. Caribbean Canadian might be more geographically accurate? For one thing, I'm one of those Black guys whose mother tongue is, as displayed above, French. As a result, I can't puff up my chest and retort, "I'm from America. I was born right here, you yokel!" if a bearded man or red-cheeked white woman frowns at my accent with a "Where you from, boy?" I'm from elsewhere. (The "boy" on the other hand, will still get you a well-earned invitation to go do something very unpleasant to your own body.)

Because of this wrinkle of having been born Haitian, raised Canadian, and having adopted America as my third home in adulthood, conversations both about and around race have always been a fixture of my life. My Blackness is what you might call a little scattered. It took me a while to get the hang of it. Lots of books were read, and I'm still learning to this day. This can create complicated ripples around both white and Black people. Hell, I might make some egregious errors in this open friendship of ours.

But, being Black is my default state. There is certainly no bravery or artistry to it. I don't power up a crystal, and there is no *Sailor Moon*–type animation sequence: I only exist as Black. My skin is a blunt and obvious rock dropped into the lake of the world. Most of the time, I don't have to do the work of sorting it out, as someone or something in the world will take it upon themselves to tell me exactly what shape my Blackness should take and if I'm doing it right or falling short. The world can be very good at doing that. So much so that I used to think that it was irrelevant to even concern myself with it at all.

That approach would work until the moment it didn't and awareness of my race suddenly filled the room. In the space of a conversation, I would find myself filled with Black thoughts, Black history, Black joy, and Black rage. Because race is one of those things that categorically does not matter between friends until it does. Until it becomes the most important thing in a room wherein every syllable feels like a potential misstep that might take down everyone in it. Hold your breath. Backpedal carefully. Look for a shift in tone. Hope for an exit.

Please don't say something that makes it impossible for us to hang like this again . . . Please don't say something that makes it impossible for us to hang like this again . . . Please don't say something that makes it impossible for us to hang like this again . . .

I've experienced these moments many times, across all three countries I've called home, and these are what have inspired this book.

And we might as well address it here: of course Black and white are not the only two races out there. They are the only two races that have had primacy in my life: the one of the guy who brushes his pearly teeth across from me in the bathroom mirror; and the white one, which has primacy in the world that same guy goes out into every day after rinsing and spitting. These are therefore the two that will be given the focus here. That is simply because they are all I'm comfortable writing about.

Now, this is the part where you might bristle and say, "Actually, Ben, there is only one race . . . the human race."

I only ever hear that inspirational throw pillow from white people. You're well on your way to an All Lives Matter Facebook post there, champ. The rest of us, on the margins, know that race is "a thing." Certainly a thing worth writing about.

Oh yeah. It should be said that, at some point, that mint-breathed guy in the mirror chose to become a writer. Look, I don't quite know how, either. It's weird for me, too. At first, there was fanfiction. Xander trading bodies with Angel and gently having sex with Buffy over the Hellmouth during an apocalypse: 56,000 words. NC-17. These borrowed stories became original ones in the form of my own novels centered around Black teenagers very loosely based on my own experiences, heightened into entertainment and clean three-act structures. What you're reading now are attempts at unvarnishing those experiences. Well, some of them, at least. This is a tell-some, not a tell-all. Writing is messy, and race is messy. It seems like a match made in heaven.

"Writing," Toni Morrison once said, "is really a way of thinking—not just feeling but thinking about those things that are disparate, unresolved, mysterious, problematic, or just sweet."

It might not be as lofty as that. Maybe I became a writer simply because I could neither sing nor dance: my attention seeking required the props of pen and paper. It's safe to say that we would not be here if I were good at playing the stock market.

One last thing: there will be no expertise here. That is Ta-Nehisi Coates's lane. That *GQ* model with the brain of a philosopher and the soulful gaze of a majestic national park deer. (*Between the World and Me.*) Likewise, if you are looking for effortless six-foot-two-inch-tall Black guy swagger and prose that will explode your stomach, see Damon Young. (*What Doesn't Kill You Makes You Blacker.*) Media confidence and literary steadfastness? Roxane Gay. (*Bad Feminist: Essays.*) Consistent hilarity? Samantha Irby. (All of her books. Every last one.) Ibi Zoboi is saving the next generation one book at a time right over there. The list goes on. Bookshelves are peppered with extraordinary, generation-defining writers tackling race. Their canon is necessary and powerful . . . and . . . this ain't it, chief. I have more to say about Token from *South Park* than Martin Luther King Jr.'s last night on earth. For that, see Katori Hall's extraordinary play, *The Mountaintop.*

As your new Black writer friend, I will also give you a few book recommendations along the way. Especially when you don't ask for them. I will then resent you when weeks and months pass without that recommendation being followed up on. Eventually, I will bring this up in the middle of a disagreement about something else entirely. "You never check out the books I recommend to you!" I'll bellow while we wrestle on the sticky floor of a pub. That's the sort of fun, volatile friendship you're in for here. I can be a moody motherfucker who was born craving the last word in every argument. (See also: *petulant* and *insecure.* Hell, all in all, I might rate as "most average human" in a package that happens to be Black.)

"Getting to know you is easy at first then completely impossible," someone—who you will meet as "Mia" but whose name is not actually "Mia"—once told me, sitting on my bed watching me fold clothes into boxes, which was their way of helping me pack for a move. "You're like a layer of whipped cream over a steel door."

It was a colorful metaphor that stuck with me partly because I might have phrased it the other way around; I fancy myself a thick steel door hiding nothing but fluff inside. I'm sure you'll have an opinion by the end.

All of this is to say that I might have already bamboozled you, as the Blackness that follows is purely Ben shaped; the expectation that you were getting an easy sidekick without an inner life was perhaps slightly exaggerated. Know what you are in for: there might be a needy, anxiety attack–riddled blerd ("Black nerd") with a bottomless pit of very polite rage at the end of this friendly introductory fist bump.

ONE

SURE, I'LL BE YOUR BLACK TELL-ALL WRITER

NEW YORK CITY, NY
YEAR: 2018
POPULATION: 8,398,748 (BLACK POPULATION: 24.3 PERCENT)

I AM TWENTY-NINE years old and officially settled. My bank account has—hold for applause—a third and fourth digit that don't disappear as soon as the rent clears. The rent, it should be said, clears every month.

I live in New York and teach at my old college. A college professor, of all things. It's one of those things that just happened. Teaching, as it turns out, is just a matter of lying and pretending you know what you're talking about while also believing the carefully constructed lies students feed you in return. The slew of emails asking for extensions, regrading papers, demanding seats in workshops due to extenuating circumstances, et cetera. They are endlessly creative little liars these days, and writing is just lying with a few adverbs thrown in for good measure. I'm grateful to get a consistent flow of interesting students in my classroom each semester. (A coworker told me it's gauche for academics to badmouth other institutions. I would follow his advice if he didn't teach at that Instagram filter with a real estate portfolio, NYU. No offense to the actual students of NYU. I speak only of your alma mater. I'm sure you're all individually nifty.)

Outside the ivory tower of academia, I've monetized my emotional stuntedness and published one young adult novel and submitted the outline for a second—real books, with spines, acknowledgments, and everything. The one-star reviews are long, which thrills a strange part of me. I'm verified on Twitter and appropriately pretend like I don't care that I'm verified on Twitter when students bring it up.

Tonight, I'm hanging out with Marty somewhere in Brooklyn. His name is not Marty, but since this is a book other people will read, all the names here are lies.

My dog, left back home in Harlem tonight, is adorable. She's a rescue, but I was shallow about it: I scoured the internet until the cutest orphan was available. A better person would have been happy giving a home to a pitbull with attachment issues, but they really shouldn't let mutts with attachment issues foster mutts with attachment issues. A lab mix—heavy on the lab—for me. Blue, previously Gilmore II, previously Buddy. She belonged as a puppy to a medical student who got overwhelmed with school and wanted her to have a good home. I've tried.

I've figured out my look: unpolished hipster. It's a generic look, if not for my being Black, which adds polish to everything in New York. "A touch of street," to quote an old girlfriend who gave me a chain once. I wear blazers and cardigans when I teach, Jordans when going to park cookouts with Black friends, and boat shoes when attending Caucasian-heavy rooftop parties. I know no one is paying attention until someone ends up paying attention.

I like my roommate-less apartment. Not to be *that* guy, but in New York City, that's half the battle. A tiny sliver of the world to call your own, even though the monthly $2,100 rent reminds you that it's absolutely not. Living in New York means becoming an expert at maximizing the space between your toilet and your sink. From coffee maker to meditation corner, there's honestly so much potential in that crease. In my neighborhood, Hamilton Heights, a few blocks away from musical sensation Alexander Hamilton's old pad, that's a very good price. It's not that quiet uptown, but a very good price nonetheless. Every night I hope the owner doesn't sell.

I meet friends for drinks now. Individually, mostly. I don't have a cohort and have given up on looking for one. Single-strand acquaintances work best for me.

I imagine—as one does—that if I were to get shot by a cop on the way home (it's very cute you think there would need to be a reason) that I'd earn a full obituary. Local professor, published author, beloved something or other . . . *Look at how cute his dog was!* That's worthy of a hashtag. My reveries are sudden and violent like that: morbidity that slips into a kind of sentimental snapshotting of my life as it might appear on the front page (of the *Post,* not the *Times*: I'm not an egomaniac) in past tense.

Marty is the first friend I pitch this book to. Well, friend by proxy. Marty is Canadian and moved to New York City after a stint in San Francisco, working for a rideshare company whose app you most likely have on your phone.

I like Marty. Marty is the same age as me, with a thicker

French-Canadian accent, blond, good-looking, and short. I like my very good-looking white friends to have noticeable flaws. At five-feet-nine myself, the two- to three-inch height difference I share with most friends leaves me with the literal short end of the stick. That said, Marty has very square shoulders. I slouch and slump while he manages to stand tall, despite being five-feet-six.

At our second bar of the night, what I'm working on as a writer becomes a natural lily pad for our conversation.

So, I go through it; through this. I tell Marty about the chapter headings you will find in this book, in their ill-formed stage. The notes written on my phone, the self-sent texts. Loose threads of experiences that shared a commonality (me: Black; world: white) but no thesis and with enough embarrassment and awkwardness along the way that an editor—and eventually a reader (Hi!)—might see something worthwhile in it.

"It sounds interesting," Marty says politely afterward.

"Write what you know, right?" I shrug, because self-deprecation is how I've learned to deal with this author thing (see also: *Ivy League thing*; see also: *graduate school thing*).

Marty nods, and our conversation moves on.

Despite his slacks, stock market sheen, and grade-A posture, there's a reckless side to Marty that I admire. He doesn't like to go home early. He casually makes plans to meet around 10 p.m. on Saturdays, and the third bar isn't automatically the end of an evening to him. Marty likes his pub crawls. He tells stories— barroom legends that get better with each telling—of nights that turned into mornings and of backseat bodily fluids encountered as a driver in San Francisco. Some of them might even be true.

In truth, I'm not sure how much I like Marty. I'm also not sure how much he likes me, to be honest. Stick us in a dungeon with electrodes applied to our nipples and interrogate us, and we might rank each other a four on a ten-point scale. "Yeah, he's cool" might be something we say about the other person to some third party that we one day learn we have in common.

Guys don't need to like each other to hang out in this loose way. We can be amicable without being tight. Hang out for drinks, then go weeks, months, without texting before hanging out for drinks again, never getting closer.

I've come to realize that liking someone—truly delighting in seeing their face, hearing their voice—is not a given in adult friendships. Adults have ritualistic catch-ups that involve Google Calendars and an internal downgrade of what it means to be friends. No one is spitting into their palms and giving each other high fives within five weeks, know what I mean?

Adulthood cedes passion to banality, ushering in "Let's have dinner and catch up" rituals of going through the motions. Young friends love each other. It's why I enjoy writing them in young adult books. They tattoo each other's names on their wrists, and sleep in the same bed, and dislocate shoulders pulling each other onto trains.

The tragedy of a guy like Marty in a city like New York is that he moved here too late. The reckless twentysomethings who could have been his tribe have settled. Marty moved in just late enough to be lonely. It's a common problem in New York, at least for naturally social people. Marty would be most at home with a bunch of bros around a big barbecue, alternating between tank tops and shirtlessness, but he's yet to find that kind of friendship here.

Hang out with him, our mutual friend Georgie messaged me over Facebook. Stop cancelling, you hermit! Georgie likes to joke that I'm gay in a way that felt loving in high school but feels actively problematic now that she's a thirty-year-old married well-to-do Montreal lawyer and I'm a Manhattan bachelor staring down the barrel of my thirties.

Admittedly, I *am* a bit of a hermit. Despite the gasps that my rent may draw from non-Manhattanites, it's a steal for my apartment's interior and this rapidly gentrifying corner of West Harlem. I like to enjoy it. I've finally reached the age group that matches my indoor low-key interests: TV, writing, trying a recipe out of nowhere. I fill up my social tank by hanging out with Marty once in a blue moon, sometimes once a season.

It takes effort to hang out with Marty. Marty wants a ride-or-die bro: someone to forge more barroom legends with. Unfortunately for us both, I'm not as good of a wacky sidekick as I used to be these days. Marty smells like recreational cocaine—sweat and gasoline—without having ever talked about recreational cocaine near me.

So, instead, Marty and I intermittently hang like this. We talk a lot about his dating life. Which app, what girl. Marty likes Asian women, which he attributes to his time in San Francisco.

In another world, we might be closer friends. Or, we might dislike each other in some sharp, noticeable way. But we haven't hung out enough for that to be the case. We're stuck in the middle ground of near-thirty-year-old men looking for something. Really, our closest point might be that we would both feel bad being at home at 9 p.m. on a Saturday, single and living in Manhattan, albeit for different reasons.

At our third bar, after a game of ordering pickleback shots at every stop, Marty looks at me, a bit glassy but still holding his alcohol leagues better than I hold my own. The booze has started to peel away some of the veneers of polite restraint from our conversation: it feels easier.

"About your book," he says, a good two hours after first landing on the appropriate lily pad and shouting out of necessity because, well, loud West Village bar on a Saturday night. "Aren't you afraid people will think you hate white people?" he repeats after a failed first attempt.

"Nah," I shout back.

It's a ridiculous thought, and I can't help but think he's completely missed the point. I haven't even started writing more than just notes, I explain. This is just a seed. Books are extremely long processes. I say this with the expertise of someone who has now written two young adult novels. He stares at me, a half-smile on his face.

"I don't hate white people!" This could become exasperating.

Someone hears me, and it's a silly enough thing to say out loud that Marty and I both laugh.

"It *sounds* like you hate white people. A little."

"How?" We're both talking seriously but through bursts of laughter, which is how we're able to talk seriously in the first place. Picklebacks are truly disgusting.

"You're writing about all the white friends who think you like them . . ."

"Not all of the people I write about are my friends."

"Right, right, but some of them are. Some of them think you like them."

"I *do* like my friends," I defend, trying to keep my tone light.

"Right, okay," Marty says with a dismissive wave. Marty doesn't always like snarky Ben. "But you're not just like, 'I like Jean-Martin, Jean-Martin is so great' for three hundred pages."

My default language has become English over time and exposure, but Marty's brain still fully operates in French, hence why
his hypothetical names are thoroughly French Canadian. *How Bilingual Are You?* had been one of our first conversational lily pads,
back when we only had Georgie in common.

"You're going to criticize these friends," he continues.

"But you actually consider that racist? How is that racist?"

"Did you talk to them? These white friends you are going to
write about? Are you going to ask them before you trash them?"

I shrug. I hadn't planned on it.

"See?" he concludes.

Despite his lack of an actual argument, I detect a touch of
smugness. That might be unfair. He might just be a good-looking
white guy smiling and happy to have been heard. It's sometimes
hard to invent a difference there. He does not sound concerned
that he will be included—zoink!—but rather offended on behalf
of people who look like him and might be.

"Well, I don't consider writing about them racist," I say, feeling
cornered, though still unclear as to his whiskeyed objections. "I'm
just, I don't know, sharing my experiences. I . . ."

I have something to say, I want to answer. *Something that was
born in Haiti, raised as the only Black guy at Saint-Esprit Elementary,
the Black Ivy League student, the Black professor, the Black Airbnb
user, the Black writer.*

But Marty might be right. I might just be looking for an outlet
through which to make cheap jokes at the expense of a class that
cannot be wounded or marginalized. It wouldn't stop me, mind
you, but I really should know my own intentions.

". . . I just want to write it," I say instead.

Writing is selfish and I never feel as powerful as I do when doing it. Even if all these labels are fragments of different chips on my shoulder, I get to milk that sucker, don't I? My ancestors were goddamn fractions.

"It's not fun, you know?" Marty says, conceding, but not back-tracking, while we stay on the same conversational lily pad for a beat longer than I'd want.

"What's not fun?"

"Being the white guy in all those stories. The default bad guy every time."

Maybe we're both a bit drunker than expected. Maybe Coors Light would have been preferable given our level of nonintimacy.

He shrugs, wanting to have fun again, and I'm there with him. "I guess I just don't think about race as much as you do."

It should be said that I'm known to have an expressive face. Flip to the back cover. It's a very Play-Doh–like situation. Unless I'm actively smiling through it, you're likely to know what I'm thinking. Once again, my face betrays me.

"No, see!" he says loudly, trying to be heard above "Californi-cation," which someone has apparently paid their life savings into playing on the wall-mounted jukebox. "That face! That's what I mean. It's like we have to be the villain of every story."

A vaguely snarky reply forms in the back of my mind. Pickle-backs are disgusting but not that strong. Instead, I sublimate the urge, making a mental note to write about this later: the writer's talent for literary revenge. *The villain of every story?*

Come on—how was I not going to put a chapter on Marty in this thing after a line like that? Because now, there would defi-nitely, definitely be a book.

"I'm not telling you not to write it," he says, shoulders unchar-acteristically sagging. "It sounds interesting."

"Then what are you saying?" I say. Something about my voice must sound angry or challenging. I realize that I am suddenly angry. Angrier than is warranted in the moment, or than I fully understand. I recognize my tone before my words slip, and it pains me to have been drawn into this picklebacked outburst. Like a stovetop going from cold black stone to bright red too quickly.

"Sharing my experience." He smiles. If he was smug before, now he's a little uneasy, having sensed my discomfort. One of us has to give the other an exit, but I'm tired of being put on the defensive.

"Of it not being easy to be a white man? With dual citizenship, a six-figure salary, and a freaking motorcycle in storage somewhere in Brooklyn?"

"Correct. It's a burden." He smiles, and we both laugh. That's the exit, and we take it.

The evening doesn't descend any further into hostility. We hang out as usual. He takes me through his dating profile, explaining his logic in photographs. As it turns out, there's a very sound White Man logic to all these boat photos, but that is not my story to tell. In the back of my mind, a weirdly defiant voice decides to write my first entry about my friend Marty.

This is a stove I want to touch.

THINGS YOU PROBABLY SHOULD NOT SAY TO YOUR BLACK FRIEND

We should begin by setting some boundaries—y'know, for the uninitiated who normally don't think about race too much. To paraphrase an old significant other who would not tell me who they were texting and giggling with in the middle of the night, right next to me: "Boundaries are good!" Our friendship, after all, is newly minted. Consider this a preventative chapter. An abridged catalog of things not to do. If we were to meet in person, we might go through these as flashcards with a stack of books over your head and a pencil in your teeth. Yes, there will be a quiz, and yes, as you will see, I've heard variations of all these things before.

"Can I touch your hair?"

Situation in which this might arise:
I've been rocking the same haircut since I was twelve, and at some point, while standing in line at the movie theater, you might find yourself drawn to my plumage. It's inexplicable. A slight twinge in your hand. *Is it a Brillo pad? Is it soft or coarse?*

Why not?
We already know the answer to that one, don't we?

If respecting the personhood of others isn't enough for you, how is the fact that I'm now bravely in my thirties and that a breeze could jump-start my receding hairline? I feel it receding at night. Who knows where your sticky little hands have been or what hair-receding toxins they carry? Six feet away, please.

And if you must know: I condition every other day. It's softer than a Pikachu's underbelly. Not that you'll ever know.

How your new Black friend might respond:
"Can I play with yours? I want to do a whole 'Singin' in the Rain' number under the dandruff."

"Did you see that? That couple was looking at us. They're mad because we're interracial."

Situation in which this might arise:
At a restaurant with your Black soon-to-be significant other. Or almost-significant other. It's that delicate week where labels haven't been applied yet, but they've been purchased, and you're not on Tinder anymore because if one of their friends saw you, it would be an unspoken betrayal.

Why is it wrong to point this out to your Black friend, date, or lover?
Well, as the Black person in that scenario, what are you expecting from me here? What do you want me to do? Do I go over there? Do I tip you back and French you in the middle of a restaurant? Do I pull my shirt off in one motion, oil up my belly, and motion for said couple to throw down, right here and now? I'm just left wondering how often you're scoping the room for intolerance while I'm making a case for my being a romantically and sexually viable human being, which is already an intricate dance with lots of arabesques.

"Why, I don't care if you're blue, green, red, black, or yellow! It's all the same to me."

Situation in which this might arise:
Um, the roomier corners of a very simple mind?

Why is it wrong to say this to your Black friend?
"Why, I don't care if you're Tom Brady, Peyton Manning, or Tim Tebow, it's all the same opening act to the halftime show to me."

Cool story, and I see what you're going for here, but, um, yeah . . . I'm Black. Dark-skinned Black, if you want to go there. You should see that. In America, a "race-blind" world simply amounts to a white world in which the rest of us are quiet with pursed lips, not making a fuss. As your friend, I will go to that lame work party where I don't know a single soul with you so you have "someone to talk to"—you should likewise be willing to occasionally be discomforted by the racialized reality of our world for me.

"I'm just not attracted to Black features when I swipe on the apps. You get it, right? It's not racist; you and I are friends."

Situation in which this might arise:
You generally being a bit of a douche, slightly tipsy, and a lot single.

Why not?
Congratulations: you've just voiced a preference no one asked for followed by three inaccurate things in a row! My smiling in those moments does not make us friends. Sometimes a smile is the safest way to briefly show fangs.

"I just really don't think about race."

Situation in which this might arise:
In the middle of a conversation about some instance of racism as we watch TV. I'm upset. You shake your head from side to side, confused and angered at the state of the world. *How can anyone be so racist?* you might say. *People should be judged by their character, not the color of their skin.* And then you drop the above platitude

with a look meant to reassure me that you are a good person . . . only to look worried as I turn toward you like a velociraptor who just heard a pin drop in the other room.

Why not?
I understand what you're trying to do, and I know you mean well, but race, that pesky ole thing, exists independently from you, regardless of whether or not *you* exercise the privilege afforded by not having to think about it.

How your new Black friend might respond:
They don't. At that point, I'm left with no choice but to fade away as if someone with a time machine just prevented my grandparents from ever meeting.

"So, what: I just can't say it? Even if I don't use it as a slur?"

Situation in which this might arise:
You're usually drunk. So am I, for that matter.

We're at the corner booth of a pub, and we're getting *real*. The devil has retained your services and you take the task seriously. It's just a word, after all? We give it more power by not saying it, no? We should take that power away? "Devil's advocate here," you will eventually preface before asking me to share in my *nigger*-using privilege. Just a little smidge. You just want a taste of the high.

Why not?
. . . Look, I'm not your dad. But it says something that you would want to, no? That out of the 218,632 words in use in the English language (171,476 in current use and 47,156 obsolete words), *that*

one is the one missing from the vocabulary for you. That without it you feel censored, unfairly treated, maligned.

Not *defenestrate* or *petrichor*—which, sidebar, is the best word in both definition and phonetics and refers to the smell of earth after rain—but *that* word.

Nigger *as a noun.* **Nigger** *as a pejorative.* **Nigger** *as a modifier.* Let's consider this question instead: Why does your vocabulary feel incomplete without it?

Whatever the case, it kind of kills the premise of this entire book because, *nah, friend*, I won't be your Black friend if you only want a Black friend to give you a free pass to use the N-word with the larger Black community. Also, I can't just unilaterally grant you an N-word pass. I have to submit requests to Michelle Obama's office, Whoopi has to see it . . . it's a whole bureaucratic nightmare for me.

How your new Black friend might respond:

Everyone reacts differently in the moment. Another Black friend might take a swing at you. I prefer full dissociation. I sip my drink, purse my lips, and just zone out. I itemize all the mugs in my cupboard while you make your argument to complete silence . . . *The chipped one, the one from college, the set I split with my old roommate* . . .

Most white people will eventually, hopefully, get the message and back down. Some of them will come to it on their own with a vaguely embarrassed, "Well, I don't know . . . maybe I just don't get it." Or "I don't want to say it, I'm just wondering . . . drunk, I'm actually just drunk, Ben."

Some white people may be emboldened by this silence. They

feel challenged by it somehow. "Like, 'nigger,' there! I said it. Nigger! You're here and I'm still here, you're still here. What's the big deal?"

And that's how you get deleted from my phone on the way home and muted across all social media platforms ¯_(ツ)_/¯.

"I could never date a Black chick. Just a preference."

"I love Black skin. I don't get racism. There's nothing like that ebony complexion. Gimme some more of that Nubian goodness."

Situation in which this might arise:

Trick question. <u>There is no situation where it is appropriate for this to arise—no matter how close we are.</u>

How to respond as a Black friend:

Your PornoTube preferences are between you and your religious institution. I am not here to discuss, massage, understand, or grant absolution for your interest in "race play," racial fetishizations, or your sexual preferences and predilections. I cannot be the racial representative of what you thrill yourself to. Just living my life over here. Like, dang, I didn't even ask you!

"Are Black guys really . . . bigger down there?"

Situation in which this might arise:

Surprisingly many. Y'all get comfortable very quickly asking that one. I don't know, maybe it's my face. To give you an idea, I'm thirty-one while writing this, and I've gotten this one at least eight times.

Why not?

I mean, want to check my calves and teeth while you're at it? Honestly, who raised you? Give me their email. I want to send Susan a strongly worded email.

How your new Black friend might respond:

"Yes."

"White privilege isn't a thing, Ben!"

Situation in which this might arise:

You come across a meme making fun of white people on social media. It bugs you, but you can't quite place why. It's a weird pebble in your shoe that 178 people have already shared this meme mocking a White Guy outfit/album/practice/way of life you find perfectly suitable and may even identify with yourself. ("What's wrong with drinking a White Claw in a Patagonia vest?") You swallow it until you come across a news article, hours later, condemning white privilege . . . or even just pointing it out. The comments are filled with people enumerating various manifestations of privilege that you quietly defend in your mind because, you know, you just don't think that much about race.

You shake your head. You were just mocked, and then people accuse you of having it too easy! What the hell?

White privilege, you assert, implies a boat full of Leonardo DiCaprio clones and a seven-digit bank account. You have neither of those things. Chrissy Teigen won't even return your direct messages. You have bills and a backache and feel unfairly targeted by this insinuation of privilege that you do not have. So, you fire a DM to your friendly Black friend, who shared the image in the first place, intent on blowing his narrow mind.

Why not?

Yes, white privilege is absolutely a thing and yes, you absolutely do have it. That's a nonstarter.

I don't blame you for not noticing it. I don't notice my credit score until it's time to look into taking out a loan. It's a protective, invisible barrier that you don't notice because you've had it your entire life.

Many good-hearted people are taught to see racism as individual acts of meanness. A cross burning on a lawn. A shouted or whispered slur. A crumpled résumé of a job candidate named DeShawn. Those are out there, yes, but this concept also extends to the system that gives dominance and preference to a societal group—your group.

I might trash your DM, but I do understand your frustration. When you have as much freedom to do what you want, think as you want, and move as you want, when this privilege has been imbued in your education, your work, your neighborhood, and then reflected into your mirror, your television, your laptop, it can be hard not to take criticism of it personally. Even if you wanted to turn off your white privilege, it's not something you can turn off without some advanced Ramsay Bolton flaying of your Caucasianness.

Now, that's not to say that a guy who sheepishly introduces

himself as "Hi, I'm Todd, reluctant beneficiary of white privilege, and would like to apologize for my race" doesn't creep me out.

I'm not going to be friends with that weird dude! That's the same guy who wears a THIS IS WHAT A FEMINIST LOOKS LIKE T-shirt, or goes to Gay Pride parades for the express purpose of taking photos with scantily clad women. Point is, acknowledging white privilege doesn't mean you need to follow it up with performative white guilt in search of absolution. I'm not going to be your priest or therapist: work that stuff out elsewhere.

How to respond as a Black friend:

With a book recommendation.* In this case, we'll go with *White Privilege: Unpacking the Invisible Knapsack* by Peggy McIntosh. She's a terribly smart woman—white, too, if that matters—and writes about this exact thing from your exact perspective.

*Please note that any book, hardcover graphic novel, or DVD borrowed from me will require you to take a photo of yourself holding the item in question. This will be stored on my phone. The photo is then moved to the desktop of my computer, so I don't forget. I've lost over twenty books this way, and shit gets old. Like, I miss my books, man. You people cannot be trusted.

TWO

TEN THINGS TO KNOW BEFORE
BEFRIENDING ME, OR "WHICH BLACK GUY ARE
YOU GETTING?"

Good question! The first and most important lesson is that no, not all Black people are alike. By now, you've probably realized that you're getting a specific type of Black male here, so let's cover the basics. I'm a type J, which is somewhere between an Enneagram 4, a Charlotte from *Sex and the City*, a Slytherin, and a Ross from *Friends*, all with a Littlefinger rising.

By the title of this very book, you know that I am happy—thrilled, even!—to be your Black friend. Whether yours is already a thriving multiethnic social circle or this whole racial disparity thing is a completely new experience for you, it's all good. For the next few hundred pages, I am committed to being an honest, fun Black friend to you. Think of me as . . .

- The Turk to your J.D.
- The Wallace to your Veronica Mars

- The Gerald Martin Johanssen to your *Hey Arnold!* (with a much less bawdy haircut. That boy did not love himself.)
- The coworker Deacon to your Doug Heffernan (CBS's *King of Queens*)
- The Falcon (aka Sam Wilson) to your Captain America . . . and later on, Bucky (Sidebar: Isn't that some refried bull? Veteran superhero, head of Super Agents at the espionage agency S.H.I.E.LD., and bird telepath went on to become the sidekick of the resurrected 1968 sidekick. Give the Falcon his own movie, for God's sake.)
- The Lee Jordan to your Fred and George Weasley (Don't recognize the name? Revisit your Harry Potter canon, friend. He was that blink-and-you'll-miss-him Black character who was described as the "twins' best friend." That's right: the Weasleys were such peasant wizards that they even had to split a Black friend.)

The list goes on and on, but needless to say, you and I are joining a rich tradition here, buddy!

Still, friendships are a two-way street. After thirty years on this planet, I'm fully aware that a friendship with me comes with its own non–racially themed challenges. I can be a difficult person. (I know, I know: you're now holding this book, mouth thoroughly agape.) The point is that you should broadly know what you're in for.

The following tidbits of self-insight are brought to you by a medium amount of introspection and two therapists totalling five sessions, one of which was subsidized by a very generous Groupon. Think of this as a disclaimer, a *caveat lector*.

1. I CAN OCCASIONALLY BE MEAN?

Or, I should say, "I *am* occasionally mean?"

Let me explain. It is my personal belief that there are only two kinds of people in the world. Only two, no more, no less: naturally nice people who force themselves to be mean to survive and, alternatively, naturally mean people who pretend to be nice.

That's it. Eight billion folks; two piles. These are all synonyms for the two kinds of people who make up humanity here at the top of the food chain. Being mean is not an act, it's a natural, default state that some people tame better than others.

You are either a bit of an asshole with a heart of gold, or the nice person who exerts a lot of energy on fighting their default setting of "asshole" that if left unchecked can lead to them being a phenomenal piece of trash. Most interpersonal conflicts come from people misreading one as the other.

In my case, after a lot of flip-flopping, I've confidently settled on the certainty that I'm a mean person who *tries*, and mostly succeeds, in not leading with that easy, mean foot.

I avoid conflict. I smile a lot. I funnel it into snarky young adult characters who have the freedom that comes with being fictional. But in the real world, mean is the other side of snarky that you occasionally tumble into while trying to make everyone laugh with a joke.

I'm the guy who, in a mutual moment of comfort with someone, guards down, laughing and joking over beers, will make a casual observation, only to look up to find myself staring back at the devastated face of a friend, flushed at the cheeks and shocked at what they've just heard. I've gone too far without even noticing it and will proceed to feel terrible about it for the next two to five years.

A horrifying example was the night that I—on the verge of tipsiness—casually told the roommate of a good friend in college who was complaining about the fact that every guy in her life was a disappointment that it was at least nice that her new boyfriend looked so much like her dad because she could now work through the issues with someone she can legally bang.

. . . Oh, come on: don't look at me like that. That's funny! At least two people were chuckling. I think. Anyway, I was subsequently banned from ever stepping foot in their suite again. I realize I shouldn't have made the comment, but I mostly stand by that one. Daddy issues recognize daddy issues, Lola.

2. WHILE I CAN OCCASIONALLY BE MEAN, I AM INHERENTLY OVERLY SENSITIVE. AND PETTY.

In the third grade, I remember shoving my friend Simon for some slight or another that I've long since forgotten. Whatever it was, I shoved first. After a beat, Simon shoved back. I instantly crumpled to the floor with teary eyes. Why, Simon? *Why would you shove me? How could you?*

My skin isn't paper-thin: it's porous. It's a wet page torn from a hotel Bible. It's a sail made of tissue.

One of my primary school teachers, Mrs. Ivette, once scoffed at one of my drawings during art hour. It was a good drawing, all right? Have you ever tried to draw a bicycle from memory? It is *shockingly* difficult. Go ahead; grab a pen and scribble it in the margins of this very book. See? Hard. Anyway, I was just a ten-year-old trying my best. And this raven-haired harlot in dangling earrings and conservative cardigans leaned over and said—in French, as the entire world was back then—"That looks like a baby wheel tied to its mama. Try a bicycle next."

The other kids in our classroom all laughed in unison in that specific way classrooms of fourth graders laugh in unison, all sounding alike and then stopping all at once. It echoes.

In my hyperactive mind, the story does not stop there.

Twenty years later, I'm driving on a highway when I spot a car by the side of the road. I slow down. I normally wouldn't, but it's one of those listless drives with a destination but no timetable to keep. I offer to help. She's hesitant, as any gray-haired woman in her sixties would be, but I smile and have a high voice and she's relieved someone came riding down this road. "Oh my god, thank you, so much!" she might say as I begin to change her tire, carefully mounting the new spare. Naturally, I recognize her before she recognizes me and, as I slowly tighten the lug nuts, with each rotation bringing a new layer of hope to our interaction, I lead the conversation away from points of commonality through which she might place my face. I'm from Portland, USA, and passing through, I'll say. My parents are Nigerian.

In this fantasy, I carry a pocketknife, and a quick, subtle jab is all it takes to deflate the tire while chattering about this imagined life. "If only you had a bike," I'll say coyly, getting back into my car as the horror of recognition finally dawns on her face.

It's been over two decades. The details get more vivid every time I imagine this scene. The confusion in her eyes that gives way to recognition, then deep shame. The shape of her mouth about to say my name as I glance at my rearview before stepping on the pedal and driving away as wolves howl in the distance. I cackle and laugh after letting out a scream of release into the night . . . You can freeze-frame the movie right there and fade to black and white; my story has come to a worthy conclusion. Roll credits.

I'm very aware of how messed up that is. I don't even own a car. Or an active driver's license.

The brain space that vivid fantasy occupies would be best served by something else. I could play the stock market with the time and energy I dedicate to unproductive pettiness. Then, with my newfound wealth, I could show them all . . . You see? It's endemic.

3. I WAS RAISED BY POPULAR CULTURE

My brain was first wired into Creole and French concurrently in Port-Au-Prince, Haiti. English came later and through the small, fat-backed television in my childhood bedroom. That's where I would shut out the world and soak up the banter and rhythmic timing of late-afternoon sitcoms for hours. Awkward moments—like a breakup, or an emotional conversation—come with a tiny caveat of "Wow, this is such a powerful season finale" in the back of my head. My high school friends are carryovers from season 2 of my life, and the folks I see once in a while without a last name may be saved as "First name—GS" on my phone: *Sean—Guest Star.*

Speaking of popular culture . . .
Why do white guys love to list members of the Wu-Tang Clan?

(I have more questions about white people, believe me. If this is off-limits—like my hair—please let me know.)

No, really: they throb at that. To be clear, I am familiar with the members of the Wu-Tang Clan, but white guys love to stand in a circle, or sit on lawn chairs at a barbecue, and try to list all the members of the Wu-Tang Clan they can remember, glancing to me for confirmation each time they get one.

This has happened to me three times in my life. Two barbecues, one Montreal–New York road trip. Two white guys, hairs of varying shoulder-length, looking like roadies for Five for Fighting, deciding it would be fun to "go through the roster."

I promise you that my stare will be blank. I know them, mind you. *Ghostface Killah, Method Man, U-God, RZA, Raekwon, Masta Killa, Cappadonna, GZA, Inspectah Deck*. No Googling required. I just won't give you the satisfaction of bonding with a Black guy by listing members of the Wu-Tang Clan.

4. I'M FLUENT IN WHITE WOMAN

How fluent? Let's just say I've gotten used to the nails-on-a-chalkboard refrain of a white person telling you how much they love Beyoncé.

I was emotionally raised by the white women of the small cable-ready television in my bedroom as an only child. My inner monologue is Emily Gilmore, my astrological sign is Wisteria Lane in retrograde, and my spirit animal? Cersei Lannister, son.

Much like Tarzan had to meet other humans to realize that it was kind of weird how he could walk on his knuckles and slide across vines, it would be years until I realized that being raised by the WB, CW, and having an idyllic memory of the Gilmore girls was not a conventional experience for anyone, let alone a Black male.

5. YOU WILL OCCASIONALLY BE TESTED

Candidly, I **(and many other Black people)** secretly think—fear—that my white friends might be a little racist deep down. It's a thing. After a few false starts, friendships that turned out to be too problematic to endure, you find yourself waiting for that other shoe to drop. There are informal tests along the way; little tests neither of us are aware of until they've been failed. For example, the shoulder tap at the bar nodding toward a group of Black women entering the establishment and going, "Lucky night for you, man!" (What the hell was that, Brock? *Did you just assume my taste in women?*)

One definite test manifests in how I come to meet your other Black acquaintances. Casually, at a birthday party? Awesome! Bumping into you on the street? Great! Getting a DM with a forward of your other Black friend's funny tweet with no explanation other than "YOU TWO SHOULD HANG"? . . . Not great.

It's completely fine that your wedding—all 240 Vermonters—only has a handful of nonwhite guests. You can't control that! But if Jamaal, your only other Black friend from college, your spouse's coworker Latesha, and I make eye contact the moment we walk into your farm-to-table reception and find ourselves navigating toward the "ethnic" table in the corner, I guarantee we will proceed to abuse the open bar heartily bonding over this crap.

6. SPRITUALLY, I LEAN "COWARD"

In the world of men, there are teeth-showing growlers, and brawlers, and hunters, and gatherers. I have no delusions about my role—my basket of berries is freaking cute, all right? I decorated it with pretty flowers, and you can find me in the nearby creek, humming a song to myself while the village is getting slaughtered across the meadow. I'll tearfully decorate their graves later.

To give you an idea, I am currently writing this book at the height of the COVID-19 global pandemic. There is a stay-at-home order throughout New York, and NYC currently owns the dubious honor of being the hardest-hit city *in the world*. Sure, I may get overtaken by a sudden dry cough and fall prey to compromised lungs, but I am *not* dying in a street fight because someone stepped on my Jordans and I felt disrespected. Nor am I the Black guy who takes it upon himself to die first by flipping his baseball cap backward, grabbing a log, and going to check out the strange noise at minute thirty-seven of a horror movie. Hell, no. *I choose life.*

I may get my feelings hurt from a comment made at the bar, and in turn mumble something about you (see #2 and #1, in that order) but you won't find me swinging the first (or second, or third) punch. Nah, dude. Will I duck behind someone with their back turned to the mayhem, hoping you'll accidentally punch them and that the epicenter of the brawl will happen there instead of on my beautiful cheekbones? Absolutely.

I prefer to think of it as a really specific survival instinct in a deeply unfair world, y'know? Say what you will, but the coward lives.

7. I'VE LIVED A PRETTY BORING AND LINE-TOEING LIFE

On a related note, the amount of hood struggles you'll find in these pages is minimal. There's a fair bit of poverty, but it's the deeply ashamed immigrant kind where your mom bursts into tears when you try on baggy jeans at Walmart and shoves you back into the dressing room, whisper-seething between clenched teeth that "They'll think we can't afford belts!"

I've never really had "beef" that did not involve Wi-Fi and harshly worded direct messages. I write very long emails, but these fists know no rage.

I've never smoked a single cigarette my entire life. Part of that comes from being born of that generation that saw their first cancer commercial before being offered their first smoke. By the time someone extended their dad's cigarette my way, I had the defense mechanism of mocking their peer pressure, lifted from a commercial about how to resist peer pressure. You're dealing with a very good boy here.

8. WHAT DO YOU DO, ANYWAY?

These days I'm a college professor and a working writer. Occasionally books, occasionally TV writers rooms. Writers are sensitive creatures. They're opinionated, have an unearned sense of superiority, and have already thought out their answers to their inevitable future *New Yorker* interview. I'm absolutely no exception in this, save that I'm *actually* awesome. I am a peacock of glory, the embodiment of a Kanye West song given lungs, and as a result have very thin skin when it comes to criticism. Very thin.

So, don't criticize me. But also, don't praise me in a way that I might misread as condescending, either. You should understand that I can handle the worst of your criticism but find no need to issue any of it, ever. (If you're a writer yourself, that sentence makes complete sense to you.)

9. YOUR 420 TEXT WILL BE IGNORED

The presumption of weed is something that Black acquaintances have had to deal with from the fourth grade on. People aged ten to twenty-eight will assume you to have access to a never-ending supply of weed they can hit you up for. You'll get "'Sup, dude!" and leaf emoji texts from numbers you don't recognize on April 20. A smooth-faced guy in a plaid shirt will break from his pack of TODOGs (Tims or Dans or Grants) at the back of an Austin bar after psyching himself up with a few Natty Lights and feel completely justified in hitting you up for weed. "Do you have any? You holding?" he'll whisper. You'll consider rushing to a nearby 7-Eleven and buying all the oregano you can and making him empty his bank account at the ATM for the privilege. But that would take effort. "No, sorry, dude," you'll simply say before returning to your Tinder date.

While I've smoked in my lifetime, I've never owned much weed or cocaine or any of the harder stimulants that *Law & Order* reruns told you that my pockets are layered with at all times. My weed consumption is not a lifestyle. It's an occasionally offered distraction, and often an attempt to fit in: part of the cost of having so many white artist types in my life.

I am not holding, okay? I do not know how to roll a blunt. I don't have anything "on deck." What is a fun thing for you (or occasionally a full-blown persona to make up for a glaring lack of personality) is an expectation of folks who look like me. Considering that weed is now on its way to being no more provocative than a stick of cinnamon-flavored gum, maybe you can go ahead and break that association in your mind? Thanks.

So, please do not text me a marijuana leaf emoji at midnight. I was the high schooler Googling "where to find weed?" in an incognito tab after being invited to a party strictly for my presumed weed-summoning abilities as a Black kid. For me, 4/20 is not a holiday. More often than not, it's a weekday, and at 4:19 p.m. I'm trying to wrap up work while browsing a food delivery service with the passion of a husband scrolling through porn while his wife is in the bathroom. Your dreaded white friend definitely has a better weed connection than me. Go bother them.

10. I'M NOT SPIRITUAL, SUPERSTITIOUS, OR RELIGIOUS

What can I say? Lent isn't my thing. Neither is Kwanzaa, mind you. I'm a Christmas boy, sure, though not for religious reasons. It's strictly an eggnog and "Ooh, pretty lights" situation. Now, this does not particularly matter to me, but I've found that it matters to some other people. I once dated someone who felt "misled and bamboozled" by my Daisy Buchanan level of carelessness toward a higher power. I like to step on those sidewalk cracks and used to sign the cross in reverse order at Sunday school to see what exactly would happen and who it might summon. I liked the stories and parables—I just never believed any of them were true. I might give them a breezy edit, y'know? Find the best plot twist to understanding those footsteps in the sand.

Now, if you're wondering what this possibly has to do with our new interracial friendship here, well, you've clearly never attempted to voice any of these thoughts to any of my aunts in their Sunday best shaking their heads at me in abject horror. To quote my aunt

Colette, whose hat feather was trembling with holy concern as she shook her head at my eight-year-old self after broaching the topic: *"This isn't right . . . The devil lives in your boy, Belzie!"*

Throughout my life, my mother's faith was important to her, so as a result I grew up respecting it without ever believing it or participating in it with any real conviction. My atheism, if we have to name it, is strictly passive. I do not preach it, and I am happy to accept your pamphlet with a nod before recycling it. Don't convert me to your setting, and I won't try to convert you to my neutral. Cool? Cool. Oh! While we're here . . .

Astrology is also not my journey.

Honestly, can we all calm down a bit with this? While I have a deep respect for theistic belief systems, I would like to erase myself from the narrative of your narcissistic sky tic-tac-toe. If a student can ask me for a paper deadline extension because Mercury is in retrograde, I get to give you a full 180-degree eye roll. At some point this past decade, *astrology* + *hiking* became a personality, and I want no part of it. Look, be your best narcissistic self, please. Heck, I get along with narcissists (surprising, right?), but Miss Cleo gibberish is profoundly boring to me. I have no idea what it says about me that I am a Sagittarius except that it has led to a lot of condescending smirks and "Ah, that explains it." Honestly, just call me an asshole and be done with it.

All right! That should be plenty. By now you should have a pretty good idea of who I am. See? It's really not that deep. So, how did I get here? What's my Black story? Well, like many Black people before me, my beautiful Black story begins with two Black people making love on a beautiful island of the Greater Antilles archipelago.

Although, probably not on an actual beach? It was near a beach from the photos, though . . . Look, we don't know each other well enough for you to ask where my father inseminated my mother yet! Rude.

THREE

THE FIRST GIFT

A familiar thing happens every May. Without warning and with far more ferocity than the usual hashtags, social media is suddenly flooded with photos of young, thriving women for twenty-four straight hours. Some of these photos pre-date digital photography altogether: they bear the grainy marks of 35mm, the soft tones of black and white, the faded sepia of the past scanned into the twenty-first century. Tangible photos that must still live on mantels and in ornate frames somewhere. One glance at the calendar and you know: Mother's Day is upon us.

You will scroll through your phone and travel all over the world through these young women in bygone-era shorts riding bikes, wearing sunglasses and throwing up peace signs, or in some cases just giving a defiant finger to the camera. A lip ring and black lipstick at a concert here, a knitted sweater with hands pulled into the sleeve on an old couch there. These women are the larval stages of future mothers.

Sons and daughters, especially those in their twenties, revel in bragging about the women their mothers used to be. Those friends who whine about having to go home for the holidays or the panic attacks experienced at LaGuardia, pantomiming the political fights they'll have with their outdated, regressive parents, atone for their filial sins with flower emojis and soliloquies. There are 364 days of ingratitude—or worse, indifference—to make up for.

It's not that these dynamic girls are gone. They've just been folded into the maternal figure whose day is being celebrated. They were precursors to the "mom" their children will come to know. The one who worries and Facebooks as a verb. The one whose voice audibly dips in voicemails because you not picking up when she called was already a dismissal: another indignity, like the carelessly strewn socks you left her to pick up or uncleaned plate left at the table when you were a teenager. It's okay, though. She'll keep giving because that's just what mothers do.

I'm no better than the other ungrateful children of the web. My social media features carefully curated photos of my mother, reveling in how awesome she is. In my case, however, it's because I know she was never meant to be my mother. No matter how easily giving and understanding and folding and cleaning and hugging and calling and worrying all come to her, I suspect Belzie would have thrived without a child and the blessing—and inconvenience—of loving me. At the end of the day, that's all my dad had on her.

How do you write about a single Black mother, without reducing her to a series of stacked tropes and demographic woes? How do you write about a philandering Black father biding his time before the next wedding without making him a stereotypical deadbeat? Like most parents, if you grant them a second look, I'm aware that both of these people are so much more than the broad sum of their demographics. People are complicated creatures, more so when they are our parents, occupying Venn diagrams where idolatry, disappointment, anger, regret, and, yes, affection meet and help to complicate ourselves.

Whatever story she had written for herself changed with me: wet and viscous, squeezing her thumb in some corner of Canapé Vert hospital where she was a beloved nurse, after a routine C-section. Not that she would have it any other way, if you ask her even today, three decades later. She has made a full performance of telling the story of my birth.

"I told my doctor," she will say over neatly served tea at our kitchen table, smirking slightly and moving her arms as she tells the story the same way she tells every guest I've ever brought home. "He was a friend, so I pulled him aside and I said: 'Listen, doc: no pushing! I can't do it. Give me the drugs and pull the baby out.'"

Time of birth: 3:46 p.m. That was it; the woman was screwed.

FOUR

SURE, I'LL BE YOUR BLACK CANADIAN

It's 1994 and I'M FIVE years old. I'm standing in my dad's office in Haiti, facing his desk, hoping he doesn't notice the dirt I've tracked onto the giant room's faded Persian rug. I rub it in deep with my foot, trying to keep my back straight.

Dad has summoned me, meaning one of our two maids hunted me down in the backyard and away from the ninja battle-field I was assembling, high on the *Power Rangers* reruns that come on once a week. I am hastily dragged by the arm to the door of the sunny room filled with plants, books, furniture that looks too heavy to ever move. There are maps on every wall, and the radio is always playing loud Haitian men proselytizing about the state of the world. Political evangelists long before YouTube will add their faces to their voices. The messaging is simple: *The world is unfair. Please subscribe to my worldview and send money if you can.*

Dad normally only calls me in here when he has to discipline me, mostly, I think, because he likes the echo, but today is different. I think today he has news. He's giddy and excited.

We do not particularly look alike but share the same birthmark on our left butt cheek. His skin is lighter than mine—as is my mom's—and he does *not* have a mustache. Nearly every ethnic father in every story of lost homelands I've read is defined by their mustache, beard, or prominent sideburns, but my dad's face is bare, populated only by a light-gray neck fuzz that disappears as soon as it sprouts. He has piercing eyes behind thick rectangular lenses housed in a thin golden frame.

"There's no future in Haiti," he declares after motioning for me to sit down across from him. Before working in the ministry of education, he was a teacher and a principal, too, I think. I can't be sure, to be honest. His story isn't mine.

Right behind his head, I notice a new map of America with the folds across the Atlantic still creased. My dad enjoys maps the way the adult version of me will one day enjoy framed stills of movies around my home and office. We're both compulsively trying to fill the blank walls with stories.

At school, he likes when I befriend white foreign children. They are the wealthy ones, well-to-do ones. And we are joining their hub, I'm told. Somewhere where the foreign white kids roam around freely.

"We're going to a place where you have a future," he continues. "Canada. I used to live there before." I'm not told before what. Presumably, just me. Mom is at the Canapé Vert hospital, looking after her wealthy patients, but I assume she's been looped in.

"It's very cold there," he says. "You'll hate that part. There's snow everywhere for half the year."

I don't have to ask about my dog, Bouli; I already know he's not coming. My follow-up questions annoy him, evidenced by his answers becoming more brusque with each of my inquiries:

". . . It's, I don't know, frozen rain. Go check the freezer. That's snow."

". . . We're leaving after Christmas. You still have a few months."

". . . Yes! Of course there's TV, but you're not moving there for the TV!"

The last is the wrong follow-up question, and I'm told to memorize one of Aesop's fables to recite for him the next day. He has big new plans, global plans, and they don't involve my watching TV all day. He settles on *"Le Corbeau et le Renard"* ("The Fox and the Crow") and doesn't notice the brown hue of dirt on his patterned carpet. I can still recite that fable to this day, but it's a party trick that only dazzles from the mouth of a five-year-old.

MONTREAL, QUEBEC, CANADA
YEAR: 1995
POPULATION: 1,775,778 (BLACK POPULATION: 7.7 PERCENT)

My mother and I leave Haiti on two different promises. I'm going to a world of well-to-do white children, 24/7 electricity without a generator, and once there will secure an amazing education, thanks to my father's incredible foresight. I'll perfect my French, learn English, and never be hungry. I was never hungry before, mind you, our house had two fridges, both full, but now, hunger won't even be a presence in my world unless I actively look for it. North America is the world of one-liter Coca-Colas and 99-cent bags of chips. It's safe there in a way Haiti isn't.

For her part, my mom is promised a life of things I won't be privy to until when we can drink wine together, years later, as we drill each other for insight on what we remember of the time.

"It would change depending on the day," she will tell me later. My mom had done her nursing residency in Switzerland before returning to Haiti and meeting my father. "Some days he said I won't need to work at all once in Canada, and other days he assured me that surgical nurses make $100,000 a year there. In both cases, there would be good restaurants every night. That was the big one. Never having to cook; only restaurants."

I suspect she always knew there wouldn't be restaurants every night. Mostly, I think, she chose to believe those promises on my behalf. I used to tell myself that this was proof of just how much she loved me, her only son. I would later realize this was only part of the truth. She loved both her son and her ambitious husband.

My father has Canadian citizenship from his former life there, and Mom and I can easily obtain citizenship through him. I learn I'm now a Canadian citizen by receiving a laminated mint-green card with a tiny red-and-white flag in the upper corner that says so. We're not trying a new country; we're emerging from a shell we will never return to.

Mom wanted Switzerland. Two of her sisters still lived there, in Neuchâtel. But Dad had lived in Montreal before for seventeen years, the entirety of his first marriage, which I will learn about later. He knows the country, so citizenship will be much easier. He's also older than her so, again, she defers.

She clings to the fact that she has a few nursing friends in Montreal, too. Haitian women who studied with her in Switzerland and then settled in Quebec with their husbands.

One of our maids cries, waving us goodbye and watching the car to the airport pull away. The other one already has her back turned to us and is walking down the road with a backpack on. It's unclear which one of the two was a thief, but for years to come, Mom and Dad will both tell the story of how one of them was a thief who pilfered them blind for years.

We spend a long time at the airport and then stay with Dad's sister, my aunt Atalante. She looks like Dad with a wig on, but pretty, too. I like the snow, but for all of its novelty, it isn't as interesting as I thought it would be when I was reaching into our freezer in Haiti and grabbing handfuls of frost from the back while standing on a chair. The cold itself is much more appealing. "Minus sixteen degrees Celsius!" someone, maybe Mom, says. I inhale until my insides are cold and I start coughing. I develop a cold within minutes of exiting into the airport parking lot by doing exactly that; breathing in the chill and letting it sit in my stomach. Aunt Atalante forces me to drink tea the moment we get to her place. A big mug and then a second one. "The last thing you need is a sick child on your hands here!"

Her apartment is worn-in and comfortable, the way small apartments become home after decades of residence. It smells like our kitchen but in every room. I'm told we've met before when I was younger, but I don't remember. I lie and say I do. She's bought me a stack of coloring books and sneakers that are too big. She likes me and my mom and invites us to stay as long as we need, but Dad is proud and has the money for our own apartment from renting our Haitian home. He wants to find one soon. A new domain that's his with an office I can be summoned to when need be.

"We're not on vacation!" he snaps when Atalante hands me a pamphlet about the La Ronde amusement park.

Dad is restless to get some momentum on this new swing at

the North American dream. I'll never quite figure out what exactly he was trying to get started. Maybe this newly adopted North American life is simply a fiftysomething late-life crisis from a man frustrated by a country that didn't have a Corvette retailer to sell him a phallic symbol.

"There have been letters for you for years," Atalante tells my dad at the kitchen table, resting a tin can of cookies between her legs and fishing a stack of rubber-banded envelopes from within the cookie tin and handing it to him while Mom watches as she makes oatmeal at the stove for us. "They've written me a lot." I have no idea who "they" are.

"These are old," Dad notes, flipping through the mystery letters, taking in the names. A perk of being a quiet only child is that adults will grow comfortable talking freely around you. You're expected to color in your coloring books and not listen.

"They wrote me, and then they stopped," Atalante says. "Because you told me not to answer." She's his younger sister, so like Mom, she too defers to him.

"Nothing from Roger?" Dad asks. Atalante gives her brother a look like he just said something ridiculous. He might as well have said, "The green giraffe ate the last cloud." That's the level of silly she just heard.

Dad gives my mom a quick look, takes the letters, and goes into the living room to read. He moves into every home like it's his own, displaying confidence and ease in a way that somehow inspires deference from hosts. Years later, I will learn that this disarming coolness also makes him an excellent card player, if an unsuccessful gambler. Overconfidence will betray you.

That night, I learn that I have five older half-siblings somewhere in this vast new country. Mom whispers it to me when I ask about the letters as she's putting me to bed. Bit by bit, I will come to piece together the tale of Nicolette, my father's first wife: how she moved to Canada with him from Haiti the first time, gave him five children here, and then died rapidly of a disease no one mentions.

Nicolette left children behind. Some grown, others teenage. The youngest was fifteen, another had drowned. I understand they became resentful orphans when Dad moved back to Haiti, alone and without warning, where he was introduced to a young bright nurse laughing seamlessly through the dance clubs of Port-au-Prince. The whispers of my father's former life are strange and convoluted. They feel like soap opera fiction. Not even a classy one. Something bawdy where puppets come to life and pregnant women are kept in caves.

My father is a man of stories. I believe all of them.

My mom's nursing friends are thrilled to see her. They invite us to their houses and I play with their children. They want to take her to this salon, or that one. Within a month in Montreal, she would have been a part of weekly book clubs and throwing parties. Her life would have filled up quickly because that's just the type of person she is; a chatty social butterfly with stories, jokes, gossip, and impressions to spare.

My mother was always more popular than me. She was an extrovert before Myers-Briggs would become a religion to the nineteen-year-olds in my life trying to turn themselves into trading cards statistics. Over time, I realized that this was also because she was a lot lonelier than me. This particular psychological nuance means that she doesn't simply *like* people—bizarre as that is—she *needs* them. On her birthday the phone would ring from morning to night with calls from across the globe. Haiti, to Florida, to Switzerland. If I never minded having a mom who was more sociable than me, Dad certainly minded having a wife more sociable than him.

⛹

"Not here," Dad declares, finally, disappearing one morning and coming back in the evening with a newspaper from a town neither Mom nor I recognize. "Montreal isn't the right place to raise a kid. You don't know this country like I do."

Mom agrees, sad but hopeful. This will be a recurring theme for her, my poor mom.

"We'll meet people there, too," Dad says. A quiet town will let us rent a bigger apartment. I won't grow up surrounded by drugs and city noises. Again she defers. He's the experienced parent, after all.

⛹

We move to the municipality of Sherbrooke, two hours away from Montreal by car. There are 136,600 people in Sherbrooke with a 2.2 percent Black population: the largest visible minority population, by quite a bit. Next are Latin Americans at 1.5 percent.

I don't know the word yet, but I learn the meaning of downsizing, moving into the third, middle-floor apartment of a building totaling six units on a quiet street. Our house in Haiti is an estate compared to the three-hundred-square-foot apartment at the corner of Fisette Street. We were wealthy by Haitian standards: a big house and electricity more often than not. (That amounts to wealthy in a country where entire families live in piles of trash.)

In the end, the maid's house in the back was a little bigger than the sum square footage of our new Canadian life. There are no restaurants every night. This new life comes with a brutal currency conversion rate; affluent in Haiti and now made lower-middle class in Canada. He would never have admitted it, but I suspect that one of the key differences between my father and me was the fact that he was, deep down, an optimist. His inner white woman, if there was one, carries a copy of *The Secret* with highlighted sections and an unwavering certainty that there's always a bigger picture at work. Thank God that genetic trait didn't imprint.

FIVE

SURE, I'LL BE YOUR BLACK FOREIGN KID

It was programmed into me early: white kids are the good kids to hang out with. Back in Haiti, my best friend at the Le Petit Monde kindergarten was Dimitri. His parents had loose ties to the Bill Clinton administration. I remember nothing of Dimitri except his blond hair, tanned skin, and this fact that his parents had loose ties to the Bill Clinton administration, which Dad commented on often. The more white and light-skinned people you had in your school picture, the better your preschool was regarded back there. That's no longer a factor in Canada. I've been dropped into a good bucket of whiteness. Tiny little pink heads peek through the banks of snow-scribbled sled tracks that flank my new neighborhood on our way to my new elementary school.

"Speak French there, not Creole," my dad reminds me in Creole as he drives me to school on the first day of second grade, navigating the new rented car and snow tires. It's his version of *Have a good day, it's okay to be scared* while Mom interviews for a job she will not get. Creole is only allowed at home, never in public. Two of my new classmates even speak English, that key to the world that Dad will later insist that I excel in. At the time, English looked equal parts complicated and annoying in my books, having all the same letters as French but in the wrong order. Some words looked needlessly complicated, others suspiciously incomplete. *Rhythm. Publicly.*

My brain was first Creole, then French. At age eighteen, sitting on the Greyhound bus to move into the United States, with Mom sleeping in the seat beside me, I will realize that my inner monologue is now in English and that while I still speak it, I can no longer read Creole without sounding out the words.

I'M SEVEN years old and now Canadian—the paperwork is in process—when Dad insists that I wear a tie to the first day of school as a "point of pride." His, not mine. The classroom is bright, with colors and cutouts on all the walls. The air smells sweet from the lingering collages the kids did two days prior to my arrival when the spring half of the second grade officially started. The teacher, Miss Germaine, is nice. That's all I remember. It takes me no time at all to realize that I'm the Black kid, singular, of Saint-Esprit elementary. This makes me the very first Black friend of seventeen white second graders all at once and, to be honest, it's fucking great.

"Can I touch your hair?" Kevin asks me at recess, right by the classroom door, brave and bold in a way only very young, very blond children can be. The other boys stand behind him, curious and excited.

"Sure!"

After that exchange, Kevin is my best friend. I want to die on a field for him, sword in hand, having served with valor.

"Can I go next?" Jérémie, a human avatar of freckles, asks. Each head pat gets me a new friend.

They all live in the neighborhood, have lived in the neighborhood since they were born, and something or someone different is still good at that age. Jérémie's followed by Eric, and then Simon who lives closest to me and with whom I will walk home from school: a straight path, nine minutes away. I don't have much to say to Simon. He's better at sports than me, but we have enough common interests to keep a friendly fire burning. The covenant of the hair touch is nearly unbreakable. Simon waits for me on his doorstep, and we walk to the school together until the middle of fourth grade.

Girls like me, too, but more slowly. My handwriting is neat and cursive and causes an "Ooooh" when I'm called to the chalkboard. We didn't learn the stutter step of blocky, lowercase letters in Haiti, and getting three rulers smacked across your hands is an amazing motivator for calligraphy.

I get a Super Nintendo on my first Canadian birthday, and Haiti becomes a distant memory. The memory of our house and its two gardens—one indoors and one outdoors—is swiftly washed away with the first mushroom Mario the plumber jumps onto. I vaguely wonder if my armless Ninja Turtle action figure of Donatello (the purple one, you layman)—who had lost his left arm and thus deserved a warrior's burial—is still in the outdoors garden back in Haiti, but don't wonder about much else.

The renting of our Haitian house will be the primary and steadiest source of income for years to come. It brings in $12,000 a year, in USD, which is a fortune in Haitian gourdes and below the poverty line of annual income in Canadian dollars. I'm told—because my mother has been told by someone else who also has been told—that this house survived the earthquake that split the country's soul apart without a single brick falling. Its big red gates now apparently belong to a bank.

For years, until something close to nostalgia begins to uncover the memory, all I will remember from that country, my mother-land, will be the grimly profound and unbearable lack of video games and cartoons.

I wear T-shirts now, and Kevin and I trade our lunches with each other and no one else.

He loves the roasted chicken legs and pikliz (Haitian pickled vegetable relish) that my mother diligently makes every night to kill time and make our apartment smell like a home. Even cold, it's adult food and objectively delicious. We make a game of trading lunches, and he gives me neatly cut sandwiches that are color coded white, pink, orange. Somehow, the cheese, meat, and bread all taste exactly the same. Dominic, a shaggy-haired boy who appreciates *Dragon Ball Z* at the same religious level that I appreciate *Dragon Ball Z*, smells the chicken and presents me with a string cheese and microwaveable pasta lunch. I nod my head at him like I'm a nun being lured into the occult.

I'm in love with Kevin, the way third graders fall in love with their best friends. We'll move into houses next to one another one day and our kids will play together. Anything that happens until then is just homework and weekends.

The pack turns. Kids like me until, suddenly, they don't. (I will update you if this phenomenon stops one day.) I don't know why.

Maybe we're all just growing into our faces and the outliers are standing out more. Or, maybe we all collectively realize that we're big kids now. At-risk youths with hoodies and new *South Park*–obtained curse words in our arsenals. Somewhere someone heard there was a pecking order and came to school excited by the idea, which spread quickly. Who knows? In my case, the first crack appears on a winter afternoon in the fourth grade during a free activity period, as we're all working together on gluing bits of cotton onto red construction paper to turn it into Santa's beard.

A North American education amounts to a lot of gluing, as it turns out.

Over my shoulder Simon shows Eric something and the two of them snort-laugh when they notice me noticing. They're each other's best friends this year.

"What's that?"

"It's a ranking," Eric says. He's learned to smirk, ahead of the curve. The list amounts to four French words stacked on top of each other with a chasm in between.

BLANC

JAUN
BRUN
NOIR

They're colors but also very clearly not colors. The B in *BLANC* has what I will one day learn are serifs. It's been outlined over with a highlighter. *NOIR* is last. There's a typo in *JAUN(E)* (yellow) because Eric is low-key inbred and will tap out in the seventh grade anyway.

But for now, I am easily upset and can't control my face yet.

Eric snorts while Simon snorts apologetically. White people turn pink when they laugh very hard, I notice for the first time. It's like the shittiest camouflage imaginable.

"It's my dad's," Eric says, shrugging.

When I point out that it's in his handwriting, Eric rolls his eyes. It's his copy but the real list is his dad's. I'm being a baby. We've grown into racial beings with an ever-expanding and contracting idea of difference and inclusion, who know how to roll our eyes. We've seen it on TV enough to replicate.

"You're being *raciste*!" I say. Loud enough for Maxime and Clémence to start paying attention. I don't know how I know that word, but I do and so do they. They share a worried look. Eric puts the paper away.

"Don't tell Mrs. Louise, okay?" Eric asks. Begs. He sounds worried, and I like that.

I wish this halved my love for them like my dad's belt did for mine in Haiti, but it doesn't. I go back to my desk and resume gluing. My Santa is flawless. I perforate pink sheets of construction paper with a hole puncher and collect the circular remains. I place each tiny paper circle around Santa's skin, made with peach-colored construction paper, and just like that they become freckles. There's no brown paper in the plastic bin from which we collect our colored sheets.

Mrs. Ivette nearly passes out when she sees it. No, seriously: in my memory, the woman needs to lean against a chair at the sight of my Santa. It's put in the middle of the Christmas array of

Santas with "RUBEINTZ," my full name, under it. It's the first
one you see displayed by the door. Simon's and Eric's blend into
the background, and although I could mock their sad artistry, it's
good enough that theirs weren't good enough for center stage on
the door. Marie-Audrée compliments me on it, which only sweet-
ens my artistic triumph. Her sweaters are always fuzzy because she
has two cats and brought them to school last year in two crates
for show-and-tell. I brazenly tell her that her hair is pretty today
while Eric walks by, and he hears her giggle. She caught him eating a booger once and he cried. I secretly—and pettily, perhaps—
rejoiced in his humiliation.

I walk home alone and wonder if this is the future Dad was
talking about; if I'm living it right now and if I'm being ungrateful for briefly considering what shade Eric might turn if his dad
belted him . . . or if a hole puncher hit him across the head. Having now Googled all these people, decades later and with a fair bit
of nostalgia, I can confirm that Eric now looks shockingly like a
penis. As if a wizard granted a penis a wish to become a real boy
but used a new wand he wasn't quite familiar with, leaving the
new forsaken creature bald with a tilted forehead and a wrinkle
that looks like a slit at the top.

SIX

SURE, I'LL BE YOUR ANCHOR BABY

My mom hails from the north of Haiti. It's a weirdly shaped country already, half of an island that looks like a hook. Looking at a map, it was always hard to pinpoint the "north" of its flat top. But it shaped her in a specific way. Her first response to trauma is to boil water because whatever happens, people will need to drink water and, to this day, water from the tap is not to be trusted. Even when food was sparse and the fridge was well spaced out, with plenty of space between each item, we also always had a carton of matches and a box of candles at the ready. The trauma she is prepared for, that she trained for as a nurse, is the obvious kind. It's wounds and diseases. It's lights going off unexpectedly, a sudden fever in the night; the sort of misery that requires you to stay up all night. She's not ready for the quiet, private misery of Sherbrooke, two hours from Montreal and her only friends in this country.

I instantly have Kevin and seventeen new stories in the form of new white friends, while she will suffer a string of private humiliations while smiling for me at night. It's clear which one of us was lied to about this bright new future.

Because of the differences in certification requirements—bureaucratic minutiae—her nursing degree isn't worth much in Sherbrooke. She can't find a job. In Montreal, she would be able to attend programs catering to immigrants like her. She would have a cohort.

She has to go back to CEGEP—the two-year Quebec equivalent of a twelfth and thirteenth grade, before university. Just for a few credits. To a seven-year-old, anyone who is not a child is an adult. The CEGEP kids drive and have purses, and Mom has purses.

It's Dad's car, and sometimes he gives us rides. Anything that conflicts with his schedule or willingness to drive requires us to get quickly acclimated to the bus system. The number 6 stops a block away from our home. Mom and I take to cutting through a parking lot to get to the stop until one day an old lady comes out and tells us with a smile that the parking lot isn't for pedestrian crossing. Mom could charm her. She's charm incarnate. Instead, she walks past the woman with her chin high and coat bundled. I mimic and follow her. *Bitch*, I think in my head.

Whatever social gene I inherited from her was first spliced with my dad's ruthless self-sufficiency and privacy, all solidified by a lifetime as an only child. I've had years of alone and nothing to compare it to. As a result, I didn't find myself dying on a vine when moved to Sherbrooke, Quebec, Canada. For a woman like my mother, used to being the life of the party, to conversation filling the house, to telling the same stories over and over with small deviations that gave them new life each time, it was more or less a death sentence.

Cab drivers lock the door when we get in, and Mom squeezes my knee without saying anything as we ride in silence. She leaves a fair $2 tip on the $8 fare.

Her outfits dull as the days pass. Her stylish vests and silk blouses are ironed and then placed back into the closet. Her gold accessories stay in their boxes and the boxes in their drawers. Some days, she'll put them all on for a Saturday trip that amounts to church basements and other garage sales. Her hair begins to thin. She spends all day looking at the photo album she brought with her. She's allergic to this future.

"Why do you write the names behind the pictures?" I ask, finding her at the kitchen table again, looking at photos again.

"Because one day you'll forget them. And when you do, looking at them will make you sad. You need to do the work to preserve the memory."

No, I want to say. You need to forget and move on, you silly woman. This is the future. It's already started and you're wasting it.

Mom's candles finally come in handy exactly once: during the vicious North American ice storm when, four years into the great Canadian adventure my father had immigrated us into, the power went out and the whole of the province of Quebec was covered by a sheet of ice, causing power lines to collapse, cars to crash, and roads to be blocked off. For five nights in the dead of a −22 degrees Fahrenheit winter, our apartment looked like the candlelit setup to a *The Bachelorette* proposal.

There's no TV to watch and fill the dead air. Dad doesn't talk, he reads, seethes. There's no such thing as a comfortable Haitian silence. Haitian silence is loud and unnatural. An aberration. The chitchat and ongoing life commentary are suddenly on mute, leaving the day-to-day motions strange and off-putting. Five days is a very long time to live without electricity in this new modern world.

There's resentment between them, but I won't know that word for years to come, so she and I sit at our kitchenette table and I take her through my Pokémon cards. The concept of an Eevee confuses her.

She frowns at Jolteon, Flareon, and Vaporeon—my prized trifecta—displeased at this bit of mythos I just laid out, but suddenly interested. She tilts the Eevee card to face her. In my mind, she likes that he's brown.

"Does he eat the stone?"

"I think you just touch them with it."

"How does a stone have thunder inside of it?"

That one stumps me.

"Maybe the stone is from a spot that got struck by lightning and—"

"—and who says he has to change?" She keeps her eyes on the phone, waiting for her sisters to ring.

"You get stronger, you survive." I'm not a baby, and in my multiplication table–adjacent mind, Pokémon die when they lose. It's a rough Poké-world out there.

"If you want to survive," she says, eyes on the side of my father's face. "You have to draw a tight circle around yourself and don't believe people who tell you that you can just reinvent yourself."

She's not talking to me anymore, and Dad's not reading anymore. It was never a big mystery as to which one of them I get my dramatic streak from. He's in the other room but also less than thirty feet away, because $365 rent will only grant you so much privacy in the new world.

"They're deluded," she says, switching from French to Creole. "Because it will probably be worse and cold and poor. Stay as you are for as long as you can, Beintz. Stay an . . . an . . ."

She taps the card twice, prompting me.

"An Eevee."

"Yes. Stay an Eevee as long as you can. Don't trust someone who promises you empty stones."

Dad's book hits the back window. In Haiti, she might have been threatened with being hit by now, but here, in Canada, she might not be. I collect my cards and go into my room with them as Dad bursts into the kitchen, snatching up his book. My favorite Pokémon is Blastoise from that day forward.

I didn't know resentment, but I somehow knew "cabin fever." They both had it—Dad for the apartment and the small life it contained, and Mom for the whole of Canada, too big, too massive, and entirely useless without friends or cousins. They needed to let out the tension and step into the arena loudly screaming at each other in that way that makes white people wish the loud foreign Blacks didn't move next door. I imagine they wish they had polite white neighbors.

The electricity comes back, of course. Spring thaws the ice. The storm was an anomaly, but the atmospheric disturbance has set in. Something's broken in Mom. She wants to go back to the island.

Dad's style of fighting is random acts of violence. In Haiti, he had belted me twice—though my butt only bled once. In a modern country, he has to mind himself. People keep an eye on rowdy immigrant men. "Domestic abuse" comes up on the nightly news once, and I want to believe it's my first Canadian smirk, right at Dad. He notices. I want him to know that I know new words now.

Mom's style is talky. *Ranty*. Even as an adult son, I'll still be susceptible to it. She'll move from room to room, muttering to herself, loudly doing the dishes, waiting for Dad to ask what's wrong, tempting him. When it finally happens, her yelling will turn into conversation and then back to yelling again. It will default to the silent treatment, and then flare up again. It's not a fuse being lit; it's gas filling a room until there's no air.

To protect me from it all, I get cable in my room via a splitter installed at the back of the living room outlet that goes throughout the kitchen and under my door. It's a random and unspoken gift from my father that is set up for me one day after school. It makes for a shockingly effective distraction. My world defaults to an audience laugh track.

I start picking up bits of English from the sitcom reruns of FOX 34, adding it to the French and Creole. *That '70s Show. The Drew Carey Show. Seinfeld. The Simpsons.* It's a two-hour block, back-to-back, a survey of American popular culture, a second education for me.

It's at that point, I imagine, that my mother realized that American television had anchored me. There was just no going back to Haiti once you'd given a kid an N64, a classroom with computers, and McDonald's twice a week. Electricity without a generator was a given.

"Don't you miss your school?" she tries one day. She's talking of Haiti. Of the private school where mediocre men with rulers send me to the corner when I roll my eyes at their mediocrity and the kid whose parents give the most money ends up with the highest grade. The smell of the latrines could stun a small horse.

Mom is ready to be a divorcée at the airport, with a polite son at her arm. There's still life in her. She's from "the north." Haitian Winterfell blood. She's used to fighting, and she'll fight her way back to Haiti and her old life or some semblance of it. I know she will, and I can't let that happen.

She tells me of her plans one night, putting me to bed. She wants us to conspire together like we do for everything. Like when

I see a manga at the store I really want and that she'll buy for me the next time she's there and leave under my bed. (A wasted expense according to him.) Now, it's my turn to conspire to make her happy. But I'm my father's child, too. Ambitious, stubborn, and greedy.

"*This* is my school," I say.

"Your school in Haiti," she clarifies, annoyed that she has to.

"I'm Canadian now." The card says so.

"Beinbeintz, please."

"No! No! You can't do this!" I say. I don't care if he hears. I know she won't belt me. She'll be the one who gets in trouble; not me. "You can't keep yo-yoing me all over the world like this! It's not fair!"

I heard *yo-yoing* as a verb on a TV show and it must have stuck. My fighting style is emotional blackmail. I'M SEVEN, or eight, and selfish for the first time in my life. Unfortunately, it's aimed at the wrong person.

"Okay, okay!" she says, crying now, too, feeling terrible. The next act she'd briefly started to plan is now a nonstarter. I feel bad, too, yes, but less than she does. It would be a lie to say that I'm completely unaware of what I'm doing. Using my words and other people's feelings to get exactly what you want . . . Puberty is still a ways away, and I wonder how much of my dad I've already soaked up.

"We're staying, Beintz. We can stay."

Haiti or Canada, nothing has really changed. She gives and she gives and Philippe men take and they take. What a nuisance it is to love me.

SEVEN

SURE, I'LL BE YOUR BLACK SON

If I was apprehensive of writing about my father here, it's not because of the emotional trauma. To this day, mine is mostly a strange indifference to him. The epilogue comes early on this one: we never quite gelled, he and I. I feel worse about the indifference than I do about the man. He might say the same about me. I'm sure that first finger squeeze in the maternity ward left both of us cold. I don't hate him. I'm grateful for what he gave me . . . I've honestly just never warmed up to him? Now, this may all sound very dark and harsh to you, who came here hoping for stories of pickup games and fried chicken from your new homie, but keep in mind that:

a. My life will grow to include a lot of male writers, often white. Fiction writers, screenwriters, both established and aspiring. So, needless to say: #daddyissues abound. So, to be clear, fellas: y'all definitely have them, too. These are often unfairly given to women in media narratives, but in my experience, daddy issues are the currency of literary bros, these former sensitive indoor kids now rocking man-buns and copies of *The Road* by Cormac McCarthy on their shelves.

Through beers, short stories, text exchanges, and chatty dashes across the highway to reach a movie theater, I've heard plenty of these moments that live right under the stories of fishing together or teaching you how to drive in the empty parking lot of a mall. That time he was too quiet on the drive to or from your soccer game. The fact that he sent you a link to a nearby law school—along with his monthly $3,000 check—and how this clearly means that he doesn't support your life goal of becoming the next king of stand-up comedy. His agreeable divorce from your mother when you were twenty-six years old, which turns you back into a teenager. I've heard it all. So, it's my turn. Emotional reparations, baby.

b. I am positive the man never loved me either. I was Robert's seventh chronological offspring. His first marriage had birthed five. There would be four more. There are a total of nine of us, last I checked. High five for potent semen there, Pops.

DISCLAIMER: If you are imagining my father right now, you're probably picturing the prototypical deadbeat Black father that so much of the media has offered us. A tank top, gold chains, lack of work ethic, getting high, and overly reliant on a societal net, dark faded tattoo ink against darker skin, with a bushel of unclaimed offspring and baby mamas in his wake.

Very incorrect.

I mean, okay, fine: maybe the bushel of baby mamas

part. The man was a whore, what can I say there? I'm not a whore, but to borrow a folksy bit of kitchen-table wisdom from Aunt Atalante, after learning of the twenty-four-year-old woman her brother had gotten pregnant after parting ways with myself and my mother:

Some people will hunt with any dogs that'll run with them.

I never quite knew if she was referring to Dad as the dog or the hunter. Regardless, my father is not the stereotype you might be imagining.

The "deadbeat Black dad" stereotype is one of the most pervasive Black stereotypes out there. It's understandably harmful to paint all lacking Black fathers with such a broad stroke, and while his belt whipping once drew my blood in a country far away, that is not the man I'm writing about here.

For one thing, the man was viciously, annoyingly smart.

Smarter than me, by a good mile, which is the only distance in intelligence that I suspect he could tolerate in a child of his: either a genius, a mile ahead of him, who could lead him to a better life, or a mile behind whom he could constantly impress and who would, like so many in his life, exist in constant awe of him. Safe to say I was neither.

His is that smartness that breeds arrogance. The type of smartness that thrives in academia; where grants, fellowships, and offices reward your intelligence and deem you an exceptional Negro, especially at the University of Haiti, and later, Canada. At some point, Germany, too. I believe there was also a stint in the Netherlands as well. How can everyone in your life not be transitory when you were so gifted and singular that your native commune of the Gonaïves started a foundation in the sixties to send you off to study in Port-Au-Prince, knowing you were too good for them? That you were smart enough not to have to go hungry with your siblings but be put in the back of a crowded bus filled with livestock and sent off to a better life? It's a true story, too. I remember the newspaper clipping in his office. That's some Lin-Manuel *Hamilton* crap right there.

There are moments of fondness. I saw myself in him when he would compulsively buy boxes of books at garage sales, bring them home, and unpack them with a hint of reverence, going on at length about the authors or topics he recognized and staying quiet, but curious, about those he wasn't familiar with. He'd read those first. I learned to admire a stacked shelf of acquired knowledge through him.

1998

Have you ever heard a Black Haitian man speak fluent German? It's very cool. It would happen occasionally around our tiny apartment. He'd be reading another dusty tome. (Unlike chess, Go, or reciting Aesop's fables, he had never expressed or insisted on teaching me. Languages were *his* thing.)

I half thought he was making it up for a long time; affecting the staccato of the German language and speaking gibberish for the proud smirk in my mom, and taking pleasure in my eye rolls, until, at age eleven or twelve, we bumped into a German family who had just immigrated to Canada, and, like us, found themselves at the *Carrefour de l'Estrie* mall, of Sherbrooke, Quebec. I don't remember how the conversation started, but at some point,

Dad and this strange and very tall man with thinning blond hair and blond chest hair that peeked through his man-cleave began to converse in German.

They did not know each other. Dad might have muttered something casual in German, the man's eyes might have suddenly widened in shock and then delight. Mom and I might have been left hopping in place for warmth, each carrying multiple grocery bags, while these two stray men carried on in German for twenty minutes and parted ways with a proud, brotherly handshake, the man clasping Dad's between his two giant white paws, crackling with transparent hair and brown spots.

"When did you learn German?" Mom pondered on the ride home, impressed like she always was. "It's like you don't even have to translate it in your mind."

"I don't."

"That's so fascinating to me," she said, arm on her window, watching him drive from the front passenger seat like a schoolgirl.

I hid it better, but I was probably as curious as she was. *Why isn't he a translator? Or an ambassador at the UN? Why did we just cash a welfare check and get groceries at Super C, the cheap grocery store with stained bananas?* I suspect he often pondered the same thing.

"When did you realize you could think in German?" Mom asked at a red light.

"Why are you asking that?" He sighed, distracted by traffic. My father saw women speaking as a time to gather his thoughts. A respite from the intellectual rigor of other men and maybe a shift to seduction, though I never witnessed that myself.

"Because you just spent twenty minutes speaking German, maybe," I chimed in from the back, a preteen aware I could no longer get the belt after being put on my knees for two hours as punishment, not in a white country like Canada.

He'd "just learned it, at some point," he shrugged off, not in the mood to talk.

Now, I realize that this was probably a lie. He probably took many courses, and after spending X amount of years (or months, or decades) in Germany, became fluent. Where and how he became fluent in the Spanish, English, or Latin, I have no clue.

Dad was an equation. Incomplete, partly because I didn't have all the integers in hand, or maybe because I resented having to solve him in the first place. Asking him any questions about his life, no matter how superficial, was like putting quarters into a very specific jukebox that would stutter through a full song, turning it into a string of words and leaving you to solve the equation and imagine the rhythm yourself.

Ultimately, the father I choose to remember was a man trying his best, falling short, who disliked not being in control and who couldn't stop being selfish in the end. Rather than a convenient stack of stereotypes, tank tops, and chains, it turns out my father was complicated, nuanced, infuriatingly contradictory: in short, entirely human. Who wouldn't have some light daddy issues every time you brush your teeth because, I'm told, I look exactly like him when he was my age.

EIGHT

SURE, I'LL BE YOUR BLACK BOYFRIEND

At school, our student body vaguely changes. A few kids leave, a few newcomers arrive. There are now a total of three Black students at Saint-Esprit Elementary. Two siblings in the third and first grades. They have each other and, presumably, their own Erics with folded lists in their pockets. I spot them across the playground while playing *ballon chasseur*—dodgeball—at recess. I refocus on the game. I can't be seen talking to babies. I can't warn them. I wouldn't even know what to warn them of.

Puberty is looming within my fifth-grade cohort. We're learning English in class. It's the language of sexy teenagers on television. In our minds, we'll soon be joining the cast of *Degrassi: The Next Generation*. I've become more Quebecois than Haitian. At home, we watch *La Petite Vie*, the hyperpopular *Friends* of Quebec sitcoms. I pay attention to hockey and feel involved when the Canadiens lose, though I still find the games too long. Celine Dion is now our household's national icon. We have opinions about her, and the amount of time she's spending in America feels like a betrayal to our Canadian household. We've made friends with other Black families around Sherbrooke, yet it still falls short of a community. These friendships are not unlike the ones you find at work: based less on a shared sense of identity than geographical proximity. Dad goes to play cards at their houses on the weekend. He's there from morning to night on Saturdays. I don't understand why Mom resents these absences so much until I realize that the difference between her and me is that I believe him.

Kevin is just another fifth-grade classmate now. We're still friends, but I no longer wonder what he's eating for dinner while I'm eating Haitian rice and fish at night. I've noticed that his blond hair is slowly turning brown, and I wish it wasn't. He and I now talk about the subtle eroticism of Ms. Pac-Man and how that fluffy tight little bow at the top of her head and those Jezebellian eyelashes and that bright red lipstick make all the difference. More complex Ms. Pac-Man feelings—simmering around the decidedly more three-dimensional forms of my now pubescent classmates—are nearing but remain at a distance, a mirage coming into focus.

Mom and I spend two consecutive summers in Florida to recharge her batteries and improve my English. These extended two-month-long summer vacations elsewhere are our household's clumsy steps toward a divorce that will flood my toes with relief.

When we come back from Florida, the sixth grade is a sudden battleground none of us expected. Bodies have changed. Previously chubby Melanie now has heaving breasts.

The boys are lankier. Some kids now look exactly like their parents picking them up from school. It's not here yet, but you can tell who will be bald in adulthood. I compare my two first-day-of-class pictures, hanging from last year and now—fifth grade and sixth. I haven't changed. I might be thicker, but it's the same thing: "boy, Black."

The starting shot for our nascent romantic aspirations is the fact that Jean-Philippe Desmarais, now taller, even better looking than before, still smart and charming, too—honestly, screw him—suddenly has an *ex*-girlfriend. No one is quite sure who the girlfriend in question *was* and how that status had even come to an end, but no one questions his explanation that she goes to another school, an exotic claim that only adds to his reputation. *Another school?* Jean-Philippe is smart and nice and doesn't need to lie about this thing—unlike say, Vincent who lies about vacationing in Miami on long weekends—so we trust it, pepper him with questions, and find that suddenly our own lives seem lacking. Behind in puberty, we start to pair up. We have to catch up, or middle school will smell it on us next year and eat us all alive.

I'm one of the kids who tries to put it out of their minds. I have other, purer interests of the Pokémon variety. I should mention that I have a Charizard. It's not a first-edition version of the rare holographic card, but a Charizard is still a Charizard. It's the elementary school version of being verified on every social media platform all at once. Kids are stabbing each other for those across North America. (Don't make eye contact with me like we're the same, you Charizard-less peasant.)

I can only keep myself in check for so long. The sixth-grade hormonal crusade hits a fever pitch when Emiles G. gets a girlfriend, too. Yes: Emiles, that chinless expanse of neck with an Adam's apple the size of a fist at age twelve, walks hand in hand with Catherine C., the skinny one who wears makeup and is on her way to becoming a chick who can hang. The rest of us accelerate our processes. The boys split apart and start mingling. Some crack jokes in class. New looks proliferate. Steven L. starts to experiment with hair gel, a swoop situation covering half his face. In a few months, he'll become "the most handsome boy in the neighborhood." The girls have decided. No one will see it coming when it happens. He can barely read in class.

We rush to learn the timeless art of seduction and run toward monogamy like someone's handing out medals. The whole point is to not be left on the bench.

I'm still the one Black kid in our grade. Somewhere along the way, I've recognized that as the opposite of an asset. I stop by the Pharmaprix one morning and start aggressively smelling deodorants. The shopkeeper assigned to follow me upon entry laughs to herself in a way that's not entirely concerned with my hearing and gives up, returning to the counter to tell her friend. I buy two sticks of Axe Chocolate assuming it's the one made for Black people. I also don't hate the smell, which may speak to some deviancy at the bottom of my soul. I've aligned with the rest of the world.

Soon, I'm officially dating Genevieve M. I give her a squeeze monster from Toys "R" Us when I ask her. She gets good grades and has long, pretty hair. She wore makeup one day and didn't anymore because too many people noticed, which may be what emboldens me to ask. Genevieve says yes and her friends giggle. I've secured a girlfriend, but I am entirely unclear on what, exactly, that means. I don't tell my parents but, later that night, I will relentlessly search the topic on AltaVista. I can't take her on trips and don't know how to procure body oils and/or what to do with them. Mom's hair stuff smells right but it's not the right type.

Dad walks into the bathroom to find me kneeling on the bathroom sink going through Mom's shelves of third-tier products salvaged from the supermarket, pharmacies, and specialized stores. She's looking for alternatives to her neat shelf, left back in Haiti. Dad raises two mocking eyebrows.

"It's for my girlfriend," I tell him defiantly, gathering as many of them as I can to carry into my room. Mom is already asleep. She goes to bed early while Dad reads on the toilet and waits for the lotto numbers after the evening news and I play video games in my room with the door closed.

He smirks at me and keeps the door open waiting for me to exit. "Is she white?" He knows the answer. I lie anyway.

"No."

In the morning, I wake up to a sheet of condoms on my desk. I won't fully understand the significance of this for a few more months.

I stuff it into my backpack, knowing that I would be in trouble bursting into the kitchen asking any follow-up questions. I'm too young to know that Mom wouldn't recognize them. I don't know what to do with them, but some of the kids at school enjoy them and seem in awe that I possess them. So, I milk it.

"You two are going to have sex?" someone asks, suspicious, inspecting the labels carefully at lunchtime.

"Maybe," I answer coolly, collecting the condoms from him and folding them neatly into my backpack's side pocket. They're my new Pokémon cards.

"Black guys have sex early," someone else says. They're on my side.

"Black guys have sex early," I repeat, emboldened.

Genevieve wants to make out, but getting me to put out is like trying to draw blood from a laptop. I want to watch cartoons and hold hands. I wish she was in love with me. Or, maybe that I was in love with her. Some big emotional swell that would be sated by holding hands and staring into each other's eyes.

She leans her head on my shoulder during recess while we're sharpening all 120 color pencils of the leather box case she got for her birthday. I didn't know it was her birthday, so I'm the one who sharpens the pencils and she empties the shavings into neat little color-coded piles. Other kids look at us and in doing so reverently learn that this is what it means to be in a relationship: arts and crafts together and minimal conversation about TV shows and music.

She sometimes says things that stay with me but that I don't understand.

"Faye and I decided that if you were white, you would be a redhead."

I still won't know how to decipher this eighteen years later. While writing this essay, I still don't.

Our wholesomeness as an age group is declining, too. *South Park* is our new religion. Even the French-dubbed version that airs at 10:30 p.m. on Teletoon is joyful to us. Dad doesn't think we need cable TV, so I learn to lie well. I chime in around Kevin's plot summary and add to the chorus of laughter.

Occasionally, I stumble too badly to recover.

"I bet you didn't even watch it!" Eric charges.

Eric dislikes me suddenly. I wish he'd ask to feel my hair again.

"You're such a liar, Rubeintz!" I won't be Ben for another six years. Rubeintz is still a name with too many letters in the middle and hard to pronounce at the end. A sandwich with German aspirations.

Genevieve and I watch *Save the Last Dance* on VHS in her purple bedroom, and she starts holding my hand. It's a harrowing tale of interracial love: the type we might have both thought we were signing up for in dating. The characters are racial mythologies serving up dramatized proxies for our sixth-grade romance.

Her, the ballerina, learning hip-hop to get into Julliard, and me, risking my bright future for a friend I grew up with and who is already on a dark and druggy path.

"That was such a good film!" She says *film*, not *movie*. And just like that, we're one of those couples who has a favorite *film*.

Years from this moment, I will somehow remember that the Black guy got shot at the end (though this never actually happened). It will confuse me that they dance together at the end as the credits roll. Every cell in my body was expecting the Black boyfriend to die. Dramatically. I'm already conditioned to expect the Black boyfriend should have died.

Even with a degree in screenwriting two decades later, I still think the movie would be stronger if Sean Patrick Thomas's character died in Julia Stiles's arms. But I do not know that right now.

We cuddle and I say something like "This is nice," like Buffy and Angel that one time. She nods her agreement and scoots into me.

"Do you have pot?" she asks, giving me Ms. Pac-Man eyes.

"What?"

"Pot," she repeats, arm locked around me and eyes bright with the intensity of someone who has finally psyched themselves to voice a long-standing query. Her eyes are the greenest things I've seen. So many shades of green . . . How strange.

No.

"Oh. Do you know where to get some?"

No again.

"I know you do. Someone said you definitely did."

Her next question being obvious makes lying a nonstarter. She's disappointed, but cuddling is nice. I don't ask who told her. I wish we could stop cuddling now. I want to go home. Mom is alone there again tonight.

One morning, the games are declared over. The sixth-grade class of Saint-Esprit primary school has a declared pair of victors: Simon and Catherine allegedly had sex. Actual sex. Both tell us separately while glancing at each other from their end of the fenced-in schoolyard, and we decide that their stories line up enough for it to be true. His performance is enthralling. He's recently become the class clown, the same way I'm the class Black guy. In his mouth, sex sounds wet and meaty. He makes a sound that reminds me of a wooden spatula going in and out of a jar of preserves.

"No, you don't understand," he interrupts someone trying to chime in, maybe me. "It feels so good. Like, way better than just jerking off."

I haven't done that yet either. I wish I was at the girls' table hearing the soft and tender version of the same story. Lots of kissing and oils that suddenly reveal their usefulness.

At home, I try to jerk off to Ms. Pac-Man. I picture her eating me whole—me falling into a yellow ravine of Ms. Pac-Man. *Mrs.* Pac-Man: her being a married woman, with a husband hard at work eating ghosts for her, from a vaguely racist conservative background who does not approve of interracial trysts, is as crucial as the bow. Yes, it appears I have some issues.

"We should move," Dad says one day. "This is not a great neighborhood for a teenager."

He starts looking for apartments in Rock Forest and will eventually find one with a spare bedroom that we will visit, sign a lease for, but never move into as a family. It sounds like a ridiculous concept; a town a few miles away that sounds like it should have a Pokémon Gym.

He's right. Our neighborhood is bad. The same kids that used to rub my head and ask me if Haiti has beaches now skip classes together. The ice rink behind the school is where they hang out, and I'm one of the only ones left skating, with the younger kids and their dads. They now sit on the side, kicking snow and passing around cigarettes stolen from their parents. Simon becomes a fourteen-year-old social smoker. I'm a good kid, so we don't talk again. The final straw is that I have a girlfriend.

"Should we have sex?"

"I have condoms."

"Do you want to?"

"Not really."

We're both relieved.

"Am I handsome?" I ask Genevieve as we sit with each other on the steps of her wooden porch. She is only the first girlfriend out of three who will go on to hear that question. She sits up and tilts her head at me because it's as strange to her as it is to me that a boy would ask that question or care.

"Well, you're Black. It's different."

"How?"

"It just is." Eventually, when I'm quiet for a beat too long, she offers, "You're a cute Black guy." I'm not thrilled that it's that easy to appease the acid in my guts.

"Okay."

"You should get dreads," she suggests out of the blue one day, I think simply because she just learned about dreads. I consider it briefly. I still see no point in dating someone. You have to find things to do and there are a lot of silences to fill that feel too intimate. My puberty is still two years away.

After three chaste afternoons of nothing on her bed, lying head to toe with her socks on, holding hands, except when she's doing homework or I'm playing my Game Boy Advance, she breaks up with me because she likes Jean-Philippe.

"I thought it would be funner to date you," she eventually says when we decide to be friends after two weeks of the silent treatment whenever we bump into each other in stairwells. For me it's drama, for her, it's sheer disinterest.

"I don't know . . . You're kind of boring," she elaborates, though I have no idea what I am expected to do with this epiphany.

"Oh."

"Dating you is, like, sweet. I thought it would be something . . . I don't know. Different."

"I get it."

We hug. It's a mature breakup, and we both want the easy swagger of little kids who've had a mature breakup.

I look at myself in the mirror that night and do a five-minute monologue to myself, cataloging every facet of my dullness. *You couldn't keep Genevieve M. interested. Genevieve M. with the horse stickers and literal ribbon in her hair. You're not just boring. Vanilla is boring but vanilla is still a flavor—a popular flavor. People want their bathrooms to smell like vanilla. You wish you were ice cream, son. You're the ice around the goddamn container. The sticky condensation that leaves a residue on people's fingers. Why couldn't you be Lil' Bow Wow, Will Smith, or Basquiat?* Google becomes your best friend in understanding what you're supposed to know, like, watch, and listen to. Even if you don't abide by them, it's vital to at least know all the standards you're falling short of.

NINE

HOW TO GO THROUGH LIFE WITHOUT DROWNING, PART I

I'M THIRTEEN and my aunt's kitchen is huge and bright. My mom's relationship with her sister is nothing like the dutiful weariness and point keeping of my dad's relationship with his sister, Aunt Atalante. Mom and her sister will occasionally hug each other out of nowhere and for no reason at all, and you can tell they're sharing a memory that doesn't need to be voiced. My aunt, uncle, and three cousins live in a gated community in New Port Richey, Florida. Their house is big, with ceilings you can't touch even by stepping on a chair. Their children, my cousins—two boys a couple of years older than me and a girl, four years younger—are cool, and I like them as much as I envy them.

I breathe in the AC not only because it's hot outside (sweltering, really—God, Florida), but because it's wealthy, valuable. Something I can internalize and take back home. We go for long drives to giant supermarkets and malls, sampling this American life two tax brackets above ours. My aunt's a nurse and my uncle works at a store. Somehow, that's enough, because it's 2002 and that's how the economy works.

I like to rub my hand against their marble kitchen island, like some half weird nephew, half enthralled Gollum for no reason other than that it feels fancy. Our kitchen counter back home, waiting for me in seven weeks when we go back to Canada, is barely a shelf, cluttered with a dish rack, spices, and pots, a laundry basket. No inch is spared. I suspect my uncle thinks I'm wiping my greasy hands off on his marble counter. I'm not. I'm trying to remember it to take some part of the tactile memory home with me.

Years later, I'll find out that their home looks exactly like every other in their small gated community: valued at roughly $300,000; and that, while a wonderful house, is not the rap video I remember—but for now, I'm thirteen and I'm enthralled. It's the American Dream™.

My cousins are ungrateful, I think without ever saying. When Melissa, nine, rolls her eyes because she doesn't get the remote, or cries when she sits pretzel-style in the living room in pink shirts, getting her coarse Black-girl hair roughly combed out, I want to grab a wooden spoon, smack her twice, and tell her we've decided to ship her ungrateful behind back to Haiti where she'll clean marmites all day with increasingly coarse hands.

"Why can't we move here?" I say without thinking to Mom at night in the guest bedroom we share. I know she secretly thinks the same thing but knows better than to say it aloud. She doesn't have the luxury to entertain these kinds of thoughts.

She answers in French or Creole, speaking of the language barrier, the work she doesn't have, the visas we don't have. The schooling I would be too behind in. Occasionally, she runs out of arguments and will throw a "What would your dad say?" in there.

Right. Him. From the listless Q&A chitchats on the phone, I know that he doesn't miss us any more than we miss him, but we pretend for each other's sake that he does.

When I stare at her, she follows it with a more logical argument, aimed at overturning my adolescent hierarchy of needs.

"We couldn't live here. We'd have to find another apartment. One without furniture or TV."

"You're right, Mom," I eventually say. The lack of TV is the first real flaw in my elegant plan to pack up and move here.

Still, that won't stop my hand from rubbing the marble at breakfast and dinner the next day. Once she's used to having me around, Melissa—ever observant—draws attention to it by saying I'm making love to the marble. Impertinent American child. Respect your elders.

No one knows where she's picked up those two words "making love," but my uncle hates it. My English is still bad, and my cousins amuse themselves by teaching me "bitch" and "pussy," so I certainly can't be blamed. When Tuxedo Mask kisses Sailor Moon on a fade-out of a Toonami block of cartoons on Cartoon Network, I tell her they're off to make love with his penis and her vagina, and luckily, Melissa is not a narc yet.

We spent a lot of time in that kitchen, distributing takeout for this temporarily seven-person household of my aunt, uncle, three cousins, myself, and Mom. The adults sit, the children stand up. Or, maybe it was the other way around. Either way, chair-to-ass parity was never achieved that summer.

It's in that high-ceiling kitchen of the gods, with pizza and Crazy Bread being passed around, that I heard about Julie Smith— my cousin Ricky's classmate who died while on vacation. The news of her drowning was currently making the rounds of the eighth graders and had landed in Ricky's MySpace. We took the news as somberly as we could considering Julie Smith and I had never met. Julie Smith was young, and we, their children, were young, and that was enough for Mom and my aunt to be devastated.

"So young," Mom said, eyes on me.

"Can you imagine?" Aunt Louisa said, eyes on Melissa, nine.

"How did she die?"

"She drowned," Ricky explained.

"In a pool?"

"No," Ricky said, done with his Crazy Bread and ripping Melissa's in half, always a good older brother. "At a lake with her family."

It was almost imperceptible, but the next series of looks Mom and Aunt Louisa shared—pursed lips, tilted chins, and raised eyebrows—carried within it an entire conversation that in my mind went a little something like this:

What was that child doing in a lake?

"Vacation."

White Nonsense.

White Nonsense.

I don't like you at lakes, my mom says without saying. *I'd fall apart if you drowned.*

I commit then and there to never drown, thinking of excuses to use in the event of lake invitations in an imagined other life.

You'd fall apart if I drowned.

Mind you, this all happened in my head, while fully fondling some marble, so perhaps that look never actually took place.

Despite it being penciled in on all of our calendars, we didn't go back to Florida the following summer. Two plane tickets amount to $1,000. Sometimes, it's as simple as that. Still, my relationship with swimming was problematic from that day forward. It will remain that way through college and into adulthood when I finally remedy the situation. We'll get there.

TEN

SURE, I GUESS I'LL BE YOUR CLASSIC NAME-BRAND COOKIE

Located on the South Shore, the Collège Français was a barely private secondary school. Despite being nestled in the suburbs of Montreal, the midsize school managed to be as diverse as any future New York City subway. For roughly $2,000 a year—perhaps even a bit less, it's hard to remember—the illusion of a high-end education was something most working families of immigrants on a budget could afford for their children. They imagined us, their kids, learning to speak a perfect idealized French, free of accent, in white and forest-green polos with dark blue slacks and black shoes.

We were the at-risk offspring of immigrant men. The truth was, we were all misshapen and greasy, finding our way around each other, too afraid to embrace any real delinquency and content to curse a lot. Boys were too shy to shower together, and after gym, our classroom smelled downright spicy. Our jocks played soccer: the varsity suburban Quebecois kind. Each day, I ride the bus to school and listen to my iPod. It's during that stretch of time that I discover what an Oreo is.

My middle school's Black kids tended to come in three common subcategories: (1) the Thugs, (2) the Oreos, and (3) the Immigrants, which referred to the international kids from our student body; those Black kids who came from faraway countries where the rest of their families resided. Foreign Black. Different-language Black. Dashiki Black.

If you didn't fall squarely into one of the three, you would be designated according to your nearest classification. In the tenth grade, for instance, Leo was our African. He was tall, dark-skinned, and stoic with a heavy African accent. People liked him well enough from afar without having much to say to or about him. His name was solely omitted in the class-wide Attractiveness Ranking of the boys the girls did one day. Leo belonged to the "Immigrants," and while I was an immigrant myself—born and raised in Haiti until the second grade—I did *not* want to fall into the same bin as Leo.

People only paired up with him for team assignments when they had to. "You're not friends with Leo," Maxime, a kid from our grade, once complained. "You're an ambassador to him." I took it as an unspoken compliment. I wasn't like Leo; I could be befriended by the Maximes of the school on equal footing.

I stayed away from Leo. Two well-behaved Black kids with good grades start talking and pretty soon, they're declared best friends and teachers put their desks together. They're on the second page of the school pamphlet together with their thumbs up and the word *Diversity!* floating over their heads. Hell no. I would not be a Leo. I would make that horny attractiveness list, goddammit.

For my part, I liked anime and manga, was completely uninterested in sports, and my favorite music was "basement white boy" punk rock (your Weezer, your Sum 41, your Panic-punctuation At The Disco) so naturally, I fell into category #2: *Oreo*.

My Blackness was not "fake" in my mind but secondary; an aside to the equation. I didn't quite know what to do with it, and to the eyes of many, my interests did not align with it. It was easily disregarded by friends who did not necessarily have the highest regard for cultural Blackness.

And I, in turn, would smile through the parts of myself that were cringing, because all a kid wants is some friends. (People in search of an easy label to place on you love to guess an accent, by the way. After four identical conversations in a row, you kind of just want to yell, "Haitian Canadian—eff off.")

In the ninth grade, our history teacher, Mr. Mirault, is a large, once-redheaded man whose hair has turned completely white and who freckles easily. I almost wish we still had gluing hours so I could replicate him in construction paper, bringing him to life as I did Santa Claus.

Mr. Mirault loves Black students. He loves all ethnic students, but Black ones in particular. We have a special place in his by-passed heart. He pats my shoulder when we file into class with him. The man had a history of humanitarian work that lived in framed photos of himself surrounded by Black children in front of brightly painted buildings with patted dirt as floors. I suspect he saw us, his Black students, as Dickensian street urchins, nebbish and impossibly earnest, pulling at his dress shirt for White Man Wisdom.

On movie afternoons, his go-to choices are *American History X*, *Malcolm X*, and *Hotel Rwanda*. We end up seeing that last one twice. To him, a teaching career was the continuation of a life-time of good work to make us rowdy immigrant children aware of racism. The man has a particular glistening hard-on for Black-on-Black genocides, subcategory Tutsis and Hutus. Every documentary on the Rwandan genocide is screened for us while other sections, away from his well-meaning supervision, get to watch *The Matrix*.

"Racism is a poison," he says, making benevolent eye contact with the only Black kids in the room of twenty-six bored preteens in the throes of puberty, me and a girl named Sora whom I do not like. The two of us share awkward looks when the movies turn gruesome and Mirault loudly moans his disapproval, stopping short of winking at us.

As a modern boy with a Playstation 2 back home, I resent being reminded of this type of Blackness out in the world once a week for ninety minutes at a time. My classmates' occasional yawns and glimpses at the gruesome footage of a movie like *Hotel Rwanda* feel personal. I don't want them to imagine this as being my past. My house had two gardens. We had maids.

I hate being associated with the Blackness Mirault traffics in. I don't understand how this amounted to a history class, so I skip five or six classes in a row. I sit in a bus stop around the corner from the school building and read the mangas I've stuffed into my backpack until my mom finally gets a call.

"School is *not* optional, ever," my mom rages at me that night, angrier than she's ever been. I slam the door to my room like a properly misunderstood teenager and she rants while ironing my uniform and then we don't talk for two days. We're a household of two, which feels right even in moments like this. Linkin Park gets it, and everyone else is a poser.

I never again miss a single class with Mirault. I practice zoning out and nodding along to his rants while he makes meaningful eye contact with me, clearly wishing my insides were chocolate-stuffed instead of the regular standard Nabisco white filling.

It's not always hatred or disdain that makes your skin crawl. In fact, sometimes, it's the exact opposite: Some people will easily love your Blackness. They will respond to it, gravitate toward it, see it before they even see the rest of you. And once they see it and classify it into their preferred category, they won't bother to look any further. The rest of you is just a skeleton holding up that beautiful Black skin.

ELEVEN

HOW TO GO THROUGH LIFE WITHOUT DROWNING, PART II

As it turns out—and without taking away from the tragedy of those who've lost loved ones to drowning—it's fairly easy for me not to drown.

Occasionally, it takes renewed commitment.

When I sat in front of *The Shallows*, a 2016 survival horror movie in which Blake Lively plays a surfer stalked by an unreasonably persistent great white, my sympathies were with the shark. The apex predator belonged in that water: Blake Lively did not. I could not buy into the fiction of this seven-foot-tall blond woman desperately trying to survive through the night. You could have been home, Blake. You're playing a beautiful young woman, full of life . . . Go get some takeout and go home: Why are you in the ocean by yourself? Why didn't your mama say no? Blake didn't respect the water and thus had to pay for her sins.

To this day, I tend to victim-blame people who come back from vacation with green hair or complaining about anything other than getting sunburnt at the beach. Slipping on a rock while climbing waterfalls during your spring break trip to Cenote Tres Oches of Homún, Mexico, and breaking an ankle? Why were you there? Who told you that would be a good idea? Were you taking a selfie? Like, why would you put yourself in that position? Respect the waters, for they are deep and insidious.

(This will all be 40 percent more poignant if I end up drowning one day.)

I'M FIFTEEN, and Francis L. invites everyone to his parents' cabin in the middle of the summer. I'm invited in the sense that I was included in the email that went out to thirty-eight people. The few who were omitted are purposeful and fuel hours of suburban high school gossip across phones and passive-aggressive Facebook posts. We get bored in the summers.

My mom is initially thrilled. She's always happy when I get out of the house and socialize. She doesn't want our fatherless home to leave me asocial and misshapen. I understand where she's coming from; I'm already getting fat. Like me, she takes a lot of comfort in the few instances in which I socialize on a large scale like this. The occasional big party, or a night out to Montreal in a group with three girls from the nerd lunchroom table we share. The table of high school girls who discreetly carry notebooks dedicated to tracking their diets and lemonades laced with cayenne pepper to school and where I'm always welcome and feel at home.

"Go! Go have fun!" Mom says. She's working now, and no longer just sits there watching me go to school with crisp freshly ironed clothes.

"It's at a lake," I say. "In Magog."

My mom's eyes widen.

It's an unspoken rule of our new two-head household. Local pools in backyards were fine. They're communal holes—relatively safe, transparent, uniform, guarded—in which I'm free to paddle around; but natural holes, those always get that look from her. Julie Smith's memory has not faded.

"You'll go to the next one," she says, apologetically. It's fine. I'll go to the next one.

As it turns out, being an only child comes with extraordinary pressure not to die. I sometimes wonder if my mother's Black worry was any different from the worry of mothers everywhere. Probably not. My friends' white moms probably also worried about the strange bodies of water their kids would occasionally wander into without supervision. Maybe every mother carries that same burden of worry, regardless of race or creed. Maybe what was different in my mother's case was the additional dread that having taken a Black child from Haiti only to have them drown in a lake of Magog, Quebec, would indeed be nothing short of "nonsense."

TWELVE

BOOMERANGS COME BACK

I'M FIFTEEN and, somewhere between Linkin Park and My Chemical Romance blaring, with some mainstream Kanye slipping in, and the near-constant state of boyish self-discovery that I find myself in within my bedroom, I don't see it coming. *Him* coming back, that is.

"Why are we talking about Dad again?" I ask bluntly with a frown when he comes up in too precise of an anecdote, free of vitriol, around the dinner table.

"He called," Mom says, and I spend my day steeped in enough gossip to know that tone, complete with a sly private look, like a teenager keeping a secret they want you to ask about for the thrill just so they can deny it.

Goddammit. Between high school, the emergence of man tits, and this powerful new advanced form of pubescent horniness, my mind had been elsewhere. Harboring crushes on classmates, talking with strangers on the internet, the wholesome tenets of teenagedom had distracted me from the return of my father to our lives. The better life he had promised us from his office in

Haiti had been cashed in without him. His presense was no longer required! The teenage iteration of these complex thoughts was a groan and slamming of the fridge door followed by a weekend of unsupervised Kazaa pornography. (God, you don't know what Kazaa is, do you? Illegal. It means illegal. Please stop attacking me with your insufferable youth.)

I hated the looming intruder he now was, crawling back toward what was supposed to be our doorstep, hers and mine, two hours away from the one he'd left her in. I hated how I had to pretend to be happy to be a family of three again, mourning the awesome single-parent-and-emotionally-thriving-while-being-fully-broke family of two we previously were.

When I tried to prevent it, it was already too late. I began eavesdropping on the other phone (one landline but three phones because my mom liked one in every room) occasionally—fine, compulsively—fearing the worst. They had been talking on the phone for weeks. Not like teenagers do after school, crapping on classmates, but instead talking about things like finances and rent. How the money he was paying in rent for his sister's basement in Cote-des-Neiges, Montreal, where he had been staying, after having burnt out in his most recent attempt to leave wife and child/children behind and start over in Haiti with a new younger woman of means, could serve *our* household. Careful use of pronouns was always one of his strong suits.

"I could fix that," he would say of a sink he couldn't fix. "I buy a lot of paper towels. I can drop a few rolls by." To her, it sounded like a new and better paper towel than the ones we dragged home on the bus, two rolls at a time every week because buying bulk is a luxury meant for car owners. I pictured gray, rough, industrial towels and remembered how our quilted toilet paper would turn single-ply the second he moved back in.

They gossip. Bits of gossip about people they knew or still know. How other people heard about us and liked to gossip—getting back together would show them.

Mom liked the familiarity because otherwise she'd be sitting alone at the table, staring. Being a little sad never translates to being a little happy for her. She always wants to be happy; *only* happy. And a little bit of sadness is not something you just live with. You chase it out with radio, TV, phone calls, and neighbors. *Baye audience*, in Creole; shooting the shit. Strangely enough, I had never accounted for the fact that my mom might love, genuinely love, her husband.

"Don't make that face," she would say when I glared at her after I hung up the phone she would push into my face to make me say hi to him and tell him about my schoolwork.

"He's your father. I can hate him but you can't. You should remember the good times." People always say that, failing to acknowledge the main flaw in that advice, which is that those "Good Times" file cabinets are sometimes filled with faded facsimile receipts; small moments that can be presumed to have been there at some point but were not properly preserved.

"Life would be easier if he was here with us, no?"

She partly meant money.

He had his retirement fund, a steady check every month from his first stay when he taught high school in Canada.

"I have a job," I say. "I chip in." I shouldn't have bought the iPod. It reminded her she lived with a child who didn't like to make conversation.

"He has a new car." A dark burgundy Subaru that looked wealthier than its leaser. That car was the only thing on the pro/con list I saw of value in Robert's return to our lives, considering neither Mom nor I knew how to drive.

"I like taking the bus," I try, but eventually, after two dinners at Au Vieux Duluth, my favorite restaurant chain where as a child I was once berated for wanting ice cream on top of my $14.99 plate of shrimp on my birthday, I lose the battle.

Robert begins to plan his move back in with us.

Three-person households work best with a common enemy, and it was clear that I alone would be waging the battle against Robert's return. The condo was ours, with many asterisks, loans, and co-signees; he would have less power, he would be more polite. Her logic was both sound and stupid considering the man we were dealing with. No zookeeper puts a lion in a panda habitat thinking the lion will mind his manners.

"I love you, son," he said at the door, with his two bags of dirty clothes, ready to settle into the guest bedroom upstairs and inch his way back into our new life. He'd flamed out in Haiti, and his offering to the teenager he was coming back to Canada for a trial reunion with was a sloppily folded red *101 Dalmatians* T-shirt and a pair of matching shorts I used to wear when I was a toddler. He extended them from his backpack at the door, as if he'd rehearsed it in the car and couldn't wait for a more intimate moment.

There was something in his voice. It wasn't fondness, not quite. It was the memory of fondness, an echo. He might have believed it, too, I now realize. Holding that bundle of clothes, sweepingly extending them to his fat offspring, he might have actually believed he loved me or wanted to so badly that the difference between actual love and wanting to love was now negligible.

"I don't have a bedtime anymore," I answered from the top of the stairs, annoyed by how moved Mom looked by the awkward declaration. You have to set boundaries early with vagrants you take in.

"Well, we can discuss it," he chuckles.

"No," I repeat. "There's no bedtime here."

There was a brief flicker of disdain in his eyes that I know that high school me, all greasy forehead and hoodied, standing at a meaty five-feet-eight and 180 pounds, would have happily returned, but with Mom looking at both of us—her family—he eked out a truce with a forced laugh. This theater encapsulates our following year of vague animosity skirting one another's existence around a condo in Greenfield Park, Quebec, seven minutes away from Montreal.

"I don't have a bedtime anymore" was a catchall for all the things I couldn't explicitly say at the time.

I don't go to bed at 9 p.m., because I have real homework now. Stuff you maybe don't even know. Mitosis, motherfucker. Do you even know mitosis, bro?

I'm going to watch so much European porn with the door to my room wide open. Do something about it. I dare you.

No, you don't. Why are you lying?

You wouldn't be here if she was stronger, and we both know it, old man. Aren't you embarrassed? You dreamt bigger than us and failed. How many new siblings do I have now?

I don't pout. The three of us converse without communicating. He assumes I'll be applying to McGill soon. The local college with affordable Canadian tuition. About $5,000 a year for Quebec residents, or something.

"I'll help you fill out the application," he says one day, and Mom smiles. "If you want."

"Thanks, Dad."

"If I was around, I wouldn't have let you two buy this condo," he says, looking around with vague disdain at the home he was borrowing, turning the tiny guest bedroom into his office.

"The location, the layout," he sniffs. "It's all wrong."

"It's all wrong," I repeat casually, eating cereal, standing by the fridge, floating above my body vibrating with rage.

Mom smiles and cleans the kitchen counter more ferociously and pretends she didn't move heaven and earth to get us this little corner of the world, being dismissed in her own kitchen. She doesn't look up. She doesn't have to. Making eye contact with me at the moment might incinerate her. I blame her, not him.

I make myself smaller and bigger all at once, staying in my room and spending a lot of time on the internet. I keep my paychecks from work to myself entirely. The fighting starts again and I don't even bother listening in. I don't enjoy reruns. I order delivery, collect it at the door, and eat it in my room over SAT prep books as I plan my exit. Every SAT practice test taken in my room is another spoonful of dirt I'm shoveling out.

When I reemerge from my room, five months later, fatter and a bit feral, to eat dinner at the kitchen table again, Dad is gone. Back to Haiti again. It was a mutual decision, I'm told. People don't change. None of us had. All three of us had stayed the same as we were in Sherbrooke, only now older.

I must have said goodbye, I simply don't remember it. I move his furniture to the curb that weekend without Mom having to ask. She makes my favorite chicken and prepares my favorite potato dish in the oven that evening.

"He was mean," she says while we're watching television one night, mostly just not to stare right at each other now that we're back to two. "So effortlessly mean."

"He's gone now," I summarize and wrap up all at once. I hate reruns.

"We were supposed to have more children here," she says a few minutes into the nightly news.

"What?"

"Once we were settled in Canada." She shrugs. "That was the plan. To give you little siblings to look after. Only children grow up crooked."

It sounds like the slightly awkward translation of some Creole saying.

"You'd have been a good big brother." She smiles, patting my neck, sad but smiling. Would I have been a good sibling? Maybe, maybe not. One of the perks of being alone is that there is no one around to reflect how crooked you are. I like that open space that lets my branches flare out in awkward and contradictory directions.

Even before it was made into a literal exit, my father always lived *elsewhere*. This elsewhere-lived was in the maps in his office, the books on his shelves written in languages I couldn't understand, the next wife he hadn't met but believed to be a given when the time came. The man I knew dreamt big and, for better or worse, always put his dreams first.

Occasionally, Dad has aspirations of Haitian politics and connections. Of being the next Aristide or Lavalas. Big loaded names that the Haitian diaspora still gossip about to this day. People worthy of worship in their communities. Dictators who put burning tires around the necks of dissidents. (It's the harsh side of Haiti that our big red gates protected me from as a kid and that he sought to raise me away from, and I get that and am grateful for it.)

For the record, I sincerely do not resent him for leaving. Nor are there any lingering questions in my mind. I almost worry that I should probably have cared more, at some point. The indifference sometimes feels too vast for comfort. Though ultimately, I much prefer to be left with the shoes to fill than the feet here to fill them. People come into your life for a reason or a season, right? The season was my childhood and early teens, and the reason was to give me the world. (On top of the whole, y'know, conception thing.) The man was a proud mountain with greed in his eyes and fire in his belly and I'm grateful for the sliver of whatever it all amounts to.

Black communities, especially in America, are often put on trial for the literal sins of their fathers. It's that familiar refrain of "Where are these thugs' fathers?" "No wonder they're all rioting in the streets!"

That notion is not only overly simplistic but largely inaccurate. It also dismisses the presence and agency of non-head-of-household Black fathers who continue to parent through cohabitation, visitation, mentorship, providing important albeit nontraditional support. And that is without even getting into the fact that these Black men getting incarcerated or killed at a systematically higher rate all over America also have children at home whom society will not think twice about until it is time to punish them for the sin of having been raised without a nuclear-family-model father figure. I am not equipped to pull at that thread in any coherent manner, so allow me to recommend some books.

BOOKS YOU SHOULD READ IF THE BREEZY BEACH-READ
TOPIC OF SYSTEMICALLY BROKEN BLACK
FAMILIES INTERESTS YOU:

- *The Color of Law: A Forgotten History of How Our Government Segregated America* by Richard Rothstein
- *The Myth of the Missing Black Father* by Roberta Coles, PhD (editor), and Charles Green, PhD (Disclaimer: This one is a big ole expensive schoolbook, but it is a very important one.)

THIRTEEN

FROM ANOTHER MOTHER

I'M SIXTEEN again, looking ahead to two full months of summer vacation before the eleventh grade, and ready to be a man. Now, this requires a few precise things, namely facial hair and a job. I have no facial hair yet. It will burst out of my face at age twenty and not a day before. One of the two will suffice for now.

My head is almost perfectly spherical these days, my ties are flat and wide. They look borrowed but were actually purchased online.

I get very few callbacks, but one gets traction quickly.

The man who interviews me is Black. I know this because throughout our four-minute phone interview he senses it in my voice and asks me point-blank before moving on to the next point of my overstuffed two-page résumé filled with interests in things that don't interest me in the least, like "kayaking" and "world issues." The energy would have shifted if one of us had been white. I wouldn't have been told to come in.

Upon arriving at the grocery store for more interviewing, I further learn that he is in his early thirties, has a closely shaved head, easy smile, and, if I had to guess, works out a lot without dieting. His handshake is strong, and I admire his posture.

None of his co-managers, cashiers, stock people, or the receptionist is Black. Yet, he is at the front of the poster on the bulletin board at the lobby of the grocery store, crossing his arms confidently and showing all his teeth.

"Rubeintz," I say. "Or Ben." *Pick your own name,* you tell yourself. *Isn't that what immigrants do sometimes? No one is stopping you.* "Thunderous Nomad Knight" was a close second.

"Roger," he says as he introduces himself and escorts me through the aisles. "Let's go up to my office. I imagine you already know what a grocery store looks like."

He has tired eyes but the vibe of someone who comes alive on specific occasions—his arms are extended to encompass everyone into the office photo framed in the corner of his small, well-lit office.

The interview goes well. I have the conviction of the well-researched sixteen-year-old with dreams of a GameCube, Xbox, and PS2 all lined up under my bedroom television. The job itself amounts to designing the weekly flyer for promotions and posting them both online and in print. The branch wants a local identity on top of the safety of being a countrywide retailer.

I flip through the Bible-thin pages of the weekly flyer, with deals in red blocky font bursting out of yellow thought bubbles.

"Yeah, I can definitely do this!" I say, trying to be charming. "And I'm not just saying that because this is an interview and stuff."

Two dollars over minimum wage. I'm sixteen, without experience, the position is low enough and temporary enough that I want it. I don't risk running into anyone from my high school there.

"You're four years old, dude." He smiles. "How do you know Photoshop?"

He's funny.

"Up until last year," he explains, "we didn't even have Photoshop, or, like, a Facebook page. Just some fucker playing around with printout pages and an X-Acto knife and glue stick."

I get the teenage thrill of hearing an adult casually curse and instantly decide that I like him. I would like to work for him, chit-chatting like this all summer.

"Photoshop, a Facebook account . . . you're turning this place around." I smile.

It's emboldened and dickish but he takes it in good humor and laughs. He doesn't have a ring on his finger and there's no framed photo of himself with another person claiming ownership sitting on his desk. I suspect there would be stories of dates.

"I should hire a white kid," he eventually sighs, at ease after a few questions about my favorite subject in school.

"Um, what?"

"If I hire you, everyone is going to think it was because we're both Black," he says. "Trust me, it's a thing."

I nod. The logic tracks. I'm already learning about the real world. He leans back into his swivel chair and assesses me with crossed arms, how the visual might play out.

"Okay, first the name, now . . . Weird question," he interrupts. "But, what's your father's name?" His eyes narrow into focus and he stares directly at me.

"Robert."

He repeats the name. "Robert . . . Do you have an aunt here?"

I have aunts. Everyone has aunts. Well, I suppose the children of only children don't but they're—

"Atalante," he continues before I can work out the math. "Do you have an aunt Atalante?"

"I have an aunt Atalante," I finally say, having completed the equation.

Neither of us says it. He has an aunt Atalante, too.

Again, for context: I'm my mother's only child and my father's seventh chronological. He had six from his first marriage and two from his third, after my mother. So, nine legitimate children in total. A few not-so-legitimate ones, too, I imagine. Don't pick up my father's used condoms if you're ovulating.

"Well, shit," he eventually says, stunned, through a laugh. "Shit!"

I don't say anything. I wish this was an interview again.

Do half-brothers share the same blood type? No, right?

Do you watch anime? Who do you like more, Naruto or Sasuke?

Do you miss your mom? I heard she died. How much of you dies when your mom dies? 95 percent or 99 percent?

I'm sorry she died and your dad left for Haiti to find a new wife. I'm sorry he nutted and now here I am.

"I knew you were around," he continues. "We all heard when he came back. I just . . ."

All? Does he mean his siblings? Our siblings?

He glances down at my résumé for the last time. ". . . I thought you'd be younger, I guess."

"Yeah, um, you too."

I suddenly feel a reckless sort of pity for him. Roger was the youngest one from the previous collector set. He was the saddest story I'd picked up on overtime.

When Dad left for Haiti, Roger had moved in with one of his mother's sisters while my dad got to work wooing a newly available twenty-seven-year-old nurse who turned out to be my mother. There were rumors of Roger getting kicked out by his aunt, doing drugs, getting arrested, falling off the map. Things that my dad could be blamed for. Instead, he had ended up here: working at a grocery store. Fed and reliable, wearing dress shirts with rolled-up sleeves.

"Do you think we look alike?" he asks, still glancing at me as he escorts me back to the front of the store, hands in his pocket. The interview was over a million questions ago. He doesn't seem upset. Just curious.

"I don't know," I say. No, we don't.

A strange bit of math occurs in my head. I'm better looking than him, which means that my mom was better looking than his. That's how genetics work, right?

How many times did he belt you? I want to ask. *You can have him back, y'know: we don't want him.*

Since that episode, I've gotten into the regular habit of look-ing up my potential siblings online (basically anyone with the last name Philippe who lives in one of the cities he's frequented) and imagining the narrative of their lives without engaging. There are a few. Very round heads, our bloodline. More questions.

"Dad sure is something, huh?" He exhales, staying inside the lobby as the glass doors slide open for me.

I give him an extended handshake that he returns, back straight and professional again.

He smiles and gives me a curt head nod. "Well, good luck with everything. Let's stay in touch, yeah?"

"Definitely."

My mom's prettier than yours, dude.

I don't tell Mom I had run into this boy, now a man, that she had occasionally mused about being a stepmother to had Dad only brought him to Haiti with him.

I spend that summer working at a bookstore in downtown Montreal. It takes an hour to get there each day, but I like the smell of new, unboxed books and the downtown hustle. I never hear from him again. The man had, like, a chip on his shoulder about the whole dad thing. You hate to see it.

Hi, Ben! So, um, I think we might be . . . half-siblings? Should I reach out? I have proof?

Yikes. This is awkward.

Honestly? You wouldn't be the first. And while I might even believe you, I promise you that #FathersDay trending on social media is no reason to send me an email. You won't find what you're looking for here. We got his good hair and piercing eyes: that's enough of a beautiful bond, right? Let's not ruin it by getting to know each other. I've got limited emotional bandwidth at this point. Think of us as Sand Snakes scattered to the wind. (If you do not get that reference then you do not read the A Song of Ice and Fire series and you already will never be my family.)

I nevertheless wish you all the happiness in the world, though. Really! It's very cool that you're Dutch.

FOURTEEN

I WAS PROMISED BALLPLAYERS AND RAP STARS, ADDICTED TO THE LIMELIGHT

Somewhere along the way, I also discover I'm smart and head off to Columbia University. No, scratch that.

You don't just head off to an Ivy League college with a 6 percent admission rate and 10.9 billion USD endowment. You also don't just "discover" that you're smart like it's a mole on your lower back while brushing your teeth in the shower one day. That was just a needlessly self-deprecating lie.

Take two: I'm fucking smart and I get into Columbia University.

If it sounds cocky to say, I apologize, but a non-negligible percentage of the world thinks my skin color puts me closer to a monkey than to a human and I'm writing this at a time during which the most powerful politician on earth routinely makes sweeping statements about the IQ of my entire race from his ketchup-and-tanning-spray-residue-coated phone. Now, I will own up that I am categorically not "street-smart" and I've given entirely too many digits of my credit card number to telemarketers before realizing what was happening and throwing my phone across the couch with a delayed gasp, but I could down a bottle of Bacardi 151 and tank that asshole in an IQ test. I lucked out and got the type of smarts that does well enough on standardized tests.

I never doubted I was smart. The more stupid people you interact with, the easier the fact sits with you. Honestly, spend ten minutes reading replies on Twitter and you'll want to submit your brain for both study and display after your death. Even when shoving a wrinkled C– calculus quiz into my backpack in a flush of embarrassment or breaking into frustrated tears trying to put together an Ikea bookshelf. In those moments, I doubted the existential soundness of quadratic equations and the insidiousness of ready-to-assemble furniture from the dastardly Swedes, but not my intelligence. I sometimes wonder if all of Robert's children across the globe share this weird confidence. *Sure, our dad was a big ho, but we sure read them books güüd.*

It's more accurate to say that I committed—during that all-important window from ages sixteen to eighteen—to the incoming wave of standardized exams, R-Score (a nonsensical Quebec grading system), and GPA that all amount to a North American education. My smarts paid off. I'm good at all-nighters and I don't have much else going on. Video games have gotten dull. And just like that, the future is unlocked.

DRIVE-BY READING RECOMMENDATIONS:

- *SAT for Dummies*
- *Calculus II for Dummies*

Okay, real talk: those yellow For Dummies books saved my GPA so many times, I cannot even tell you. They are better written than most academic textbooks out there. Sure, the cover is embarrassing, especially when you have to purchase it in person, but whatever your ethnicity, there is no shame in being bad at math. Especially calculus. My God, can calculus gobble it. Derivative these nuts, Isaac Newton and Gottfried Wilhelm Leibniz. You too, Archimedes. Get in there; don't be shy.

To this day, I don't think I've wanted anything as badly as I wanted one of those big envelopes. In the end, I get three big ones and four small ones that regret to inform me they're blah blah blah . . . I don't even open them. The written rejections will be reaffirmed via email later, anyway.

The other two big ones are good, really good, but without need-blind financial assistance for international students—which Canadians very much are—they are nonstarters. (Mom has $700 in American dollars in savings, and that makes it a good year for us.)

In the end, Columbia is the only yes without asterisks attached, and for a brief second, opening that "Congratulations!" email, my atheism wavers. Columbia University was the one to hit me in my toes at the mailbox. I read that email and felt it in my actual toes. Blame Rory Gilmore and seven consecutive seasons of *Gilmore Girls* slowly indoctrinating me to the privileged elitism of higher education. Blame *Gossip Girl* and all the establishing shots painting Manhattan as the mecca from which all rap songs were born. Kanye West's entire discography becomes my song in one envelope. My high school and CEGEP friends are already downgraded to good acquaintances from my past in my mind.

I needed a story, my own story, away from Robert's brood and Mom's dashed dreams, and it will now be an American tale. *I'm* Fievel Mousekewitz, and I'll belong there.

I'm Pam Beesly going off to an arts program in New York City instead of staying in Scranton and getting saddled to Jim's insecurities. I'm Jon Snow ranging north toward the unknown wildlings. (Technically south, but you know what I mean.) I'm Dolores riding a speedboat away from Westworld hidden inside a different robot's body.

Mom's and my aimless search for vague upward mobility finds a brand: *the American Dream*. Not North American, not French Canadian. American.

The one with the Second Amendment; 'Murica with the giant houses and crowded inner cities. 'Murica. Land of Oprah and Madea. Struggle and opportunity in equal measures at every corner, where your life might be a sad ballad, or a chart-topping song, or elevator music. If you don't know what your Blackness means yet, I highly recommend moving to the United States: they will tell you very quickly.

To ensure that your Columbia University ID is awaiting you at a kiosk on College Walk in a few months, you are to send a photo ahead along with the letter accepting said future and all the stories waiting for you inside of it.

The photographer at the local Quebec pharmacy back home, 370 miles away, is meant for bigger things, and reading over the instructions carefully, he looks at the clock wistfully. There's a bandaged tattoo on his arm, peeking from under his Pharmaprix polo, still fresh and not ready to be uncovered. I'm the last in line and he wants to go home. "It says I'm not supposed to use the flash." I come out as an outline more than a person. If the purpose is identification, then I'm the most recognizable, featureless blob of blackness that appears to possibly have ears.

"Is that okay?" He sighs, dreading that it won't be. "Dude, I'm a Rorschach test," the current me might say. But I'm grateful for the big envelope waiting for me at home and I don't want the universe to punish me for forgetting my station at the photo kiosk, so I nod politely that it is.

"What's it for?"

"A school ID."

"Shouldn't you be taking that at the school? McGill? Concordia?" he inquires, slipping into his coat.

"Columbia University."

"Cool, yeah, I love BC," he says, thinking British Columbia. "I have cousins there. It's not very diverse, though."

I stare.

"Anyway, yeah, you'll be fine with that photo. It's just an ID. Good luck."

I lick the envelope and then lick it again, sealing the rim tight before also wrapping the sides in scotch tape to make sure nothing slips out. It's my ticket to America, the place that has been advertised since Haiti. Canada with jazz fingers and a snazzy jacket. The land of Martin Luther King Jr. and civil rights where all the television I watch is made. America: land of dreams where they also gendered the green M&M and made her horny for some truly inexplicable reason, I think, munching on some M&Ms on the ride home that night.

"This is a gift," Mom repeats at various points that summer before I head off to Columbia, sometimes out of nowhere. To herself more than to me.

We take a Greyhound bus from Montreal to New York City. My aunt and uncle will meet us there the next day, flying in from

Florida. They want to visit the city and my mother's English isn't that great.

"It's a very fancy school, Belzie," Aunt Louisa says. "You can't show up there and not be able to communicate. It will look bad on all Haitians."

My own English doesn't factor into the equation—I'm the teenage package being delivered, after all—I shouldn't have the responsibility of translating my own drop-off. My aunt puts family first in a way I don't always understand but will always envy.

We get into Port Authority, Manhattan, New York, at 12:23 a.m. Some timestamps you make a point to remember. My two bags are filled to the limit, leaving the nylon stretched and tearing. Mom has packed candles and matches in all the side pockets. One of them will break apart on the elevator ride to my dorm. She spent the summer overwhelmed, both happy and sad, all at once, because her son got a full ride to Columbia University, in America, and away from her. Ultimately, the woman will never experience a single shred of doubt in her faith, let alone contemplate atheism, because of that fact.

The cab screws us over, and a simple ride from Port Authority to a Days Inn on 94th Street costs us nearly $60. I like being screwed over by a New York City cabbie on my first night there. It's already a story.

Mom and I share one room with two beds on a smokers' floor because of some mixup in the reservation. We smile and I bump my head into Mom's shoulder on the elevator ride up to the small bedroom via a cigarette smoke–drenched hallway. The hotel could assign us a smoker to puff a cigar into our faces all night, we would not care. *This is a gift.*

"Do you wish your dad was here?" my uncle asks me as we move me into my dorm the next day with my mom and aunt lingering behind.

It's not a strange question from an uncle. I understand his need to ask it. "A little," I say with a performative small shrug of the shoulder. I don't, but I know it's the answer he wants to hear. I occasionally ask about him to be viewed like the sort of kid who asks about their dad. A good person. It's a script.

My dad is back in Haiti now. He has already met a new wife. She, too, will be moved to Canada. The third wife to be sold the same dream, only at an even younger age than my mom was. He doesn't have new stories. Just the same one he replays over and over again, expecting a different outcome with new players.

Mom and I say goodbye at Port Authority later that evening as she takes an eight-hour bus ride back to Montreal, alone. My uncle and aunt offered to accompany us, but Mom and I wanted our last bit of time alone. She has a nursing job waiting for her. She's the private nurse for a woman suffering from advanced arthritis in the neighboring town of Brossard, Quebec.

She will fall into a depression and find her way out of it. I won't hear about it until it's an anecdote she can wave off in mid-conversation. That time she broke her thumb as a kid. That time she stayed in bed for twelve days because I got busy and we didn't talk for twelve days. But for now, we say goodbye in the grimy basement of Port Authority, by Gate 2 where French Canadians can be heard buzzing in line.

The last thing she does before we part ways is sign the cross on me twice. First, she draws a small one on my forehead with her index finger, and then she covers my whole being with a second large one, touching my forehead, chest, left shoulder, and then right shoulder.

"I don't believe in this," I say, annoyed and now officially adult, in a fresh Columbia University sweatshirt.

"You don't have to." She shrugs as she does it again, like she did when she was tying my tie before sending me off to my interview with my half-brother three years ago.

"This is a gift," she repeats in French-Creole hybrid, which is all we still speak to each other.

I watch her go with the ID card in my hands. The ID card is an impeccable laminated card that will let this blob of black be identified anywhere on campus. Rubeintz B. Philippe, not so much. I look at the requirements for graduation, and I decide to keep it. For three years, security guards will look at me and frown when checking into dorms, friends will laugh at how I could be any Black guy.

I ride the subway back to campus alone. I have to read a chunk of *The Iliad* before a general assembly for my Literary Humanities course, and begin a lifetime of missing my stop going uptown and backtracking on the downtown train, pretending that was the plan all along.

Some people say New York City is overwhelming to newcomers, but it isn't to me. It feels right. The bustle reminds me of the flashes of Haitian markets on the edge of my mind, only with fewer women carrying baskets on their heads. I feel safer in the crowds, that mass of bodies pouring out of trains at Times Square and 42nd Street, than in the wide, empty suburban streets of Sherbrooke. There are stories here. They've been waiting for me.

"C'est un cadeau."

FIFTEEN

SURE, I'LL BE YOUR WOKE BLACK FRIEND

I spend nine days with a roommate who is very nice but plays a lot of early-morning tennis, which is certainly a lifestyle choice. My only memories of him will be half-asleep glimpses of him spreading out his wet towel to dry at 5:30 a.m., after a post-run shower. He is the only human being I've ever seen chug a solid banana.

I think we were expected to be friends because we are both international students, but we truly have nothing in common. He is white, tall, with a square white forehead and white barrel chest, looking like an Eastern European model from the Winklevoss collection. His accent and mine don't harmonize.

"My family comes to New York every summer," he says as we politely reconfigure furniture. "I've been here since June."

"My mother and I took the bus one day ago," I answer.

He looks confused.

"You said Canada."

"Yeah, it's around ten hours on a Greyhound."

Opposites don't always attract or repulse: sometimes they just smile and nod a lot.

I want a single very badly and end up doing a room swap two weeks in with someone who desperately wants a roommate for the full college experience. I do, too, but not all at once, not if it's farting in shared air and wondering if I snored the night before. I have a man's body now. The beard is almost here and the pubes need trimming. I need a single room. I'll become friendly at a slower pace that doesn't have me excuse myself to the library four buildings away at 11 p.m. when I need a long poop that requires enough privacy for self-actualization.

My years as an undergraduate student of Columbia University are best summarized as a series of questions rather than stories.

Was my admission a fluke? Will everyone be cartoonishly rich? Did everyone here already read *The Iliad* in high school? Should I get an internship right away? Shouldn't Viacom be rich enough to pay all of MTV's interns something? What does "making connections" even mean? Am I smart enough to pull off a triple major in economics, creative writing, and sociology? (No.) What is "Four Loko"? Is that James Franco? Will you please get this Four Loko away from me before I vomit at the memory? How many meals can you afford with $17.84 in your bank account? When was the last time I spoke to Mom, again? Wait, what do you mean graduation is in three days? Why are all these blue-haired fiction majors now comparing Wall Street incentive packages or heading to Harvard Law? What's a life plan? Where can I get this wrinkled graduation gown pressed in two hours? What is this salty water in my eyeballs? What's supposed to happen next?

If I mostly remember college as a series of questions on fast-forward, the city of New York itself, on the other hand, provides some much-needed answers. It doesn't matter if you don't know who you are when you get here: the pressure cooker of New York City will tell you. I'll leave the mystique to HBO's programming and simply summarize New York as a magical place where three days without a belligerent person screaming at you on the subway is a good streak. You're very proud of living in a city surrounded by so many art venues you only visit when people are in from out of town. You will spot someone you know and like coming your way down the street and pray to *God* they don't see you. You regularly mismanage your small amount of money and end up buying a $14.99 notebook at Strand Bookstore even though you have a stack of cheap $2.99 ones at home because, presumably, this is the one that will finally make you a real writer. New York City is about three years of reading on the subway and never once making that stupid "Hot Dudes Reading On the Subway" Tumblr. Like, not even by accident. Bah! I'm telling you, it's a conspiracy.

Finally, New York—at least the New York of that time— was just so many plastic bags. A plethora of plastic bags. Grocery stores, pharmacies, food delivery: it's constant. You bring your reusable bag to the store and before it's even out of your hand, the cashier has already double-wrapped your stick of gum in two bags. You become vaguely environmentally conscious. Or, at least environmentally aware. On the other hand, you also harden yourself to walking by a string of twelve beggars without taking your headphones off. That's not necessarily a good thing, but it's needed here. You become lean, frugal, subway hard and Central Park– sunset soft, all at once. Here, you're allowed to live as a Black guy instead of experiencing being the Black guy. Trust me, the difference between the two is a canyon.

Years later, at my graduation, my uncle will admit that he was terrified for me upon dropping me off. *"You were just a fat, sweaty little boy! I was sure this city was going to eat you alive. But look at you now. You survived!"* he'll say with a proud hand on the shoulder of my graduation robe.

My extended family isn't always great at compliments. Anyway, graduation is getting ahead of ourselves.

THANKS, OBAMA

My first year of college, the air of New York City was thick with Obama. This was 2009 Obama. "First time around" Obama. The HOPE™ of what could be if a Black man somehow became president of the United States. That blue-and-red "Hope" poster was already peppered across dorm rooms alongside the likes of Malcolm X, Toni Morrison, and MLK.

Despite being an international student who cannot vote, I easily get caught up in the Black & Proud Obama frenzy, which unites everyone from the Black Student Organizations to the nineteen-year-old socialist poets in hoping for a Democratic victory. Barack Hussein Obama was a Black friend to all and, within this Ivy League bubble, we are all rooting for him. Obama had himself attended Columbia years prior—an experience he apparently abhorred because he has, to this day, never given a speech there—but we still take any credit for him. We, Columbia University. We, Democrats. We, Black people everywhere.

Columbia is hands down the most liberal environment a minority student can ask for after the Sherbrooke years. It's the land of calls to action, often against the very institution we all so proudly moved into not too long ago. There are Reserve Officer Training Corps protests and hunger strikes held by children whose ID cards grant them access to state-of-the-art food halls where we throw away the patty of the burger to lessen the total calorie count, all half a mile away from a then-rapidly gentrifying Harlem. That dissonance is rarely malicious but will often be lost on a lot of the peers I interact with.

"I almost wish he hadn't won," sighs my floormate Benjamin—white, tall, with theater aspirations and the talent to boot—watching CNN in the common room, the day after Obama's election.

"You literally put his poster on our door, dude." His roommate Chris, another transfer, laughs.

"Yeah, I know," Benjamin muses aloud, still watching the TV. He seems conflicted by his own opinion. "I just don't want him to sell out."

"What do you mean?" I ask, genuinely curious.

"You don't become POTUS without serving a lot of masters."

There's a silence I don't understand until all eyes are on me. I start to notice that I'm still, somehow, often the only Black person in the multicultural hubs I find myself in.

"Don't say that!" Min, a second-generation Korean American girl from one floor below, instantly chastises. It's as if the N-word has just been dropped. She likes talking to me when we cross paths in the kitchen and we mutually bemoan our dual unpaid internships and the fact that simply being students without working on résumés would somehow feel luxurious.

"Oh, n-no," Benjamin catches himself, suddenly dark pink because he's one of those white people who come preinstalled with a very clear color chart. "I didn't mean, like, *master*-master!"

I know Benjamin didn't mean anything by it, but I've been a

college student long enough now to be performatively offended on behalf of a cute girl. Benjamin goes to bed early.

When the small group shrinks down to Min and I, I again receive her well-intentioned sympathies and later, on that same couch, her woke fellatio as reparation for a slight she hadn't committed and that I hadn't felt. Later that night, I receive a text from Benjamin, hoping there are no hard feelings. The next time we cross paths, I salute the Obama poster on Benjamin and Chris's door. I'm starting to get this country.

Columbia's larger Black ecosystem is also thriving and disparate. No two Black people here are alike. Well. That's not entirely true. Some of them are figurative clones of one another, hailing from the same corners of the map, having the same interests and championing the same causes. Fortunately, however, these profiles are varied and I meet my fair share of jocks, artists, activists, Black Republicans, fellow awkward half-bakeds looking around with big eyes and scurrying back to their dorm rooms. "Black" is no longer the first word that defines these people to me. And amid all the interpersonal growth and kindred spirits, I also meet some powerful douchebags at my Ivy League college; the type who leave you lemony fresh for days. And some of them happen to be Black! There's a new thrill to being able to freely dislike other Black people without any hand-wringing. We might share a common Blackness, but some of our lives and interests look nothing alike. And here I have the freedom of knowing they won't be the only Black person I meet that day, that week, or that semester. It's a brave new world for me. The guy clipping his toenails in that morning lecture on the Social Imagination? My God, can that proud Black brother suck it.

SIXTEEN

SHERMAN KLUMP v. BUDDY LOVE

I'M TWENTY-ONE and just like that it's already time for junior year of college. I'm also the skinniest I will be for the next decade. It's my reward for having previously gone through every last human emotion while standing in unfamiliar pants in front of the full-length mirrors of the American Apparel fitting rooms. Weight loss is something that happens in the space of a few sentences in books: Why buck the trend? I'm skinny!

See also:

Fit. Compact. Lean. Lissome. Archeresque: pertaining to the body of an archer. Svelte. That's right, I said svelte, motherfuckers. A tight little bod for my five-foot-nine-inch frame. If this were a movie, the part would need a recast or an ungodly amount of CGI. I've transformed from, well, not Sherman Klump (though entirely too close for my taste) to something closer to a soft, less chiseled, and less confident Buddy Love.

If you are frowning in confusion right now, Sherman Klump was the chunky, prosthetic-made "Before" to the slim and sleek "After" of Eddie Murphy with a mustache in the 1996 hit *The*

Nutty Professor. The transition from morbidly obese to fuckboy before there was a term for it is triggered by an untested serum he becomes addicted to. How dare you not know this off the top of your head, friend? As a child, I didn't so much watch this movie as exhaust the VHS tape to within an inch of its goddamn life.

Now, to be clear: there are Sherman Klumps out there who love their bodies as such and are as sexually confident and viable as Buddy Love in the one scene where Eddie Murphy had to have abs. It is nothing short of awesome to love your body that way, and I admire it. I simply didn't love mine; it was surplus and felt that way.

I leave all my tightening size-36 pants bundled up in a drawer of my childhood dresser as I instead pack for life as a slim upper-classman. Fresh packs of medium-size black T-shirts and black size-32 jeans that fit loosely. Mom watches from the doorway of my burgundy-painted bedroom that, unlike my waist size, will not change an inch for the next decade. She is less sad that I'm leaving and more concerned that I am thirty pounds lighter than when I first arrived home.

She thinks of me as anorexic and weird now: a shallow New York City deviant. It's feminine to diet, after all. What is a man who doesn't eat? What man portion controls? Philippe men are stout. It's the state we default to. Endomorph body types, brah. "Often pear-shaped, with a high tendency to store body fat." The junk amasses at the trunk, which, if left unchecked, will absolutely get in the way of funk. (Hehe, I just laughed typing that out.)

"A real Haitian man needs heft," she admonishes, unfolding and then refolding a nearby towel and watching me, while we wait for my cab to the train station.

Is that what she was trying to raise all along? I wonder but don't say as we hug goodbye for too long. She still cries whenever I leave but there's no devastation in it anymore. I know that within two days, her voice will already have that tinge of annoyance when I call while she's in the middle of a story with someone on the other line. ("Yes, yes, I love you, too, call back in forty minutes!")

Let's be clear: I didn't diet that summer. I strategically underfed myself. Something about being surrounded by prep school varsity students and rail-thin English department writing majors for four semesters had created some self-consciousness on my part. Imagine that.

I initially flirted with reinventing myself as bulky before opting to shrink myself instead, tired of having the voice of a man, the face of a twelve-year-old, and the body of a weird adult with thick thighs and hints of shadows under my tits when I'm shirtless.

I'm defiantly lazy and resort to guerrilla mind tactics. I go to bed hungry and take two Sleep Well melatonin gummies to fall asleep faster, not thinking of the hungry maids left in Haiti. I also hold on to the memory of James, tall and skinny James, sitting next to me in a slow sociology seminar and how in a lull he was suddenly transfixed by the bulkiness of my thighs. How wide they are next to his skinny and hairy white ones, in cargo shorts. The guilty embarrassment in his eyes when we made eye contact is enough to slam the fridge shut and go back to bed. There's not enough dedication there to call it an eating disorder, but years later, a girlfriend will hear this story and diagnose me as having had a summer of "disordered eating." (Yes, she will be white. And from Massachusetts. With horses. Don't look at me.)

That's so problematic, Ben!

Did you just transfer here? Did you just open the book to this page? Of course it is. Look, from the vantage point of the year 2020, I acknowledge there is something deeply problematic about writing all of the above. I fully realize this and apologize . . . It was a different time. Our iPhone 4s only came in black and white with screens that did not even stretch out to the edge; we were body-negative savages, all right.

Why even include it, though? Why make some of your readers feel like there is something wrong with body types that do not adhere to—

—Oh my god. Fine. Stop yelling at me.

Let me start over, then: it was my beautiful summer of self-care, and broccoli suddenly became delicious. I laughed rinsing carrots and ran in slow motion on a beach, flanked by golden retrievers in matching bandannas. I learned to savor the subtle nuances of a crisp stalk of celery. And what do you know? The weight just disappeared! I did this for me and only me. It was never about the number on the scale or any Western standard of fitness or attractiveness. I was not at all chaotically horny and looking to be looked at by people who looked through me before. Better?

(I truly have no wisdom or objectivity to add here. To this day, I will approximate the calorie count of a single cupcake at 10 calories or 3,400 calories depending on my mood and personal fulfillment. I'm the kind of person who furiously does fifty pushups and then spends forty minutes digging fingertips into the doughy fleshiness of my arms in front of the bathroom mirror, feeling for the new muscles I've been granted for my hard work and dedication.)

Regardless of the state of mind then, I return to campus with abs. Four of them, never quite six. It's nowhere near the shirtless Black teenagers doing pull-ups on city scaffoldings, glistening with backs that look like litters of puppies wrestling to burst out of brown latex, but I'm happy with the results that I will never be able to replicate again once the weight comes back. But for now, it's 2010, and I return to campus eager to make new first impressions.

The luck of the skinny and pretty people is already on my side. My new dorm room is a gigantic single in 600 West 113th Street, commonly known as "Nussbaum" for the bakery deli on the ground floor and home to an Egg & Cheese on Everything Bagel you would flick a baby hard on the nose for. Not that that's my breakfast anymore. No. I'm skinny now: for a semester I will belong to the tribe of Columbia that studies in navy hoodies after ordering egg-white omelets with roasted vegetables, a green juice, and rye toast, no butter.

👥

My casual friend Sabrina is mixed—half Black, half white—and has lived an international life, too. She alternates her summers in either Berlin, where she is familiar with all the cool spots, or in Japan, where she is discovering them and will be spending the next winter semester.

Sabrina is the first of seven people not to recognize me on Move-in Day.

I wiggle my eyebrows at her in friendly recognition at the corner of Broadway and 113th Street, which she notes but stares through, carrying a box and a full backpack.

I'm still groggy from the lengthy Greyhound bus ride back into America, pushing a heavy blue bin of my minimal possessions up a sidewalk ramp in a sea of moving students and resident advisers, but I hear it.

"There's your friend Ben," says her friend Angela, who will also double as her roommate for the next five months.

"No, it's not," Sabrina says. "You think all Black guys look the same."

"No," Angela says, annoyed at both having been corrected and accused of something so ugly all at once. "That's Ben."

"Um, yes, it is," I interrupt with a nervous giggle, eager to defuse while Sabrina's squint gives way to shocked eyes. "I escaped the Canadian Gulag. Did you two have a nice summer?"

"Holy crap!"

Sabrina gasps and hugs me, before taking a step back and jumping forward to hug me again. On the second hug, she pats down my back, as if to make sure it isn't prestidigitation. Just like that, a summer of dry toast and bouts of medium-to-so-very-severe constipation is totally worth it.

"No BS," she asks right away, "what did you do?"

I give her the Kanye shrug. I guess my pants are a little baggier, now. I hadn't noticed. S'all good, shawty, know what I mean? No effort or body image issues were involved in the making of this thoroughly average bod.

"They have gyms in Canada, too, Sabrina." Angela smiles, eyeing me up and down, looking vaguely approving of what she's appraising.

"I mean, I might have done a few late-night reps." I shrug, caught in my lie.

That's how guys of all races and creeds lose weight, after all. In underground fighting rings like Ryan from *The O.C.* did when mourning his high school sweetheart, the tragic Marissa Cooper played by the even more tragic Mischa Barton. They "hit the gym" and do incline hammer curls to become Tough Mudders, whatever that means, I'm still not sure. Cool T-shirts, though.

I don't tell Sabrina or Angela that I'm, in fact, the other kind of guy. The one standing in basketball shorts in front of floor-length mirrors, pinching and folding, sucking and flexing, trying to fight off hunger with disappointment. Our kind—also found across all races and creeds—avoids the limelight of gym selfies.

"You're gonna have so much sex this semester," my friend Elliott, a thriving sociology major, says later that week. "I'm already annoyed."

Another detached shrug.

I don't mind the assumption living on in those who know me, but that's not my goal. If what closed the fridge at 2 a.m. was the grimace on James's face eyeing my thighs, what closed it again at 2:25 a.m. was a much loftier goal.

See, on my list of to-dos before the end of college was something else entirely: I wanted to fall in love. That kind of big TV-season-finale love. A thug and his woman, or two thugs, or two women after having murdered their boos and run off together. It didn't matter. I want that spark, that realization that happens deep inside your chest and leaves your skin prickly and filled with goosebumps as if a tongue has dragged all over your arms and back.

Another characteristic of Columbia was that the entire campus was always filled with couples. Heck, the entirety of New York City was, and to this day remains, afflicted with the happily monogamous. Couples holding hands in the middle of a sidewalk and swinging their arms to maximize the offense, couples leaning forward to kiss at restaurants, or couples slobbering over each other at the top of a subway entrance begging to be set on fire at rush hour.

They were everywhere. (My favorite were those carrying Trader Joe's brown paper bags together, basking in the simple domesticity of a salad-mixing Jane and their simple-minded sourdough-bread-baking John.)

I wanted to be one of the obnoxious chosen ones. After all, I already knew my heart can be cold. I knew that two countries ago. I wanted to confirm the opposite now. The logic was that if I could will myself to be skinny, how hard can that be?

As you might have already picked up on, I'm occasionally very dim.

SEVENTEEN

IVORY SKIN, EYES OF SOMETHING GREEN

Two months into junior year, I'M TWENTY-TWO STILL, already sliding back up toward 160 pounds, and watching *Gossip Girl* in my dorm room on a Saturday night. Take a moment to absorb the full sadness of that image. It is a mirror image of my being eighteen and watching *Gossip Girl*, and later, twenty-nine and watching *Gossip Girl*, only then it will be in preparation for my college syllabus on *Gossip Girl* as an aspirational cornerstone of teenage media content for a class I am teaching on American TV Drama. Life is a boomerang that keeps regaining velocity by bouncing off the face.

The night's episode is appropriately set at Columbia and involves secret elite societies and a showdown at Fashion Week. I had a lot of expectations of Columbia University and, beyond the books, postcard-worthy campus, and the prestige of an Ivy League, a lot of them came from *Gossip Girl*. You can't blame me here. I was raised in the era of *The Gilmore Girls'* Life & Death Brigade, a time where every other teen movie had a casual mention of Yale University's Skull & Bones secret society, where the

Illuminati's hot teen offsprings have orgies on their way to Ibiza every weekend.

College had delivered on many fronts, but not that one. Columbia may have prestige and reek of privilege, but one thing it is not—as the pungent clouds of body odor in Butler Library during finals week will attest—is glamorous. For one thing, the only notable secret society—St. A's—was a boring collection of European students and WASP kids who referred to their parents by their first names, blew mummy and daddy's money on coke, and went into finance. Moreover, the only famous person on campus at the time was actor James Franco trying to prove something by simultaneously attending NYU, Columbia, and, I believe, Yale. At any rate, I never even bumped into him. Who knows? If I had, I might have prevented *The Disaster Artist*.

The semester was well underway, and there were no real updates to my love life. Unfortunately, this new slim body did not change the operating system. I still didn't have the verve of guys who take photos of their dicks with their pants around their ankles and holding their long tank top up between their teeth in front of a stained bathroom mirror.

I mostly like people; I just tend to be bad at them in any romantically combustible context. My flirting game was still, by modern human conventions, limited. In social situations, it often amounted to paying casual compliments like, "Oh, I like your shoes" and then fifteen seconds later adding, "I'm not gay. I mean not as a full orientation. It's all fluid but, like, sexually, I like women," all delivered with unwavering eye contact.

And then two days later, in the middle of another conversation about coursework, I would slip in a "And, by the way, the shoe thing the other day was not sexual. Like, the actual shoe would not make me climax without your foot in it or anything. Cool! Goodbye forever!"

College students, as it turns out, only throw two kinds of parties. The intimate kind, that never include more than a handful of close friends, and the open-door kind, where everyone is invited and the point is to crowd the space to the point of discomfort. Kesha blares so loudly you feel it in the foundations, you can't move ten feet without navigating past twelve sets of elbows, and every line has to be spoken twice over the sound, and even then all you can do is nod a reply to whatever it was that was asked because you'll never hear it.

I turn off *Gossip Girl* and decide that's the sort of party I need tonight. College, dammit! New York City! I'm wasting svelteness while people all over the world are spending their Saturday nights on treadmills or eating small portions of oatmeal and whey powder trying to achieve this.

A few minutes on Facebook and I find out there's one happening on the northern outskirts of the campus, teetering into Harlem. I wasn't invited but "everyone's invited!!!!" I know "everyone." I have a class with "everyone." I could be everyone's plus one.

I wear a leather jacket and push my way into the wiggling mass of people, throw a few 'sup nods at people I don't recognize, and a girl with a red Solo cup yells, "Woooo!" when she sees me. I yell, "Wooo!" back. There's always a fun, loud girl yelling "Woo" at the door. They're a precious resource to the world; a burst of cheer that lets introverts and maladjusted people think they can actually do whatever it is they are trying to do in spaces like these.

I'm an asocial social drinker who spent many formative Saturday nights indoors during my teenage years. I watched *SNL* live with a stack of mangas at my side when I should have been tipping cows over. This means I've been improperly trained in the art of drinking, which in turn makes me the lightest of lightweights; slurring after a peach Bellini is my weight class. *Woo!*

I look around for an entry point and catch snippets of conversations. "I hear he pokes holes in condoms, dude," a guy whispers to another, and I will spend the rest of my life, up to this very manuscript, wondering what was the tale of this sharp-penised gentleman.

"It's all over Facebook," a voice whines on my right.

"You're being dramatic," her left-side counterpart says. "It's not all over Facebook. It's one post on one person's wall. It's not like the masses are talking about it."

"People are saying she has chlamydia on Facebook," the left voice, soft like summer rain, says with a smile, leaning into me without boundaries like I'm a conspiring cousin at a wedding. This voice belongs to, well, I can't use their real name, so let's say, Jolene. Ivory skin and eyes of emerald green. Jolene enjoys attention, makes poor spur-of-the-moment decisions, and falls in love too easily, as Jolenes tend to do. I won't say that her beauty is beyond compare, but she is very, very pretty.

"Jolene!" her friend exclaims, pretending at slapping Jolene. "You bitch. I don't have chlamydia!" Jolene laughs and hugs her friend—Olivia—defusing the anger. She has sweaty brown hair and enough freckles to look French.

"Ben." I surprise myself with my casual, first-name-only introduction.

It's "Ben" because I don't use "Rubeintz" anymore these days. I've never had much attachment to ID cards. It's supposed to be a shuffle of the letters of both of my parents' names. "Robert" + "Belzie." A strangely creative choice, but one I'm grateful for considering the first choice was apparently "Junior." "Ben" works. Short for one of my middle names, Bennett. I like being a simple one-syllable. You could recast me as Todd tomorrow and I wouldn't mind. Names are just one-word bits of fiction, after all.

"Jolene," she says, simply stating her name, and it feels like a line from a movie, which is fine because I'm working with the entire CW catalog in perfect recall myself.

"I'm Olivia," the possibly chlamydia'ed redhead at her side says, taking it upon herself to complete the circle of introductions because she still thinks this is a triangle, though I banished the thought the moment an STI was mentioned.

Conversation with Jolene, with occasional attempts to join in by Olivia, is easy. We're head turners tonight; an inciting incident at the corner of a party. This is exactly what I had launched myself out of my dorm room in search of an hour ago. I suspect Jolene likes being seen talking with a Black guy. I like being seen chatting up a pretty brunette, whose voice carries over the music, swaying her hips occasionally but not quite dancing.

"Dude, what are you going to do with a degree in creative writing and sociology?" Jolene asks. She uses *dude* a lot, as though she has cracked the code of speaking guy.

"Write creatively about society, duh."

Or, herd stray writers into functioning social groupings. I haven't decided yet.

"Ha! You better you marry rich, dude."

I wink and it's more of a brazen closing of one and a half eyelids but she laughs out loud nonetheless.

"Oh, man. Can you imagine!" she asks Olivia without necessarily waiting for an answer. "My mom would make you sign a brutal prenup, sorry."

I learn that, at twenty-two, Jolene proudly describes herself as a secular humanist, which makes me both performatively groan and is also an inexplicably huge turn-on. She and I continue like this, laughing out loud at random interludes of a conversation that requires less and less of Olivia. We let her jokes fall flat and refocus on each other, stifling a giggle at her story and then bursting out into laughter at the silence we created around it. Poor Olivia. Don't feel too bad for her: she was the type of twenty-something who called her singing "her vocals."

Jolene tasks the two of us with guarding the door to a nearby open dorm room's open bathroom. It's a two-person bedroom left ajar for convenience while its occupants join the party, which is entirely their fault.

"You're going to need diapers when you're older," Olivia mocks. "You just peed an hour ago!"

"Shut up. Also, you two aren't allowed to fuck without me," Jolene warns, before closing the door, already pulling up her skirt.

Olivia takes this as a challenge and tries to kiss me and narrowly misses only to end up licking my ear. Her tongue feels grainy and harsh against my skin as though it might lead to zits.

"Um, I'm, thank you, first of all, but I'm not looking for anything right now, sorry," I say, and I wonder if all my lines are lifted directly from television.

"Whatever," Olivia scoffs.

She is embarrassed, and when Jolene exits the bathroom with fresh makeup on and a toilet flush echoing behind her, Olivia announces that she has received a text that 1020, a bar at the corner of Amsterdam and 110th, is where she has to be tonight.

"This place is dead," she says, no longer watching me. "I'm bouncing. Later."

The invitation is not extended to the two of us. She dismissively hugs both Jolene and me at once, squeezing one of each of our shoulders without bringing our three bodies closer. We watch her walk off in what could be construed as a huff.

"We were like twins last year. Inseparable," Jolene says, shaking her head, as we watch her go. "I don't know what happened."

I shrug, not wanting to appear too thrilled that her friend is gone. No, I don't want to make out with you, Olivia. You seasonal-arc villain. You're a temptress, a foil. This is not an episode of *Gossip Girl*, seedy and tantalizing; no, this is a rom-com.

"This is going to sound mean but," Jolene starts as we naturally navigate out of the party after waiting a few minutes, wanting to avoid an awkward run-in on the ground floor, "do you ever wish we could just meet a whole new set of people every year? Not just college but, like, our entire lives?"

"New stories." I nod. New first impressions each time until you get it right. Until you find your tribe. Who wouldn't want that?

"Dude, yes, exactly!" Jolene exclaims. "I just keep meeting the same people in different outfits."

Belzie would like her, I think. *We fell in love drunk one night in college* is a pretty good story. I'm fascinated by the life she's led, where she might have been at the exact moment I was reading a book or defeating some final boss on my bed in high school, or on my knees in Haiti.

"Hitchhike? You hitchhiked around Los Angeles all summer?"

"It was Santa Monica Boulevard and in broad daylight!" she defends. "People were super nice.

Jolene is that secular humanist majoring in economics who occasionally dabbles in commercial acting.

"One couple even went into the lot and dropped me off right at my audition. People are nicer than you think, Mr. Sociology."

She and I roam around the well-lit and well-guarded enclave of the Columbia University campus. The campus is never quite empty; the patterns just change.

Once we tire of walking, we sit on the steps of the Low Memorial Library, overseeing and tracking the foot traffic of people returning from parties toward their dorm buildings. We get to know each other that specific way people who interact from 11 p.m. to 3 a.m. get to know each other.

Our conversation dissolves into tired nonsense, so much empty bubblegum pop that Willy Wonka might seek legal action.

"I think I'm in love with you," I say without thinking. How many other things in my life had I not willed into existence by speaking them out into the universe?

Jolene lets out a cackle. "Go home, Ben," she eventually says, which I somehow still find endlessly charming and clever. In a few months, I will think of it again and make it my Twitter handle.

"No," I insist. "Marry me." I suddenly stand up only to get down again and on one knee. "This is now a proposal."

Jolene pinches my cheek and pulls me up by the forearm.

"You're a puppy."

"And you're reckless," I say, still drunk enough, as she leads me across campus toward the East Campus.

"I'm reckless," she agrees with some satisfaction.

"Well! What's more reckless than marrying a guy you met three hours ago at a party?"

It's dramatically elegant, sober or drunk. I was a Canadian in need of a visa, after all. Jolene watches me for a moment, enjoying weighing a sudden proposal. It will never be clear to any of the parties involved how serious I was about this marital outcome at twenty-two.

We make out waiting for, riding, and subsequently exiting the elevator up to her dorm room on one of the top floors. Her roommates are either gone or asleep and every window in the suite is outlined with dimly lit Christmas lights. Jolene's breathing is ragged and her cheeks shine pink when we tumble into her room. We tumble in only because we've both seen people passionately tumble into bedrooms before and it seems hotter than simply walking into said room. Both of us are performing for an audience that isn't there. Her desk is cluttered with nail polish bottles, and the circular mirror above it has words like *CITIZEN* and *LOVER* written all over it, some in lipstick and others in black Sharpie. It's perhaps one of the various art projects she had mentioned earlier.

"Do you have condoms?" she asks.

"Yes."

Leather jackets come preinstalled with condoms. If you own one, go check the pockets right now. There are a few LifeStyles peppered throughout.

"This is just friendly, right?" she verifies, throwing her wallet and purse, and kicking boots off.

"Yeah, of course," I lie.

Wrong! I'm still waiting for an answer to my proposal. I'll tell her about Robert with my head on her lap someday. We'll whisper while the baby sleeps in a tiny but well-situated apartment in the West Village we can both afford.

It is hot and more angular than not. Everything is pressed

together, generating the uncomfortable heat of unfamiliar bodies pretending otherwise. I'm sweaty, but sweaty at 154 pounds is a lot different than sweaty at 192 pounds; a light mist as opposed to a swamp with a shopping cart in the middle.

"Pin me down," Jolene demands.

I have no proof of this, but I have the distinct feeling that she watches more porn than I do, which is a daunting statement considering my porn consumption is at a twenty-two-year-old-male-college-student-without-roommates level.

"Squeeze my tits," she moans.

We are billionaire Chuck Bass and millionaire fashionista Blair Waldorf, in the back of a limousine. I'm Dan Humphrey and she's Serena van der Woodsen. I'm Nate Archibald and she's Juliet Sharp. I'm Nate Archibald and she's Bree Buckley. I'm Nate Archibald and she's cougaresque duchess Catherine Beaton. Jesus, that show never did figure what to do with Nate Archibald, did it?

"Squeeze my fucking tits," she breathes again, sounding annoyed.

Isn't that what I was already doing? *Stop thinking about* Gossip Girl, *you repressed catamite!* I curse myself. *Focus on the moment. That is what this is: a moment.*

"Yes, baby, slam that Black dick into me."

I oblige as best as I can. Jolene is still in character, moaning loudly. I think she's trying to wake up her roommates.

"Like that?" I try.

"Yeah, just like that. Drive it deep in there."

I'm a bad actor. I don't have the hips or the gusto for her verbs. I want to right-click and downgrade "slam" to "bring" or "throw." I wish I had access to all the synonyms needed for this. Fat or skinny, I really should never be naked. It's awkward for everybody involved, and I somehow still maintain the energy of someone wearing ill-fitted clothes made of itchy fabric.

"Yeah, baby. Rape me. Fucking rape me with that Black dick."

"Why are you stopping?" she asks, breathless, which I can't help but note with some pride before all the uglier feelings catch up to my brain.

"I'm not . . . doing that, though," I say. "The r-word."

This is less chivalry than the accumulated pamphlets and tutorials and campus discussions on the nature of consent. Only yes means yes.

"I know that," she says, and when I remain motionless, she sighs heavily and pulls her arm out from under me.

She runs her fingers together over my head like she's sprinkling magic dust. "I hereby grant you full consent to ram that Black dick in me."

Forty seconds ago, it could have been cute. In the moment, I had almost forgotten I was the owner of a Black dick.

"Okay," I say and we resume.

She uses the word again and I shut it out of my brain and focus on the feeling instead.

I notice how quiet the room actually is beyond the sound of our two bodies. My nails are clogged with dirt, but I can't recall from where. They were clean when I left my room. I wonder if my ice cream is melted. That mini-fridge can't be trusted.

"Harder, fuck! This is so sick, but I want it so bad."

I'm focused on the feeling. I don't dissociate but instead, find comfort deep within my own body. The heartbeat, the chemicals, the buildup.

Is this still sex? She's a really good actress for a secular humanist. I don't want to be here anymore. Eventually, the mattress shrieks under us, because I could not possibly have made such a weird sound. The condom has hopefully served its purpose and she hasn't impregnated me.

"Well! That was a fun honeymoon," Jolene says, satisfied or playing at it. She begins to move around the suddenly overwhelmingly bright room, flooded with the neon overhead lights from the East Campus dorms. She doesn't redress and transitions to a pair of PJs with snow cones all over, tank top, and no bra. I'll be gone soon.

"Yeah." I smile, zipping up the leather jacket to my neck and stuffing my hands in my pockets.

"Dude, are you all right?" she asks.

"Yeah. That was great."

"God! I'm a really bad host," she whispers. "Be right back."

I take this as an instruction to stand and wait alone as she checks the hall and softly slides the door to the room shut behind her. "Softly slide": another good synonym a few minutes too late.

I fixate on her closet, which I am certain is filled with cops and her dad, and her uncle, and her cousin, the one who went to juvie and has a chain wrapped around his fist, all waiting for their cue to come out. I'm sure the pickup truck is revving up downstairs, gun rack loaded.

"Don't judge me, dude." Jolene laughs, startling me out of the violence with two filled glasses of water. "It's a ridiculous show but actually really fun."

"What?"

She nods over to the shiny poster on the left side of her closet that I had somehow missed. Serena, Blair, Nate, Jenny, and Chuck, the entire statuesque white pantheon of Manhattan, alongside the season 1 poster of *Gossip Girl*.

Her eyes widen at the recognition in mine.

"Holy crap! Dude, do you watch it?"

"No, sorry. Not my thing."

We were writing different stories tonight. The water smells bad and goes down warm. I walk back home sober and imagine the eponymous song playing over the credits. All things considered, Dolly Parton gives that Jolene way too much credit in that song, man. I bet you Jolene hugged her and said "OMG, I'd never take your man!" over and over, believing it herself. And then one night, she got bored on the toilet and texted this guy something like "How goes the domestic bliss?" Just for fun. Just because she now knew she could.

I stop halfway up the stairs to my suite and backtrack to the Nussbaum Deli on the ground floor, where the 6 a.m. workers are filling baskets with the morning's bagels. I order two egg-and-cheese bagels, on my way to my room, no longer a virgin.

EIGHTEEN

SISTER, SISTER

Black Girl Magic. You've probably come across the term at some recent point in your life. Ten years ago, most guesses as to its definition would have included the word *voodoo*, but as one Beyoncé Giselle upgraded from musician to Destined Child That Was Promised, Bringer of Black Light and Azor Ahai for an entire generation of Black people, the definition of Black Girl Magic got a parallel media boost. Instagram posts, throw pillows, *The Real Housewives of All Over* drunkenly slurring it while twirling in their reunion episode gowns . . .

The Document of Record for all that American Black culture that I always found myself a few steps behind is the website Urban Dictionary. It's as valid as the *Oxford English Dictionary* as far as these things are concerned, constantly updating itself with thousands of votes on slang and entries as varied as *wypipo* (white people) and definitions of first names written by horny teenagers with too many feelings about said first names.

(I have a particular fondness for the definition of Ben: *An amazing guy, one of the sweetest you'll ever meet. He is quiet though, until u get him alone and he becomes the funniest and cutest guy ever. He gives the BEST hug!!* . . . Poor bastard was definitely openly sobbing while typing this with one hand.)

Their definition of this Black Girl Magic is:

> *The art of pure, unadulterated dopeness that every black woman exudes, which beholds not only her internal and external beauty but demonstrates the glory of God the creator.*

> *Example: That girl's dark skin is so beautiful, nothing but black girl magic!*

Usage in popular culture: Most Real Housewives of Atlanta and Potomac describing themselves at one point or another. Apologies: I don't mean to further politicize an already fraught book about race identity in America by bringing up *The Real Housewives of Potomac* (. . . but I never trusted Monique and Candiace had it coming; there: I said it).

Everyone loves themselves a good BGM moment these days. I don't remember where I first learned it, but I do remember the first time I shared its definition to an unimpressed audience while making the bed of my old room.

I'M TWENTY-TWO and it's senior year of college. I've gone up to Montreal for a spur-of-the-moment weekend visit. Subtext: I just had a sort-of breakup, the Greyhound from Port Authority to Berri-Uqam station in downtown Montreal is nine hours and $69, and I miss my mom. She insists that the perfectly made bed "sat too long" since my last visit three months prior so we set to remaking it with fresh sheets from the dryer. There's a béchamel potato casserole in the oven that I'm already counting the calories of—just the right amount of a lot for the occasion. She is happy I'm home, as she never fails to be. As for the Black Girl Magic of it all, the whole thing amuses her when I bring it up as the latest bit of pop culture happening in America these days.

"That's adorable." She snorts, tucking sheets on her corner and passing her hand over it like a diligent iron.

"It's not adorable, Mom. It's about resilience!" I say. To me, it's still a pearl of wisdom from the edges of social media that is not yet on T-shirts in Walmarts across the continent. "Like, that special resilience Black woman have, to go through the world of sexism and racism and come out the other side without showing any flaws."

It's not only Urban Dictionary, a website curated by fourteen-year-olds; my overall liberal arts higher education is paying off at this point. I've read, studied, and SparkNoted Angela Davis and bell hooks now. The situations in which I will abstain from bringing up the fact that I've read, studied, and SparkNoted Angela Davis and bell hooks are few and far between.

"So, am I Black Girl Magic?" she says, pretending to throw a long mane of invisible silk hair over her shoulder.

"Not with those edges," I say and subsequently receive a duvet to the face. There are brief moments of equal-footed friendship between us now.

"In my days, you went home crying, screamed into a pillow, tore off the page from your notebook they wrote on, and started all over again the next day . . . but now it's Magic. That's cute."

There's no bite to the *cute*. See also: *inoffensive, sweet,* and *delightful.* The weariness in her voice is something I won't soon forget. The way she says *cute* wearily makes me think that she's recalling a memory. It is dripping with personal experience. In the grand scheme, I know it wasn't that long ago—a couple of years at most—that she was in a Canadian classroom where something like that could have transpired as she had to relearn all of her skills in the exact same language she had mastered them in in Haiti, simply to prove that she could keep doing her job as a nurse, only now to white Canadians. All the while, I was probably in my own high school classroom, fetishizing vague notions of a brighter life in the United States. (And yes, I'm aware that my mom is awesome and that I very often don't deserve her. Hush up.)

To this day, it's hard not to see Belzie's point. The effortlessness that the term demands of people, women, whose existence is at the intersection of sexism and racism, struggle and oh-screw-you struggle, feels like a bucket of cotton candy while your stomach is growling for dinner. After that conversation, it will take a few more years of walking around the world with a dick for me to come close to understanding—and by this I mean, not very close at all—the width of the chasm that separates Black men and Black women in America.

Now, if you happen to be a Black person reading this book, you will, I'm sure, have picked up on an absence by now . . . a gaping hole that may in hindsight explain a few things. Because, save for a very patient mother, *where* exactly are the Black women in this strange sheltered boy's life?

A side effect of attending primarily white schools in my early life is that there were no tables at the back of Saint-Esprit elementary or Seminaire Salesien at which to find a bunch of Black kids whose lunches smelled like mine.

When that first table of Black kids eventually became a presence in high school, with kids in homemade dreads, hoop earrings, and a growing understanding of the hip-hop culture thriving a few hundred miles south in America, I no longer easily fit with them. I wasn't another Black kid approaching them, I was the corny Oreo, which was in many ways as foreign as Leo. Worse, because it was a choice I was making in their eyes: a judgment being passed on them from a kid with good grades who goes directly home after school. The girls at that particular table were particularly unimpressed with my being—and the quizzes were vicious.

"What's Kanye's album's name?"

"*College Dropout*."

"Do you even know the difference between Kanye and Fitty?"

"Yeah, I know Fifty."

"Ha! It's *Fitty*," Angela corrects. Her lipstick is purple, and she's well on her way to giving exactly zero fucks, sometimes throwing a middle finger behind a teacher's back in class to make her friends laugh. "Not Fifty; Fitty."

"I bet you he knows Celine's last album, though," her friend Karine adds. "What was Celine's last album, Rubeintz?"

"I don't listen to that crap."

"Bullshit!"

Celine Dion's last album at that time was the conceptual bilingual *Miracle*, by the way, featuring the single "*Je Lui Dirai*" or "I Will Tell Him." She's cradling a green-haired baby on the cover, which was kind of weird. Good stuff, but the 2007 followup *D'Elles* is where I'll really feel it, y'know? (Get off my jock, all right: Celine has bops.)

Mind you, there should be no shame in having known that, but there was. Deep shame. As it turns out, that table of people who look exactly like me was just another place to perform under duress for social oxygen. After a few weeks of trying to sit on the edges and already worrying about my growing man-tits, I stayed away from that impossibly intimidating table of young Black people with the confidence of outraged women, ready to pop off if tried.

Instead, I listen to Black podcasts alone out of an ill-formed need for Blackness I can't quite put into words yet at that point in my life. Blackness I can soak up from the outside, without eyes turning my way. I browse through the Blacker corners of social media and YouTube, like a student who missed the first week of class, hoping to catch up by taking diligent notes and raising my hand high each time. I'm an Oreo that aspires to be chocolate flavored.

It will take college and the easy lowercase diversity of New York City for a few key Black women—who I'm not related to—to make strong lasting imprints on my life. I don't meet them all at once, but one by one they trickle into my life as if they had all been in a waiting room, dreading the work to be done when they would be called to bat. In short succession, I meet the first two Black women I can call "sis" and mean it. And these relationships are game changers in many ways.

The first real one is Nina. I'M NINETEEN when we meet. She is bright and friendly and to my everlasting luck, after trading a few emails in a creative writing workshop, she has simply decided that we will be friends. I know this because she knocks at my dorm room door one night with two cupcakes from Magnolia Bakery in hand, and she says:

"So, I've decided," she says, brightly. "We're going to be friends."

And just like that, we're friends for the better part of four years. We study and write essays together in empty classrooms when the campus libraries get too crowded. I nag her to come with me to my favorite twenty-four-hour grocery store for late-night runs, which is my favorite time to do groceries. She texts me to drag me out of bed and come escort her home from a bar when walking half a mile home at 3 a.m. in possession of a vagina and tipsy is too reckless of a choice. I groan and kick off my covers and head out in flip-flops, knowing my "Black guy in a hoodie" bubble leaves me safer, if not impervious. It's what you do for a sis.

Nina and I are never roommates but she keeps a lamp in my room because my bedroom has horrendous neon overhead lighting and she needs good lighting to study. Around campus, she is far more popular than me. A side effect of being friendlier, I imagine. She is the people-person to my usual gargoyle used to crouching in the shadows and jolting away the moment people get too close for my liking. I'm happy to be her plus-one at parties I'm not invited to and through her, I dip toes in the Intercultural House where Nina lives. It's one of Columbia's would-be cultural fraternities—a gateway for politically active POCs. (Think Disney World's "It's a Small World" but make it an Ivy League townhouse turned dorms in the middle of Frat Row.) Through them, I learn to use People of Color instead of Black in greater societal discourse in which other minorities might intersect.

"What's tonight again?" I say, peeking outside her dorm room to the alley rumbling with activity and international food trays. There's an open house tonight. "I was hoping to write."

"What's the word count for watching *The Social Network* for the eighth time?" Nina asks, getting ready in her bathroom, ironing her hair in a bra.

"Seventh," I defend.

"We're mixing with the larger community." She sighs. "We were all supposed to bring friends who aren't members. Jewish organizations, Asian organizations, Caucasian classmates. They said that: Caucasian classmates. Sounds like a ska band."

"Aren't you kind of phoning it in by just bringing me, then?" I say, wrapping her scarf around my head for no reason, antsy as I always am when there's a large social event ahead.

Nina's head pops out of her bathroom, eyes wide with embarrassment and a hand to her chest. "Oh my god!"

"What?"

"This is so embarrassing! Are you *not* white?" she whispers.

"I hate your ass."

She laughs, and it's the same laugh that will have Alfie, an offensively tall Peruvian senior, follow her around all night and give me the stink eye when I drape myself over Nina, exhausted by the bursts of fifteen minutes of small talk I can manage. Nina and I have never dated, let alone hooked up. Occasionally, we hold hands for no reason walking around Union Square or even College Walk, which only serves to baffle the guys and occasional girls who are also drawn to her brightness. She's more of a sister, and if she didn't look exactly like the father in the photos on her dorm walls, I might swear Robert's seed had made a pit stop in Chicago where she hails from.

Intimacy with a Black woman is . . . not deeper, but simpler— safer in a way that can't be undone from the outside. I don't talk to Nina much these days. (Tell-some, not tell-all, remember?) There's no resentment there. Sometimes people are measured by their effect in your life rather than the accumulated time, and it's safe to say that Nina changed me from feral to at least socially housebroken, no longer scared to approach these tablefuls of Black people who might find me lacking, and for that, I am forever grateful.

Around the time of meeting Nina, Morgan also comes my way. Struts, rather.

I'M TWENTY-ONE when she walks into my seminar on Japanese Monsters and Mythology, catching the eye of exactly everyone. Even the professor, a gregarious gay man, cannot help himself: "That is a *look*!" he exclaims. It might be inappropriate if the entire classroom didn't agree. Dreads, wigs, silver, black, or pink, or long hair that poofs on high when kept natural, Morgan is striking, to say the least. Morgan doesn't wear clothes; the woman has looks, *lewks,* and takes slow steps everywhere to make sure her six-inch heels don't waver. After class, Morgan and I end up walking toward and into the same building. She gives me a curious look at every light where one of us expects the other to break away but doesn't. This lasts into the 600W dorms' elevators at which point we're getting off at the same floor. We're floormates, as it turns out.

"I thought you were creeping and following me home. I was ready to mace your ass," she'll later recall, munching on fries and never gaining any weight that a lap around the park won't melt off. (Yes, she's one of those. It offends me, too.)

I've tried to imagine my life without this chance encounter and in many ways, I can't. Morgan is . . . so many things, foundational among them.

I've tried to write her into YA novels, and my approximations of her never feel right; too many contradictions that end up feeling fictional when stacked up together. She will set the grading curve in that Japanese Monsters class while also partying all over New York City. Her birthday celebrations happen at warehouses where circus performers twirl all night. Her dorm room is a truly upsetting battlefield, and she drags boxes and boxes of clothes back to Jersey at the end of every year. She'll fish into a pile of clothes, pull out a bottle of room-temperature juice, and chug while coding a website and listening to K-pop at insane volumes. I won't believe she actually turned down Harvard University because the campus was "creepy" until I see the crumpled acceptance letter in her files while helping her move.

Her vacations are hyper-researched, highly curated affairs, pulled off on a $1,000 budget, disappearing to Europe for two weeks, knowing every leg of the vacation by heart. Her friends don't like me, and I never warmed up to them. She makes no show of pretending to like mine either.

"*Why* are all your friends white, Ben?" she says, aghast, one day after I part from a study group on the steps of Low Library and she struts my way, large sunglasses on. "Who hurt you?"

"White people like me." I shrug.

"They're not known for their taste, babe." She snorts, sitting down next to me.

"Why are all *your* friends Black?" I push back, grabbing the melted Venti concoction from her hand and taking a sip from the wet straw.

"I fuck with some white people," she says eventually. "But you have to feel safe to be *friends* with someone. You in danger every time I see you, girl."

This life philosophy lives in the unwavering stare and hardened features she reserves for the gaggles of frat bros that ogle her at bars and whisper something to one another. It's admittedly pretty cool to see an entire swim team look away like ashamed toddlers.

Morgan is still in my life nine years later, which neither of us expected at the time of graduation. She'll agree to dog-sit for me for a weekend while I'm traveling and stay for fifty-one extra days when I return, becoming a de facto roommate. We won't see each other for months, and then a text request and money transfer into her account and she'll begin to design my website out of nowhere when I need one, another skill she just happens to have. Along with proofreading, interior decorating—the advanced kind, with color swatches—and the all-around uncanny ability to live a lifestyle several rungs above her income by extensively planning. The woman is vexingly good at every last thing. The cover to this book? She designed it. No, really. Conceptualized it out of nowhere as a favor for my book proposal and nailed it so hard that HarperCollins looped her in. It's not all praises either, mind you. Morgan is also—and I say this knowing full well she is reading this exact excerpt of my book and not a page more because my writing "ugh, sounds so Ben Philippey"—just the rudest woman alive to me. Occasionally, I feel emboldened by this. If Nina was a soul sister, Morgan is the type whose pigtails I enjoy pulling.

"Do you ever think about the fact that all the men you date are punks?" I declare one day out of boredom, falling back onto my guest bed, watching Morgan get ready for a date during one of her extended dog-sits at my place. She swipes left on 99 percent of men of all ethnicities because she knows she is stunning and doesn't need the seemingly neverending column of "gorgeous, heart-eye emoji" they all seem to provide when I glance at her matches. Occasionally, like tonight, a chiseled pleb or square-jawed gym owner will pass muster, taking her to some exclusive club in Tribeca.

"Excuse me?"

Morgan is occasionally a fun stovetop to touch.

"You date punks," I continue, sounding out each word. "Those poor idiots try so hard for someone who is going to save them as initials on her phone?" I continue, knowing I sound like a whiny little sibling who wants attention. "Poor little punk asses."

"I see . . . Do you want to rephrase that?" She chuckles. "I just did my eyes: I'm giving you a chance here."

"No, Morgan: I do not want to rephrase that." I have no plans tonight myself. "I said punk ass. Punk from the Latin *punkerus* and *ass* from that thing you don't wash."

I never feel any real sense of danger in annoying Morgan until I've annoyed Morgan. Her nails, for the record, are real; which I know from the numerous times they've dug into my flesh.

"OW! Uncle . . . uncle!" I say, muffled and in pain after ten minutes of thrashing. "I can't breathe, you mare!"

"You talk so much," she says, after releasing the arm twisted behind my back and letting go of my head for a merciful gasp of oxygen. "Your life would be so much easier if you were mute. Ever think of that?" she adds with a sigh and not a single hair out of place. Freaking She-Hulk. "See you tomorrow morning!"

"Remember! He's lying if he says he's out of condoms!" I defiantly shout as the front door shuts, watching my dog tail after her toward the door because she too gets entranced by Auntie Morgan. I suppose there's maybe just a bit of magic on occasion.

NINETEEN

SURE, I'LL BE YOUR BLACK GUY—EMPHASIS ON *GUY*

Nina and Morgan were only the first two. My world has become filled with Black women over the years. Friends of friends, neighbors, cousins, fellow authors, and even coworkers. Philosophically, these all amount to the same thing: *sisters*. I feel something loose in my chest when I spot them. Their existence and successes soothe something in me I can't quite pinpoint. Teaching at a privileged and liberal college only exacerbates that.

I'M TWENTY-NINE and let me be clear, 97 percent of my students are truly phenomenal human beings—be it in-progress or fully baked. I don't want to underplay that vast majority. The challenges of teaching them are interesting and the rewards immense. There are so many permutations of this career path, in which I walked out halfway through the very first workshop I ever taught in 2016 never to look back, so trust me when I say that this 97 percent is a blessing. I will never stop learning from college campuses.

. . . Three percent of them are, however, Karens in the making. There are no managers to summon yet, but professors and staff whose incompetence is baffling to them at eighteen years of age. They scoff and roll their eyes when displeased. You are their favorite professor until you say something they don't want to hear or hold them accountable, which reverts you to the gardener's assistant, messing up the shrubbery. My work inbox is a boxful of receipts of their privilege, at the intersection of adulthood and full-service nannies and tutors:

> "Additionally, I checked: there is no policy outlined in your syllabus that would indicate assignments wouldn't be accepted after the due date."

> "My only availability for office hours is Sunday from 3 p.m. to 4 p.m. Can you meet me in my building lobby at _____ by any chance? There's an office area!"

Students regularly enter my office to haggle down the word counts of their papers; a generation that knows the power of well-timed tears that are then wiped away with a smirk outside your office door once the B– is a B+. My professorial smile aims for a mixture of confidence, approachability, and occasionally a flicker of an eye twitch.

When I can't make room for one more student in my twelve-person workshop with a sixty-eight-person wait list (I'm not running a Dead Poets Society—film seminars and workshops are popular with students regardless of the professors assigned), she storms into the department chair's office and tears up demanding he rectify the situation. He does not. She allegedly proceeds to poll the admitted students on why they got in and she did not. I'm told by amused students I like that my emails are read aloud at the beginning of classes they share with her and that I'm called "an asshole!" Within the safe confines of my own book years later, I might, in return, hypothetically call her a waste of a prep school tuition whose aspirations of Greta Gerwigism will plateau at a beautifully curated Instagram album of flower crowns and hiking photos. But I'm the adjunct professor—the academic version of a starving freelance artist—and she's the undergraduate student: we both know who has the true infrastructural power here.

I tiptoe around, describing her actions as "discourteous" to her in an email and inviting her to an informal Q&A with students at the end of the semester, as a show of good faith.

Thanks, but my dad is a producer so I don't need the industry insider class, reads the short reply.

I laugh to myself reading the email in my office and briefly change my Twitter bio to MY DAD IS A PRODUCER before pesky maturity seeps in and I change it back.

On my way out that night, I tell the story to Cheryl, the interim department administrator. It's already 10 p.m., and she too is exhausted, getting the bulk of students and faculty requests all day. We are both roughly the same age and rarely get to chitchat freely without a buzzing department around us.

"That's nothing!" she bemoans. Cheryl is a Black woman and exudes an easy confidence that might serve her well in these choppy academic waters.

"At least you get to do this via email," she says. "I might already be fired."

"You're not fired."

She gives me a skeptical look. A *That's cute, child* even though we are both roughly the same age.

"This student was having problems with her insurance so I tell her she has to register online, right? It's a long pain-in-the-ass, forty-minute form, but it's all there on the portal and the deadline is tomorrow. I explain this to her, no thank you, no nothing, and she comes back an hour later with her iPad and drops it on my desk with the portal pulled up for me to fill in. She wants me to type while she reads me the information."

Cheryl is a born storyteller, but I recognize that definite eye twitch.

"And when I stare at her, on the phone, mind you, she just goes, 'Well, that's your job, not mine, so.'"

Cheryl repeats the sentence in her best Elle Woods impression. "Well, that's your job, not mine, so . . . Oof, like a twig, Ben!"

"Did you smile through it?" I ask.

Cheryl makes a face. "Barely."

"Long day, children?"

Joan Way startles both of us in the doorway, coat on and a bright scarf around her neck, ready for home. Joan Way (yes, pseudonym) is not just a professor: she is a powerhouse scholar with a résumé that was already impressive when I was born. Africana Studies, English Studies, Medieval & Renaissance Studies, Black Feminist Studies, Slavery Studies, Food Studies, Digital Humanities, and a few others.

"Hi, Joan!" I say, a little uncertain, always feeling more like a teacher's assistant than a professor around Joan Way.

She has heard nothing of our conversation, but her presence brings a slight shift to the air—that fearful trill of things unknown but longed for—as I realize that perhaps for the first time, the three Black employees of the department are in the same room together, decades of seniority between us.

"What are you two doing here so late?" Joan asks. There's always a hint of a smirk and a nod as if you are telling her a joke she's heard before but she doesn't want to deprive you of the joy of getting to the punch line.

"Um . . ."

Cheryl and I share a look of being both grateful for work and enjoying our jobs, but occasionally finding ourselves sighing those sighs, a little worn down being surrounded by so much precious white excellence and no alcohol. Joan Way lets out a single cackle before Cheryl and I can speak.

"I can't solve white people being back on their bullshit for you two, sorry."

She moves to the communal fridge and collects her thermos, sliding it into her large purse. And with that, she's off.

We then hear shouted from the hallway: "You two will be fine. Bite a pillow or something. Good night!"

Cheryl is dead. Vanquished, laughing loudly enough to be a disturbance to the cleaning staff one floor down, no doubt. That Joan Way exists and endures, in full awareness, is enough for both of us tonight.

Cheryl and I make plans to grab friendly drinks at some point soon. When I reply to that email chain after getting my grading out of the way the following week, my email bounces. Cheryl has been let go. "There were issues," I'm told when I ask.

I have no grand, unifying thesis about Black women here. Too long; didn't read? They have it much worse than Black men.

Societally, the polar opposite of the white man in America is the Black woman. What is a passive privilege built into this country's foundations to one is a series of unspoken hurdles to the other. I have read the statistics and the think pieces and glimpsed or heard some of their experiences navigating the world, but I have not felt it. I never will. Every struggle I experience comes with a basketful of GentleCare triple-ply male privilege.

And I get it: for many Black men, the phrase "Black male privilege" is a nonstarter. The logic behind that reticence is that whatever privilege a man has is dwarfed by the societal disadvantages that come with Blackness . . . That's inaccurate. You don't have to take my word for it, either. In the Renaissance Male Project, author and gender analyst Jewel Woods analyzes the privilege that us Black menfolk (guys, bros, brosephines, XYers, subway leg spreaders) have over the women of our race. And let's be clear here—it's a freaking boatload.

While we Black men might be attuned to the white privilege that we come across in our day-to-day existence, our lens tends to get blurry when it comes to Black women. Woods rightfully argues that male privilege is more than just a double standard. Just like white privilege comes at a cost to people of color, male privilege comes at the expense of women. Men are actively taking from women. (This is according to a 2019 Black Women's Equal Pay Survey by SurveyMonkey and Lean In.[1]) Black women in the United States make 39 percent less than white men and 21 percent less than white women.[2] Surely, we men can understand this without defensively throwing our arms in the air about how it's not our individual fault.

Interpersonally, Black women can experience more race-based emotional trauma in a single relationship—even in a city like New York—than I have my entire life. Without naming names: I've read the texts. My God.

Take it from a brother observing from the sidelines: the absolute amount of crap the sisters of this world go through all but *requires* dark magic to survive, let alone thrive through it. This isn't Tinkerbell dancing over your head and summoning fairy dust that smells like daylilies. It's equivalent exchange magic—the dark stuff. The blood has to be warm and the spices pungent. All the candles go off and your cough turns into a snake, slithering from your throat and hiding under a bookcase filled with grimoires. Ursula is cackling and there are poor unfortunate souls trembling in the background as body and soul are torn apart and stitched together again to start anew each day. That's Black Girl Magic— dark arts that require exhaustion of the self for a selfie-ready final product.

Can I read a book on the topic written by an actual woman, no offense? I get it, you're an ally; but a lot of this book is about your dick.

Okay, wow, rude: some of this book is about my dick. *Some.* Like, two pages total. Don't tell lies. You've been hanging out with Morgan. And, sure! These four are great and read nothing alike:

- *Black Feminist Thought* by Patricia Hill Collins
- *Women, Race & Class* by Angela Y. Davis
- *Redefining Realness* by Janet Mock
- *Killing the Black Body* by Dorothy Roberts

TWENTY

HOW TO GO THROUGH LIFE WITHOUT DROWNING, PART III

Like the Lord for some, my weird relationship with swimming was personal and something I only shared with people I trusted. That worked for a few years until I arrived at Columbia University, whose gorgeous campus in uptown Manhattan turned out to be designed to challenge all of my deepest convictions.

Anyone familiar with the Columbia undergraduate experience will tell you that it is a journey filled with construction-strength red tape at every corner.

You may be earning an Ivy degree, but know you are also entering a world in which credits are meticulously calculated, with a two-year-plus core curriculum of required classes every student is meant to complete regardless of their major, and a bureaucracy that can leave some students feeling powerless over their own lives.

The stupidest element of this academic labyrinth is hands down the Columbia Swim Test, a bizarre graduation requirement shared with Cornell, Dartmouth, and MIT. In order to get your degree, you must also—at some point in your four years—present yourself to the basement of the Dodge Fitness Center and swim three lengths of the pool using any stroke. That's it.

No one quite knows why we have to do this. There are theories that it was the eccentric requirement of a rich donor whose child had died. It might also simply be a bureaucratic justification for the maintenance of the pool. There are interviews online regularly justifying the practice in newspaper articles.

"Before I took the swim class, I couldn't even float across a pool," a student with goggles on posing in the school newspaper will say. "Now that I've taken the course, I can say that even though I'm still scared to fall into the deep end of the pool, I would know what to do."

Let's take a moment to explore how that is, objectively, some absolute bull.

First of all, engineering students in the Fu Foundation School of Engineering and Applied Science at Columbia do not have to fulfill this requirement. Should the island of Manhattan suddenly start to sink, those nerds are expected to simply build a boat.

Secondly, more often than not, it's the ethnic and underprivileged kids who end up sweating this demented ritual for four years. Most of the white friends or acquaintances I've made—especially those of the bro variety—have no problem with the swim test. They look forward to it, in fact, saving it for their last spring semester and treating the whole thing like a midday party. You'll see them in shorts and sandals, sunglasses on, headed to Dodge Fitness Center with whistles around their neck, for what amounts to a half-hour pool party.

The issue, as always, was for the rest of us. Even if I didn't protest the Army Reserve Officer Training Corps establishing a presence on campus or Iranian president Mahmoud Ahmadinejad being invited to speak at Columbia like my classmates, this was my personal societal issue that made my woke undergraduate blood boil. I cared for myself and for the Tuos—who we'll get to in a second—of the world: an underclass of insecure man-boys with body issues. They are my people, and our Elysium will come.

Tuo is my suitemate: a senior with an aggressively receding hairline and a pear shape. At twenty-two, he already looks like a midperforming car salesman with a favorite local stripper he wants to whisk away from it all. International students who don't have Jet Skis, or at least one childhood friend named Chad, approach the swim test with the proper gravitas of a requirement for their Ivy League degrees.

"I hope I don't fail," Tuo says late one night, practicing on the floor of our suite after I've dragged myself home from my typical 10 p.m. to 1 a.m. session at Butler Library, vomiting essays and reading dense sociological texts that I enjoy but forget too quickly once the A-minus-range grade clears. I'm steadily shoveling my way through a mountain of sociology credits that are slowly becoming secondary to my fiction workshops. By the end of college, this will be a fiction degree with a minor in sociology.

This poor, thickly accented man has moved the couches to the back of the common room and is actually practicing his backstroke on the floor. There's a swimming video on his propped-open laptop, and it's the most endearing thing in the world.

"You're not going to fail," I say, helping him move the furniture back as quietly as possible. Our living situation is a suite in the sense that introverts who did not want to take risks of rooming with friends could opt to live in a row of adjacent singles with common bathrooms and kitchens as shared spaces.

"No one fails the swim test," I reassure him. "They'll let you take it again, even in the summer after graduation if you don't manage to get the check mark." It's truly a ridiculous tradition.

"I have to go back to China," he answers, voice already wavering before going on to describe the nightmare that was getting a missing piece of paperwork to the school from his small town.

Somewhere in our chats, I had adopted the persona of chill, laid-back Black friend to Tuo. I know this because he had once laughed and said, without a hint of acid to his voice, that I was "the cool friendly Black guy of our suite," and something about the language, cultural, and follicle barriers had made it impossible not to chuckle along.

"It's also very nerve-wracking. Swimming in front of other people," Tuo eventually says and sighs.

He was right, there. With a double major in economics and mathematics, Tuo didn't have the time or the bandwidth to top it off with a weekly swimming course. Being shirtless and practicing your backstroke in the same pool as Columbia's hairless and chiseled swim team is nothing short of emotional trauma. I was offended on both of our behalfs.

"You have to take it too, right?" he asks. I nod for him to follow me to my room where I hand him a beer from my mini-fridge filled with groceries from the CTown supermarket north of campus encroaching into Harlem, with non–Ivy League prices.

"I have to take it."

"You know how to swim?" Tuo inquires, accepting the beer.

"My dad has a pool," I say, casually. I've gotten into the habit of lying like this sometimes around school. For no purpose other than to maybe wipe the footprints I'm leaving behind and confuse my story.

He nods and looks at me in a way that I've looked at dozens of people in my two years here—with a confused awe at what my life must default to once finals are out of the way at the end of every

semester. Somewhere along the way, I had soaked up enough privilege and cockiness that I did not plan on swimming the swim test
to collect that diploma.

"Can you not swim?"

I mean, look: if you drop me into a very still lake fifty feet or
less from the shore, I will not die. Any other situation, I might die.
But as a Black person who already has a history of family diabetes
coupled with a true addiction to sugar, I have enough of a survival
instinct to stay away from larger bodies of water. I'm *not* backflip-
ping off a natural waterfall with you, you absolute methhead.

Black people being less likely to know how to swim has everything to do with them having less access. You drop a white kid who
didn't live by the beach, summer at the lake, use *summer* as a verb,
vacation at water parks, or take swimming lessons at the Y, and he
probably can't swim either.

As a Black man who doesn't know how to swim with any sense
of forward momentum, my drowning survival tactic is to idle until
the rescuers make their way to me or to negate the risk entirely by
sitting on the rocks checking my news feed while friends jump off
waterfalls when on vacation.

Sure, I could potentially manage and waddle my way forward
for three lengths of the pool, surrounded by chiseled classmates
without hints of man-tits, but I also resented this ritualistic humiliation being levied against my freaking Ivy goddamn League
degree after dozens of essays, exams, and all-nighters.

Could I have taken the test and passed? We'll never know.

In the Japanese anime and manga *Naruto*, which introduces us to a world of paramilitary ninja villages, young ninjas are expected to take a written exam early on in their formation. Bear with me here. The exam is extraordinarily difficult by design and the whole point isn't to answer the questions but to find an inconspicuous way to cheat in a way that reflects your specific set of skills. So, the telepath takes over a nearby proctor's body and quickly memorizes the answers; the sound ninjas—there are sound ninjas—tap the answers to one another; the dog whisperer whispers to his dog; and so on and so forth. (Hinata just shows her exam to Naruto so he can copy the answers from her because she has low self-esteem and is truly a sloppy outline of a character, a fact I intend to break down over 390 pages in my next oeuvre.)

This is how I see the Columbia Swim Test. Actually taking the test was for peasants lacking in imagination. The memory of an ocular conversation between my aunt and mom had convinced me not to mess with large bodies of water and thus avoid every given opportunity to learn to swim. Resourcefulness will now be required. Yes, that is how badly I don't want to take my shirt off in front of the swim team, who would surely cease practicing immediately, point at me, burst into uproarious laughter, and then give me some horrible nickname.

My friend Colleen is getting an exemption from it because of a note from her therapist she's trying to seduce. Two boys from one of my fiction seminars who went to Harvard-Westlake talk about how they got their former swim coach to "send an email." Nora intends to play the long game and delay it to the summer after graduation and swim elsewhere in a pool managed by her friend.

For my part, there is no mind-swiping in the works. No whispering dogs, or insects, or mirrors. All I have is an ID card with a bad, featureless photo—and that's all it will take.

I meet him at the gates of Columbia, by the 116th Street/Columbia University subway station. The ad he is replying to is simple and straightforward.

[ACTIVITY PARTNERS]
"LOOKING FOR MALE AFRICAN AMERICAN SWIMMER"
(THURSDAY, MARCH 17, 2011)

Asking for a photo via email would have been a risk, but I swiped his name through social media and got the sense that we were at least the same hue. Up close, we look nothing alike. He has sharper features, is taller, skinnier. I have no doubt that he's an actual swimmer and spends a considerable number of hours at the gym. His nails are unhealthy, I notice; chipped at the base and glistening like glued-on props. You wouldn't even buy us as cousins from a crooked family tree. No Robert here.

He has acting aspirations, which my email reply avoided. It is "sort of" acting and could lead to other opportunities. If I'm ever casting a film, I'll have a proven Black swimmer.

"Right." He nods as we chitchat our way through campus, a good foot apart in height. "So, what is this?"

He's hesitant until I hold up the ID.

"A Black person didn't take this photo," he says with a snort, and it's the first smile I've gotten from him.

"Nope." I sigh, relieved.

He collects half of the money, takes the ID, which will be scanned twice—once at the turnstiles, face down, and later as he gets in line to take the exam. I picked a crowded time when, presumably, the administrators will be slightly overwhelmed by the flow of students. He stops at the steps of the Dodge Fitness Center, takes in the size of the building, and backtracks to me.

"What if they catch me?"

I look back at the school and then at him. I have no exit strategy. Just the confidence of an Ivy Leaguer getting increasingly used to cutting administrative corners.

". . . They won't catch you," I assure him.

He nods slowly. He's counting the money more than my words but eventually goes in. Thirty-seven minutes later, he comes out with a damp T-shirt collar under his zip-up. If his hair is still wet, I can't tell. He shuffles his feet while collecting my profuse thanks.

"How was it?"

"I followed your directions, found the pool pretty easily."

"And the test?"

"It's swimming." He shrugs and collects the other half of his money, vaguely unhappy with the transaction. There's no easy chatter. He's withholding now, and I get the sense that he's mad at me but won't disclose why unless pushed. I don't push and thank him for his services with a professional handshake. It's 2011 and there's a gig economy ahead—we should both get used to doing things we don't want to for a bank account that traffics in the red.

Later that evening, I will receive an email that notifies me that my swim test requirement has been fulfilled. Of course it has. You can find anything on Craigslist. Apartments, roommates, sublets, Missed Connections, fellow misanthropes to complain about the ethnic people moving in in the Rants & Raves section—or even narcotics if that is what you are looking for. (I'm not. I'm a good little boy; I'm just saying.) Even Black bodies.

That night, after reading the 1853 memoir *Twelve Years a Slave* by Solomon Northup and underlining a few key quotes for the paper I have to finish drafting that weekend, I dream of the plantations of Louisiana. Of being a cog in that system. After the day's events, the book stays with me in a way I don't like. The writing is too good, the words are too precise. Solomon's despair gets under your skin. The heat and endless fields. In a few years, I will step out of the Austin airport, committed to the rigors of a graduate program, take a fistful of the Texan sun right to the jaw, and think of this dream again.

In this dream I watch two men in rags the color of the Haitian flag run with danger behind them. They run like the ninjas from Naruto with their arms thrown back behind them. The danger gets closer and one of them, the fatter one, gains the lead, only to trip his running partner, who tumbles behind as he himself keeps running.

I wake up in the middle of the night, parched. I fell asleep without showering. I realize I haven't showered since Tuesday and it's not Tuesday. In the kitchen, I lean forward and drink water straight from the tap, maybe just for the drama of it. I notice the common-room chairs pushed aside again and take a 4 a.m. shower in the empty communal bathrooms. *Snap out of it.* I touch my lower back, wet after a shower, and try to imagine what the lash of a whip feels like. Not a cinematically directed cloud of red mist, but the actual opening gash of a whip slicing air and flesh. I wonder what holding a whip feels like; if it rings up your arm. If you care. *Snap out of it.*

I sit on my bed, wet, and finish the essay in one stream by the time the sun starts to rise. I email it to the professor, six days early and without proofreading. I want it away from me. *Snap out of it.* Keep waddling forward and pretend it's the same as swimming. Pretend there's a clear shore ahead.

The American stereotype that Black people can't swim did not come out of thin air.[1] Across the United States, more than ten people drown every day, and Black children are drowning at something close to three times the rate of white children. Sixty-four percent of Black children can't swim. These are regurgitated statistics I'm feeding you right now, yes, but that doesn't make them any less true.

This is not genetic. Our bones aren't heavier, our lungs don't take in more water. The reason is the same as for so many other things in this country: years of racial segregation. White public officials and white swimmers did not want Black men to interact with white women in such an intimate public space. Jim Crow laws, baby. Racial discrimination became normalized and institutionalized across the country.

In 1964, during a staged jump-in by protestors against racial segregation at the Monson Motor Lodge in Saint Augustine, Florida, the owner, James Brock, poured acid into his own pool to get people out. Imagine! Some would rather pour acid into their own pool than let Black people near it.

These days, it's regular gentrification that is the driving force behind modern-day pool segregation. Over the past few decades, tens of thousands of private club pools developed in suburban communities. Meanwhile, public pools, our previous notion of them, are also disappearing. Since 2009, more than 1,800 public pools have closed, and there are now more than 10 million residential pools compared to the 300,000 public pools across the country.

I'M TWENTY-SEVEN and watch a documentary on the civil rights movement. And then another. And another. When I can't find the full films, I settle for YouTube clips. I learn all these things and catch up on American history I did not have to take as an international college student. That visa was seen as overpowering the face on my ID card and somehow, these things are optional to a pristine education.

After absorbing all these facts, I feel a pit of shame at that missed opportunity back in college because that's what it was: a gift I slapped away. I look up swimming classes at a fitness center on the Upper West Side. It's relatively expensive, but I'm not as broke as I used to be these days. The class consists of twelve people. Two kids, siblings, wear arm floaties. The gray-haired woman looks shockingly like my aunt Atalante and I imagine her putting on an all-day frock the moment she gets home, hair still smelling of chlorine. Seven of us are Black.

The instructor is a young and peppy Latinx woman, Brenda. She makes us all feel like toddlers, and we laugh at our awkwardness diving under the water, holding air in our lungs. It is nowhere as stunning or fulfilling as a screening of Barry Jenkins's *Moonlight*. The eight-week process is appropriately humiliating but less so than when surrounded by Ivy League classmates.

I still swim there, though only occasionally. I keep my headphones in while changing and affect an air of casualness about the whole thing. As if I've been doing this all my life at the country club. My backstroke is coming along and it's good cardio. Mind you, I will never fully trust lakes. (Also? Abs. Like, the visible outline of abs. Purr for me.)

TWENTY-ONE

SONG OF THE SOUTH

AUSTIN, TX
YEAR: 2011
POPULATION: 828,694 (BLACK POPULATION: 7.7 PERCENT)

My time in Austin, Texas, which began in 2011 and ended in 2014, was a strange three-year stretch. In hindsight, not much happened. There is no tale of drug overdose ahead. I wasn't chased down the side of the road by a truckload of Aryan ghosts.

One minute I was twenty-two and the next twenty-five, with a master's in fiction and screenwriting from one of the most prestigious programs in America that will still have me browsing Craigslist for fast-paying gigs and guessing the email addresses of literary agents for a few years to come.

I spent three years wrestling with the promise of change and growth that being a full-time writer would, should bring. I sighed and drummed my pencil to the clock like Britney Spears in that puberty-triggering video of ". . . Baby One More Time," but the flashback and colorful dance sequence never quite happened. I went to Texas for stories, and in the end, only have a half-deck of anecdotes, false starts, and a few memorable faces. No *story*.

It's late August 2011 and I've just moved to Austin, Texas, for a literary fellowship.

Texas is a big and fictional location for me: a part of America that, until now, has been relegated to entertainment kitsch and stereotypes. But, the Michener Center for Writers is the golden ticket. It's not just a literary fellowship, it's *the* literary fellowship. The Iowa Writers' Workshop is slightly higher in the rankings but it doesn't come with as generous or steady of a stipend. Plus, it doesn't let you pursue screenwriting. You get a stipend, enough to live on full-time. It's the closest to a paid writer I will be for a few years after graduation. An old-school writer with a patron. The syllabus is ridiculous. Fairytales, Fiction Workshop, Class in America, Screenwriting. The grades don't matter; the work does.

Austin is a town at the center of cool. It's a liberal haven in a conservative state. The best of Americana. Your future is set. After this, you'll be an author. You'll have salt to your earthiness. You might develop a twang. You might drive a truck.

The New Yorker in me rolls his eyes at the WELCOME TO AUSTIN, PLEASE DON'T MOVE HERE banner at the small, colorful airport. The signage is clear throughout the airport, the men are tall, and the undergraduates are flowing in, burnt-orange shorts and longhorn paraphernalia at the ready. A bee stings me on the nose coming out of the Austin Airport, and I'm already over this wretched state that feels like a new uncharted continent.

I'm also suddenly Black again. I was Black in New York, in a way that was unimportant and trivial. Where it's rarer to step into a train without a dozen people like me. I'm not the only Black guy, by any means, but I am a Black guy, in a way that's only noticeable after New York.

But it doesn't matter, because, Michener, baby. Suck my nipples, rejection slush piles of the world! Their faculty is peppered with literary icons. Denis Johnson. Elizabeth McCracken. Zadie Smith is visiting this semester!

Their students aren't writers or celebrities; they're *authors*. With books and stuff. It's the year of *The Yellow Birds* by Kevin Powers. There's a cardboard poster in the lobby of the white, homey house that doubles as our department with a classroom upstairs. It's the sort of environment that demands to be the backdrop to deep introspection and great art.

It's a community of writers, and marketing will lead you to believe that is a good thing for us feral creatures to seek and develop. A community of peers.

My classmates are playwrights, fiction writers, and poets. Most of them are Americans. There are screenwriting courses in the class catalog, too, but no one in our incoming class of eleven defines themselves as such. The poets and playwrights, however, were poets and playwrights before they could hold a pen.

There's Obe, the sharp playwright with sinister eyes and the severe cheekbones of a budding mobster villain who tells me he's Jewish when we meet and then our second year says that he's not Jewish when it comes up again. He gives me a coy shrug and laughs to himself when I ask why, and I resolve to dislike him from that moment. Random lies as an exertion of power on other people is my stage, and I don't like an open mic-er making me his audience.

The other playwright, Rayna, is dynamic, political, and

confident with enough whimsy to balance it all and dynamic el-
ocution to boost. She teaches me how to pronounce *gauge*, which
comes ten years too late. ("Gay-jh," not "goh-j" like *mauve*. English truly is a nonsense language.) Her laugh is delightful, and
she makes precise points by joining her two fingers together when
talking. She's a graduate of Columbia, too, but older. She seems
right at home in Austin, arranging get-togethers and socializing like
a real person rather than a feral New Yorker always wary of other
people's motives and always aware of the importance of concealing
your own.

Cerim is there to network. His friendly smiles and eye contact
feel like they come with a timeshare offer in his back pocket. The
distrust starts at the back of my neck and he naturally will be the
first one of us to sell a book.

Everyone is easy to stay away from. I wish this was high school
and that I could grab my tray of whole-milk cartons and wet spa-
ghetti and take it to another table, but there is no such option. We
are each other's cohorts.

"*This,*" Elizabeth McCracken, the star teacher, says, eyeing us
all meaningfully. "This is what matters. The people. You will know
each other in a way other people can't. As friends and writers."

Three of us are Black. But no kinship exists beyond that.
There's me; Ikome, an African fiction writer who writes of Africa;
and Water, who writes slavery tales in spaceships. I wonder what
my thing is, in their eyes.

There's an underlying air of diversity to our incoming class.
Lowered standards, maybe? Pad the class with a rainbow of people, regardless of actual ability to write? For a long time, I wonder
if that's how people see me: as a token Black writer, here to provide
narratives to fit their narratives. "I don't fit here" is a better refrain

than "Maybe I don't belong here." It doesn't matter except to those of us who feel strange cashing nearly $30,000 a year from the estate of James A. Michener.

Each year, a new cohort of twelve joins the three-year program. They all feel temporary. Future likes on Facebook through whom I realize how bored of Facebook I am.

I like some of them, like Will over at the twin New Writers Project. But Will isn't as mean as I would want. Sometimes, when we hang out alone, I wish he would say viciously catty things about our classmates, but he doesn't, and it leaves me feeling bitchy, but the man is wholesome, thoughtful, with his wild uncertain twenties a decade behind him. He's the youngest-looking thirty-seven-year-old man I've ever met. He smiles and does yoga and apparently there is still room in my heart for handsome white men with long hair who smile and do yoga and write poetry. (I'm disappointed in myself, too.)

In quick succession, I receive both the best and worst writing advice of my life while at Michener. During a seminar break, a visiting professor, casually and without meaning to, successfully imparts that: "Nobody needs to see this story that's in your head. Nobody asked for it. For most of your first readers—classmates, potential agents, underpaid slush pile readers—it will be work. So, it's only polite to make this unnecessary, unsolicited thing remotely interesting."

During a workshop, a previously described classmate proposes an improvement on a story of mine they really enjoyed.

"It's such a universal story! The main character doesn't even have to be Black for it to work." Others nod approvingly. It's buried in a sea of compliments about my wit, which makes it hard to contradict. Or even register until later that night, while brushing my teeth. (Trust me: they'll all be Black until arthritis makes the keyboard a torture device, Cerim, you prick.)

On the screenwriting side of things, across campus at the Radio-Television-Film department, I'm flanked by tall beefy men in plaid shirts and impossibly specific graphic tees with cars who meet at every corner of Austin. I'm too embarrassed to ask for a ride and instead learn to love my apartment, a palace by New York–dorm standards, right on campus, six minutes door-to-door from the Michener Center with a pool.

It's right next to a bar—The Crown & Anchor—a north campus staple that, to someone else, would be the setting of a sitcom-like home base, where I meet a cast of regulars and shoot the breeze for hours in the evening. Instead, I occasionally grab Styrofoam plates of coagulated nachos and rush up home to my apartment kept at 66 degrees even in the cooler months. I'm hot all the time in Austin. Crossing campus leaves me drenched in sweat. I adopt a permanent costume. Dress shirt with a colorful undershirt beneath.

I gain weight again, so no T-shirts. I masturbate, but only at night, to keep things romantic.

The writing around the Michener program is strong but not brilliant. We're all trying and figuring it out. I'm almost disappointed that I'm not wholly outclassed. That would have been a story, too, I think. The writer who didn't have what it takes. I realize that what I want here is a story.

I write stories every week. Random tales of awkward social interactions that will eventually make up a check-mark thesis. My collection awards me a master of fine arts and nine book rejections, and one in-person rejection at a restaurant with an agent who loved the title but found the content underwhelming and presumably wanted the opportunity to tell my fully suited self in person with a cup of coffee and an earnest hug. Hmm, I still like the title, so I won't tell you here. I might use it one day. Writers are petty that way. And back there, in Austin, Texas, was when I was at my most writerly.

I avoid the program's parties and gatherings around the department. I flirt with a light depression, thinking of the other paths my life could be taking in those three years. I watch all of *The West Wing*. Twice. I purchase old DVDs of *Frasier*.

We talk about our writing habits and perform our new author identities to one another, for one another. Flirty, unassuming, friendly while secretly networking for future blurbs of unwritten books. This is the time, the arena. Writers who write about and against each other.

I want to write inky-black comedies, but instead I write dysfunctional and quiet short stories. The type of MFAs that people mock and that strike tedious debates about whether or not writing should happen in carpeted classrooms inside college campuses, or scribbled on the backs of napkins pinching your bloody nose after a bar brawl out there in the real world. The reflection paper of my thesis will read:

> *Nothing in life is as potent or inevitable as one stranger looking to another and thinking to themselves, "I like this," "I want this," "I could love this." In the stories that follow, reckless, occasionally loathsome characters run forward with eyes closed and arms open, tripping themselves in pursuit of the one thing they believe will make them whole.*
>
> *In "This is Having," well-meaning narcissist Reggie is unable to properly understand his girlfriend's*

attempts at personal growth, mistaking them for
dissatisfaction with him.

In "Arms In, Elbows Wet," Dan is prone to extreme
mood swings triggered by his pathological fear of being
left behind by the people he loves.

In "Lying Rots Your Teeth," stuttering Sammy is
driven to murder by a fraternal inferiority complex while
the universe laughs at his expense.

I spend so much time up there, chronicling the mating habits of fictional assholes in bursts of nine thousand words, that my ass feels homey. Away from the laptop, I try to remember what it's like to like people. To go through the paces of chitchat, lunch, breakfast, texting, and develop intimacy that way. Boring. I'm prickly and can't quite calibrate myself into this crowd. God, I miss New York. And Nina and Morgan.

I want a story. Being liked by people is kind of a story. That's essentially the gist of "Snow White." I begin to smile more until it snaps into a frown. Screw that. I'm disgusted by the affable foreigner schtick I've perfected. I want to be hated and fight back.

I want to be dragged into an alley and presented with a little plate of hard drugs that become the love of my life. I want to be arrested—or at least get my head pushed against a cop car.

I'm on a fully funded three-year hiatus in which the fuel is real-life experience, and I'm wasting it keeping a clean kitchen and going to bed lonely at 10:15 p.m.

I bite my nails to the stubs and Band-Aid the chapped nail beds, ending up looking like a worn-out guitarist. At night, I get restless. There's an invisible clock ticking over my head, counting down from MFA funding, twentysomething freedom, and life. In that order. I get into the habit of kicking off the covers, grabbing my keys, and launching myself into the night without a destination. 11 p.m., 1 a.m., 2 a.m. These get later and later. If you want to get hit, you gotta play in traffic. I'm looking for the sort of people looking for trouble.

I crash a fraternity party on campus where I melt into the crowd and collect high fives. "I'm Phil, a friend of Dave's," I say and then say again louder, shouting over loud music in the backyard of a fraternity house filled with twenty-two-year-olds in six-packs. Yes, *in*. Six-packs are apparel you can temporarily own. You wear them and then misplace them never to find them again. Speaking from experience here.

(Sidebar: "I'm a friend of Dave's" will gain you access into most frat parties. Dave is somewhere in the back right now and could have a Black friend. He's cool that way.)

After two beers and chitchat about the recent *Game of Thrones* season-4 finale, I head home with two new Facebook contacts that I'll never speak to again.

I want a story.

A week later, I have dinner with my classmates at a visiting professor's house. He's made too many quesadillas and wears sandals.

A classmate, one year ahead of me and already published, offers me a ride home. She seems to feel bad for me. I'm falling behind in an environment where academic success is only measured by personal and creative growth.

"No, thanks." I smile. "I have a friend swinging by to pick me up."

"Another big party?"

I shrug coyly. There's no friend. No party and no friend. I like that I might have a partying reputation around the department. I know this isn't true. But for them to notice would require paying attention to one another instead of just talking about one another, which is a ridiculous thing to expect from authors.

I watch her leave, then I start to walk and eventually keep walking. Fight face on: Why not?

A homeless person rolling a cart filled with empty cans crosses the street from me when we pass each other at an overpass. Of the two of us, I'm the stranger in the night without a destination or point, I realize. I walk on, hoping for anything that might amount to a true story I'll look back on and shake my head with a smile, thinking of my time in Texas.

One evening, I go on Craigslist and trade messages with multiple strangers. I don't have the body confidence to be the type of guy who sends floppy dick photos, biting his own T-shirt up and angling the phone just right in front of his stained bathroom mirror, so I settle for witty repartee.

A Craigslist hookup is a story. Dating app profiles are too clean, too dull for the story I have in mind. That's just sleazy enough of a good Texan tale. There are a few bites but ultimately, the most real connection comes from fakenumbersandletters@reply.craigslist.org.

We begin to email a lot, back and forth, replies coming seconds apart. The intimacy is sudden and weird enough that we're both comfortable in this format.

I've never been with a Black guy before.

Me neither. Okay, well, once. He was my uncle, though, so it was okay.

Her emoji sobs hysterically five times in a row. I'm dangerous, unknown, but witty enough to be safe.

Come over.

No. You'll twist my nipples and rob me.

It makes no sense and she laughs in writing again. I start to doze off in bed, and she sends three more emails in a row.

Wake up!
I'm bored!
I'm serious; come over.

She eggs me on to take a cab to her apartment complex, a building named Oceanwide that is nowhere near a body of water.

In a Tasmanian devil whirlwind, I'm freshly showered, groomed, and ready to be murdered at 2 a.m. The cab driver is Black, too, and chuckles, catching me fan out my pit in the car, nervous despite the AC.

"Should I still come up?" I ask the intercom outside the gates of her apartment complex. I realize it's the first time we're speaking.

There's silence. She's looking down at me through the blinds but I can't see her. I wave. The awkward Dan Humphrey wave from the first episode of *Gossip Girl*. I've practiced it before.

"Yes, one second," she eventually says.

I go up. She invites me in, invites me to sit down.

"Okay," I say, sitting on her couch with both hands on my knees as if waiting for a haircut.

She laughs, offers me a glass of fireball, and then she performs oral sex on me in her living room. I bump my knee against a crowded coffee table when it's my turn to return the favor.

"One second, okay?"

I nod.

She disappears into her bedroom and comes out carrying a bunch of framed photos facing down, looking apologetic, and then leads me in by the hand. I wish this was a real date. I want to ask her about the knitting kit, the French poster, the rice cooker. It's the brand I've been wanting to buy.

I smell Axe Chocolate on the sheets, which I'm not wearing. It's as vivid as that time I applied three coats before a party in high school. It's not the disgusting, seedy, messy sex either of us expected. There's a lot of kissing. If she climaxes, it is self-generated enthusiasm. I deserve little to no credit.

In the morning her face doesn't look like a glazed donut. We thank each other. She offers me coffee and is relieved when I decline.

"I'm gonna shower, okay?"

"Okay." I nod, understanding. I'll be gone.

I leave with a headache as the water runs loudly in the bathroom although it doesn't sound like there's a body under it yet. She has a story now, I realize, walking to the bus stop in the morning, watching joggers go by. Meanwhile, I can't tell if I'm closer to one of my own or not.

TWENTY-TWO

SURE, I'LL BE YOUR ACCESSORY TO LARCENY

Here's another thing—no, *the thing*, in fact, italics, emphasis, and all—about Black people.

No, it's not the slavery or the sickle cell or even the fact that we get to use the clear, crisp version of the N-word with a hard "er" on the tail of it. No, it's something much simpler. I'd use the word *primal* if it weren't for the unfortunate connotation.

It's that we have something in common. Something others don't. Something that deep down makes us like each other—even if only a little—in spaces that, at a glance, don't belong to us.

It's similar to spotting someone in a crowded airport whose T-shirt claims a common alma mater somewhere out East. It's the same kinship that leaves my cousin Watson up on his lawn chair at barbecues telling jokes like "What do you get when you put a Blood, a Crip, a businessman, and two guns in an elevator?"

That's the very joke that echoes in your head as you hear, "Hey, man, got the time?" in broad daylight cutting through a parking garage and then an alley between Nueces Street and Rio Grande Street.

"Um, what?" you ask, removing your headphones.

The man seems annoyed he has to repeat himself. "You've got the time, brother!"

It's an exclamation point, not a question mark, but you look down at your phone, even though your heart's beating faster and you don't know why yet.

The kinship that two seconds later makes the sudden knifepoint at your throat and the railing against your neck something less than completely overwhelming.

He holds it sloppily, leaving you more than enough room to breathe, and even to potentially shout. You've never held a knife to anyone's neck—never thought to—but you've watched enough of *The Wire* to think it ought to be placed right under the Adam's apple and flipped around to give you the edge of the blade instead. It's that exact sort of sloppiness that keeps disposable henchmen and thugs on the big screen.

You wait for the fear to kick in but for some reason, it doesn't. Under this bright, deadly, Texan sun, you're both the exact shade, so, no, brother, bro, homey, homedog, nigga, nigger; I will not give you my iPhone. You must be out your goddamn mind, *boy*. Yes, as a matter of fact, I do think you's playin' and if the blade hadn't just shifted to a more dangerous and competent position just now, I would even be inclined to tell you as much.

After a few seconds, this stupidity starts to feel a lot like courage. You start to think of a clever Facebook status update to cover these events. "It's the old iPhone. You're gonna have to mug someone new in a few days," you hear yourself scoff out of nowhere because suddenly and without much precedent, the coward has balls.

Besides, aren't you a writer? The fellowship stipend says so. Isn't there a certain romance to dying stupidly and before your time? Isn't that the story you've been pacing around for? The image of Mom choking up during the eulogy is the only thing that ultimately makes you bundle up your headphones and hand the whole thing over. She hates public speaking almost as much as you love it but would feel compelled to speak on that day. To put her in that position seems cruel, but you can't help it. You lower your voice and force every neuron in your brain to lose your foreign and harmless accent, if only for the space of the next few words:

"Twenty-nine million people in this state and you're gonna go after a brother, huh?"

He holds the phone for a few seconds as if considering a rebuttal and then hands it back to you before taking a step back to release you. In turn, you resist the urge to frantically rub your throat. He looks at you, nods, and tells you to take it easy before slinking back into the shadows.

"Yeah, you too, bro. Take it easy."

Or no, actually, you suddenly feel like turning back and screaming, *don't take it easy. In fact, go die in a fire of Klansman anger, you freaking statistic.* But you've already been stupid enough for one day—no one asked for the time in New York City. No one stops to answer. You think that back there, you would have been smarter than this.

Don't make eye contact with the two young Asian women—iPhones and clutch purses in hand—who look like they might be going up the alley just as you're coming out it. Illogical as it is, don't you owe him something? Didn't he just do you a solid? Smile at them, apologetically maybe. They should know that some of us smile and will hopefully remember it, afterward.

Get angrier with yourself with every step. There was no story here today. Nothing to update, nothing to see. Just two Black guys the exact same shade perpetuating stereotypes. The lawn chair breaks before Watson's done. Aunt Atalante shakes her head. "Dead businessman," Watson says and grins, dusting himself off and holding his side.

I've thought a lot about not including this experience here. There's something reckless about doing so. Why include a traumatic instance of "Black-on-Black violence" as a stern-jawed blond woman on FOX news might call it, while making an argument for Blackness? Why not an essay on John Lewis's legacy or 2016's Best Picture–winner *Moonlight*? Or, the vibrant, unspoken kinship of a Harlem cookout in which I end up cackling with people I did not know until moments prior and who are now my cousins?

The best answer I can come to is simply because it happened and left an impression. I remember the blade, the fear, and disappointment at the anticlimactic nature of my own death. I remember thinking of my mom and being relieved that I would never have to mourn her if I died here and now.

I did not know this man. Whether or not he likes jazz, what his family looks like, if he can swim. On that day, he was to me the very image all Black men are weighed against: a criminal in the shadows, ready to pounce and take. There was no room for interiority in our blunt exchange. I did not see the soul in his eyes. I said what I said because I was reckless and afraid, looking for survival: "seduction" instead of "fight" or "flight."

It happened to me and it could happen to you, too. A person might gratuitously wrong you, target you, and that person might be Black. You might sit in a chair shaking for a few hours. Nothing about the incident takes away from that man's humanity. He has not been downgraded to nigger for his sins. He should not be summarily executed should a trigger-happy officer walk by. I am not excusing the crime he possibly commited next or those he committed since. I am no less angry at the mugging or afraid of taking that path home for the remainder of my time in Texas. The slight trauma of having had a knife to my throat in broad daylight lingers for a few days. I may curse out the asshole a few times in the shower and pantomime the karate chop I should have given him in the moment.

But, I also get to live in constant awareness that obviously all Black men are not like this because I am what he is, something that those two young women may not get. From afar, and without seeing the blade, you may have thought we were two Black guys lurking in the shadows, planning something. Forgive us.

TWENTY-THREE

SURE, I'LL BE YOUR ONE THAT GOT AWAY

"The airport, please."

All things considered, it's something closer to vindictiveness than politeness that has me jump into the cab at the last minute and fold myself between her and her luggage in the back seat. It's only when she inches closer to her window in response that I become aware of the true time commitment of this ride-along. Like so many things in my life—Texas, New York—it seemed like a good idea at the time. The promise of a story.

But the fact was that I really was fine with this—with all of it—and when the cab had pulled up in the middle of our awkward porch-side goodbye, the opportunity to showcase said fineness one last time felt too enticing to pass up. It wasn't just a story, but a story with a clean ending.

However, the ride was now proving itself to be an extension of the weekend. There were unrecognizable bouts of dead air, the result of this third thing between us. Something thin, barely perceptible, that nevertheless touched everything. Conversation had to be consciously refueled with specific topics, and every red light and halted lane convergence now seemed like overtime to some game neither team was sure they were playing all that well.

Even the cabbie seems to notice, eventually turning on the radio to fill the lull.

I would not end college with a romance right out of a romantic comedy. Rather, I end it with a Mia. She's the closest ribbon to a sustainable romantic connection I make. We meet in a sociology seminar on the concept of the "Culture Industry" that ends up being a journey into the professor's obsession with Andy Warhol. The outline of Mia's face shines in the dark as we sit one row apart in an in-class screening of the 1995 documentary *The Celluloid Closet*. We are of that generation that simply throbs for a good "It's complicated" on our Facebook profiles.

She has flown out to see me on a whim. A few emails and she was on her way into Austin citing myriad reasons. Because she misses me. Because I was her first friend to have gotten his life together after graduation, from the looks of it (a very kind interpretation). And also because she had "some news." On the phone, it sounded like paperwork that she needed to get out of the way. It should also be noted that Mia is, simply put, rich as hell. Rich as hell in that way that waves it off as "my family's comfortable" when she opens the door to a hotel suite on Columbus Circle to study for finals because the library is at capacity.

We both take to our own window and develop a separate appreciation for scenery, feeling it important that our knees not touch. Having never been one for unfilled silences, it is still, of course, me that speaks first.

"I have you—well, your character—say this line. In this story I'm working on," I say.

"Oh?"

" *'Years from now, when you're old and wrinkled, you'll regret not having been more reckless.'* That's what she says."

She chuckles, untying her traveling ponytail to rub the sweat at the back of her neck into her hair, still decidedly unaccustomed to the South's oppressive heat. "Ben, that doesn't sound like me at all."

We take the highway, and I distract myself by trying to read the fine print of passing billboards through the hundred-degree miasma.

"Maybe you shouldn't write about me for a while," Mia eventually adds, still focused on her own brown and cracking side of the landscape. "It's not all that healthy."

"We do healthy now?" I say, motioning between us with a grin.

She reignites and extends her ring finger with all the decidedness of a middle one. The small but expensive and presumably flawless diamond catches the sun as she clicks her tongue twice. "We sure do, baby!"

This causes an exhaust-valve fit of laughter between us that seems to lighten the air and loosen our knees.

I catch the cabbie smiling in the rearview, on the outside of what to him must appear to be a pleasant inside joke between old college lovers. He seems friendly, and I wish his cabbie route extended to Sherbrooke, Quebec, seventeen years prior. I move my knee against hers, relieved when she doesn't move away. This is how I like the world; at a distance and with someone at my side.

Out of habit, I carry Mia's luggage for her. In the unbearable heat, the slight fever I've been nursing since our little balcony tryst the night before surges through my body, until I can almost smell it. I had caught a fever senior year as well. My friend David had come to visit New York, and after two days of sightseeing, I had lost my voice and skipped three days of class in the process. Mia had appeared with my favorite clam chowder soup from my favorite Columbia market deli, crackers, and takeout from Olli's, and detailed notes from the hundred-person lecture we both shared, but where we did not sit together, waiting in my inbox.

Later, she admits that it had been that night, with me freezing and in sweats shaking in her arms, that she had fallen in love with me. *You were like an ice cream cone, dripping down my arm*, she'd giggled the next morning. We don't spend much time together after that. It's one of those things: senior year is on fast-forward, the future was uncertain, I was going to Austin on a fellowship. Revisiting our old texts, her postcollege anxieties were about where she saw herself living, not what she'd be doing. Her uncle was giving her his condo. Mia is not an amoral wealthy white person. She never was. She just belonged to that tribe of people who sometimes get a condo gifted to them as a college graduation present.

The airport is, as it turns out, a place of strict emotional detachment. Even in the South. Absent are the overwhelmed sobs at untimely departures and reckless hugging at delayed arrivals that I always remembered. Maybe those memories were simply misplaced scenes from movies. Like the vivid death by cops that I still remember from the end of *Save the Last Dance*.

People yawn and sigh, seemingly at random, lost in their personal annoyances. This middle ground of "friends, really close friends" leaves us outsiders in the hustle of families, lovers, and soldiers, unsure of exactly which set to mimic. College was long enough ago for us to fall out of sync. Like a shameful percentage of college friends before us, we've lost that unique flow of ours and instead have gotten angular with each other. Passion has ceded to politeness.

"Seriously," Mia breathes, fanning herself with a magazine at baggage check-in with her hip out and left leg extended, posing for the passing security officer we both notice leering and abstain to mention. "Is it always this hot here?"

"I don't know yet. People say it cools down in November."

"It does! This is the worst we've had in a long while," agrees the wide man behind us. "You'll be pulling out the night blankets soon enough, believe me." Personal conversations are apparently open guestbooks in this part of the country.

She smiles warmly and instinctively borrows some of the stranger's twang. "Well, we're from the East Coast. Believe me, sixty's still boiling for us." The man chuckles and proceeds to share his very serious and not-at-all insane concerns regarding the East Coast.

". . . Chinese, Taiwanese, Indian, it's all over the place! It's good food, don't get me wrong, but at the end of the day, it's all borrowed, you know. You can taste it all you want but you'll never know it, y'know. Not like a Lone Star steak. A steak here is just home, y'know." The two of them drift in and out of this exchange as bags are processed and I stand on the sideline of this travelers' exchange, feeling somewhat superfluous.

"People are actually really friendly here," Mia concludes, waving as the man finally walks away, tripping over nothing.

"You know, not everyone has to fall in love with you," I say, careful not to enunciate too well.

"Please. I could be his daughter."

"Kind of my point. What's your gate number again?" I non sequitur before she can reply.

"Gate Four," she says, thumbing through her phone. "Flight's not for another two hours, though. We definitely overshot." Her tone isn't entirely free of accusation.

"Better safe," I mumble, ignoring the fleeting guilt of having shuffled her out of bed and life so brusquely that morning under the pretense that she might miss her flight. We linger a few feet away from the dreadful security check, which she doesn't expect to take more than a few minutes without layers, carry-on luggage, or conspicuous ethnicity. I'm suddenly very ready for our second farewell.

"Are you okay from here? I can't go past the TSA check." You can still be a good host while trying to get someone out of your life as soon as possible.

"Well, we can sit out here for a little while if you want," she suggests with a shrug, her way of sidestepping the actual request. "Two hours with nothing to do is a long time."

I don't point out the book or headphones peeking out of her bag and follow her lead to a set of plastic benches by the terminal map. Once some privacy is regained, the silence once again becomes noticeable and the third thing reemerges. A part of me enjoys seeing her repeatedly check the time and realize that 120 minutes alone can be very pleasant.

"Think you'll stick it out, then? This new southern life of yours?" she finally asks, shifting the bulk of the discomfort back to me. Even during the relationship, inconveniently placed during the last stretch of college, this had been an early point of contention between us. One that had led to that last big fight and *Have a nice life, asshole!*

As much as I hated to admit it, her certainty that I was too soft for the heat, isolation—"Not to mention all the football you'll have to start watching"—and overall dismissal of the idea that I might enjoy life here beyond these graduate studies had given me something to prove.

Answering now that I didn't know, that I hated how orange-and-proud-of-it everything in Austin was, wasn't an option.

"Of course! Are you kidding?" Choosing writing as a professional career path has already made me a good liar. There's no point in unraveling all that, not when the clock is ticking.

A distracted "Hmm . . ." is all she gives, loading the sound to the fullest extent.

"So where's the honeymoon going to be?"

"Tuscany."

Everything I'm suppressing must still somehow make it to my face, since she's already shaking her head with a smirk. "I know, I know."

"And how old is this guy again?"

She laughs. "Twenty-seven."

"Testicular cancer starts at twenty-eight."

She gives me a variation of the 2011 where-would-you-hide-a-dog-in-a-dorm-room-if-you-got-one-you-maniac look. My reply is a simple shrug. "I'm just saying."

She retreats into her phone, and I suddenly hate how strained it all still feels, and begin to fear that this is not fleeting but perhaps our new status quo.

The rapid-fire sex that had interspersed the visit had only occurred in sudden bursts, always bookended by separate showers. First her, then me, and then a few hours of silence with her on her laptop at the kitchen table while I read in the bedroom. Un-

til the showers themselves eventually overlapped and her impro-
vised bed on the couch remained unfolded for the rest of the visit.
That it was such a monumentally bad idea eventually became its
own transgressive form of foreplay before falling out of my mind
completely—although I noticed that, when she had the choice,
she now slept on the right side of the bed, which was noteworthy
because of the many nights I was awakened by a body rolling over
mine to claim the left side of my dorm room single because that
was the only one she could sleep on. I wondered at various points
if she felt guilty, but never bothered to ask because the truth was
that I didn't.

With two hours and nineteen minutes left to go, thanks to
some delay in Chicago, I almost wish that this politeness would all
suddenly unfurl and send us into a public shouting match granting
me an excuse to storm out. Somewhere on her right inner thigh
is a hickey, and I wonder if and how the purple bruise will be explained. Then again, she's a much better liar than him. If the brief
exposure to the heat hadn't knocked so much out of me, I think
I might take a poking stick to that bear just to see what happens.

At some point her feet eventually find their way home, tucking
themselves under my thigh when she stretches out on the bench,
slow and careful like she thinks she has to get away with it. It's
positioned like this, exactly like this, that we've had our longest,
most inane conversations, and something releases in my shoulders.

"So," I venture, giving her plenty of time to interrupt, "would
I like him?"

The Massachusetts American man of the hour with bright
white teeth in all his photos. Pink shirt on a boat, shirtless with
a strapped-on backpack on a hike, leaning in front of the Brooklyn Bridge in sunglasses, good hair. There are 1,500 of this exact

model being pumped out of the Tinder factories like *Westworld* robots every day.

She smiles, having already considered the question at length, and just as I start to dread another polite answer she begins to shake her head.

"You guys would hate each other within seconds."

She continues with a hint of pride in her voice. "Lola calls him the anti-you." I frown, unable to read which of the two men this pride is leaning toward.

I think back to that afternoon the air-conditioning had broken down, the only summer we lived together. We'd been driving each other insane all day in that cramped midtown apartment—too hot to talk, let alone touch each other—when she'd woken me from a nap by jumping on the bed with a tray of melting ice cubes in each hand. We waited for sundown, crushing ice between our teeth until our mouths were good and numb. We could have gone to her dad's perfectly air-conditioned office suite in midtown. In hindsight, it might just be one of the most amazing things that can happen to a person; to have someone kiss you so long and with so little purpose that your entire system goes haywire: hot and cold, and wet and dry, until it all stops mattering entirely. That had been my second fever in our friendship together.

"Stop that," she says, leaning forward and tugging at my ear-lobe with the bad, bejeweled hand. It's our first touch since our fingers grazed on the coffee pot handle earlier that day in a false hurry.

"Stop what?"

"You're, like, romanticizing me again. I can tell."

"And he doesn't?"

"Nope."

Eighty-four minutes left to go, and neither of us seems too concerned to continue sidestepping the land-mine topics we'd so diligently avoided till now.

"Financial analysts don't romanticize," she clarifies. "They establish and satisfy sound market demands."

"Sounds hot."

"He *romances* me," she continues defensively, adding weight to the word. "It's less pressure."

"Now, see, how can I stop writing about you when you keep saying stuff like that?" I say, leaning back to stare at the glass dome above us.

If it shattered right now, I would shield you, I think and then say out loud just to see what happens. Mia is a story that requires an ending, and this airport drop-off isn't it.

"Be still, my beating whatever," she scoffs. Yet she moves in closer, removing the buffer between us by lifting herself onto the seat right next to me, keeping her toes tucked under my thigh.

"So, why did you come out here?"

I know the pretext—that she had wanted to give me the news of her impending nuptials in person. And the subtext, too—that she missed me and wanted to see how I was adjusting to Texas after a few dramatic emails about the heat and the people. But what I needed right now was the missing piece; the logic I knew was behind it all. I'm still finding my footing, both living in Austin and attending the University of Texas, hoping that every new acquaintance will turn into a deep and meaningful connection that never quite comes. I accumulate acquaintances and classmates, but my people are nowhere to be found. Two semesters in, it's looking more and more like this is just a zip code. I'm lonely here and for better or worse, Mia is one of my people.

"I didn't want you to hear it from someone else."

I'm no great conversationalist, but it's still her turn to talk so I wait, tapping my fingers against the back of her foot, careful not to slip into a massage. This silence is entirely hers.

"I think I needed to make sure. That I wasn't making a mistake." Mia finally sighs, and just like that, the whole weekend feels like a poorly graded assignment.

"Ouch."

"C'mon, you know what I mean."

I smile, if only to reassure her, but I don't look down just yet. "I do. The ouch stands."

At some point, and without my noticing, our fingers intertwined on the back of the empty chair, and I realize I've been probing the intrusive object around her finger for a moment now. Thirty-nine minutes left, and we run out of topics again, leaving the conversation with nowhere to go but back to that illogical pearly-white wedding invitation left behind on my kitchen counter that I already know will make a phenomenal beer coaster.

"I really do want you there," Mia says, to which I snort without letting go of her hand, still focused on twirling the ring.

"I'm serious. It'll be too weird otherwise. Me getting married and you not being there." It feels both genuine and the possible setup to a cruel joke.

"Is it going to be an open bar?"

"Of course."

"Then I definitely shouldn't come."

"Oh, c'mon, I expect to be at your wedding, too, one day." There's the punch line.

"Sure. Maybe I'll hit it off with one of his sisters at the reception and we'll all move into a giant three-walled house together facing an audience."

"One sister. And she hates me."

"Well, to be fair, you did just fly across the country and repeatedly cheat on her brother."

It's patently unfunny and that's the funny part and just like that, we're both laughing again. So hard that the old man with visible sweat pits sitting on the bench across from ours whips his newspaper at the pair of us until we're both upright, pursing our lips to suppress the snickering. Wherever that guy might be at this very moment, I know that some Tuscany enthusiast who picks his honeymoon from preassembled honeymoon packages doesn't laugh like this with her. Doesn't make her laugh like this.

Her phone vibrates against the flat surface of her magazine, and she quickly untangles our hands. "One sec." The custom ringtone—something like the recording of an old woman shouting profanities from afar with two sets of giggles in the foreground— echoes an entire history that I know nothing about. She doesn't answer but begins to text right away, with a look in her eyes I can't quite place. Fondness and a hint of something else. Guilt.

"I guess I'm not cabbing it home after all," she eventually says, and it feels like she's already boarded the plane.

In one of my short stories, she's a predatory therapist and says to an increasingly unstable patient who professes his love, *"I make love; you love. That's the difference between us, Mister Simons."* It's the closing line of that story.

I follow her eyes to the faraway screen of arrivals and departures, past the TSA check, and waiting any longer might cost her the flight, so we start to move. I stuff my hands in my pockets and keep my chin pointed outward as she slips on her sandals and abandons the ponytail, combing her fingers through her hair in the glass reflection behind us, flooding the air with a chemical scent of processed lavender. Connecting flight and all, I can predict at least one lengthy armrest conversation and two business cards in her purse by the time she steps foot in LaGuardia.

"Are you going to tell him?" I ask, and for a split second, something tightens in her arms. "Anything?"

"Are you kidding?"

I might have been actually; it's getting hard to keep track. Because come to think of it, I don't want that, either. I wanted it to be ours, impervious to audience participation. A story, yes, but scribbled in the margins, in tiny print that only two people knew how to decode.

"Maybe I should sign you two up for couples' therapy . . ."

"Bread maker, blender, spa package," she says distractedly, screwing the loosened diamond back to the base of her finger. "Keep it simple, Philippe."

We stand for a moment, a little nervous, a lot unsure, and once again I speak first because something has to be said in the very next second or else I know the lavender fumes will turn noxious.

"Listen," I begin and quickly stop, frowning at the weird echo in my voice. It takes me another moment to realize that I was not the only one speaking the word at that exact moment. "If you give me a handshake right now, I swear to God I'm raising my hand when the priest asks if there are any objections."

She blinks her assessment. "We don't do that anymore; too many unforeseen incidents. Does that mean you'll be there?"

I shrug, hoping for some ambiguity. Either option seems as likely. My staying home and inhaling ice cream, sitting pretzel-style on the floor by my fridge, or my jumping on a flight for the privilege to watch my college friend—because that's what we were always described to be—get married. It's pathetic and pitiful and a slew of harsher synonyms, but I might. I might commit a thousand times over not to go but, in the final-hour coin toss, will go, no matter how many do-overs I may need; I'll overpay for my ticket, overspend on the dry-cleaning of my tux, maybe even buy a new one, and when she makes her way down the aisle, flawless, what he'll be looking for will be that imperceptible look sent my way. A hint that it's all still some middling chapter, a rest stop on respective journeys that leaves the endgame the same as it was two years ago. Sure: I'll shake the man's hand for that look.

"Be happy for me, Rubeintz." She finds my full name powerful and takes pleasure in using it.

"No."

She pecks me on the lips and pulls me into an airless hug. I imagine a tall, whipcord-lean financial analyst tripping and cracking his skull open against the edge of a conference table, halfway through a PowerPoint about market shares. My mind isn't always a nice place.

"You know I love you, right?" she adds, and if nothing else I'm grateful for the rhetorical phrasing. I want to tighten my grip but know she'll wiggle out of it first, so I settle for the upper hand of being the one to break the embrace, lingering to place a kiss into her head, stealing a whiff for the road. A loose-necked and freckled white couple stares at us through sunglasses and disapprovingly tight jaws, dragging their luggage past us. She doesn't notice, thank God.

"Yeah, yeah. Tell it to your fiancé."

She chuckles. "Asshole."

"Adulteress."

In a corner of my mind a retired couple decides to recapture something by traveling to a very specific hotel and past thick purple drapes. They rent a fully equipped room and, after changing, spend a few minutes taking in the various buckles and ropes, reestablishing boundaries and trust. They settle on the word *phosphorous*. "You know I love you, right?" the wife whispers against her husband's lips, who in return can only nod before receiving the first whip crack. My stories still remain mediocre for another two semesters of fiction workshops. I spend the Friday before her wedding trying to increase my credit limit to purchase a $586 flight back to New York plus Airbnb. I can't swing it.

On the day of her wedding, I sit for an hour in the lobby of the Austin airport, retracing our last steps, searching for any hint of hesitation in our last conversation, and trying to find, if not a story, then some trace of the woman who so carelessly let me get away. There's no grand thesis about race to be found here. Some stories live under your skin, in the red and pink of your organs. These stories are all as important to who you are, and as inextricable from your being, as the color of your skin.

TWENTY-FOUR

BLACK GHOST GOES, "BOO!"

I'M TWENTY-FIVE and I return to New York, weeks, if not days after graduating from the Michener Center. There are no ID cards this time; no one has requested my presence. A lot of my time in Texas felt like a three-year hiatus from the forward momentum that had bubbled up around me in college, though momentum toward what exactly, I couldn't tell you. The city's indifference to newcomers is already well documented in the media. Really: you are lucky if you can count on two hands the number of people who care if you live here or not. Carrie Bradshaw lied to everyone in *Sex and the City*: it's the capital of loneliness, the final triathlon of living with yourself. She was sitting at the back of all those restaurants talking to three figments of her imagination, the poor unhinged woman.

I'm one of the many, landing at JFK with less than $100 dollars cash and a shrinking credit margin. It's no longer *Gossip Girl*; rather it's every crappy CBS sitcom trying to repackage and recapture the magic of *Friends* or *Seinfeld*. Monica Geller's purple palace is not on the menu of possible domiciles.

And still, with everything ahead a series of unknowns, I return to the dating apps before the luggage carousel even starts to move and begin building fleeting connections with passing strangers' photo albums. There are tales here, I think. People to run into, montages to kick-start. Stories. I'm sure. New York City is a hub of inciting incidents waiting to happen at each corner. Although, whether they happen in person or virtually, these happenstances statistically do not tend to end well.

?

It starts with the lone question mark.

We've all gotten the lone question mark before; that nudge to keep the banter going because the road to intimacy and long-term commitment is paved with consistent check-ins and goodnight emojis.

This specific question mark came thirty-six hours after my last exchange with "OneMilkTwoSugars" (not really OneMilkTwo-Sugars), an F/25 newly minted lawyer getting the hang of odd work hours. Its subtext was clear: "Hey: it's your turn."

Our prior exchange had been pleasant enough. My work was going well; she was having Seamless for dinner again; unnecessary LOLs were had by all. After a few false starts in which we'd both had to postpone or cancel drinks, texting had become our platform of choice, and the check-ins had fallen into an almost-daily rhythm. It took effort but less so than starting all over with a brand-new match. We joked about still technically being strangers while only living seven subway stops away from each other, which in hindsight, should have been the first sign. New Yorkers are known to travel farther to pick up good Thai food that doesn't deliver to their address. But I did not reply to the lone question mark, nor to the dozen or so messages that followed. Instead, I ghosted OneMilkTwoSugars.

A Paltrow-affiliated publicist might call me "the active precipi-tator of an unforeseen, one-sided uncoupling." You might settle for "asshole." Somewhere along the way, my interest in meeting with OneMilkTwoSugars had simply vanished. It was a half-shrug of a thought process; like forfeiting a game of Words With Friends in which you had the lead, having no interest in seeing the outcome through.

Ghosting—the act of cutting contact in the midst of an ongo-ing interaction with someone you are casually, or in some cases not so casually, seeing—is nothing new, and plenty has been written about it. Many view the practice as a callous dismissal of another person's feelings: cowardly, rude, and disrespectful. On the other hand, it is also very literally just not doing a damn thing at all, something at which we twentysomethings excel.

Two days after the "?" came OneMilkTwoSugars' follow-up: "Wow. Really?"

It was passive-aggressive, but an opened door nonetheless. I could salvage this with an apologetic lie. My boss died in a car accident . . . my apartment was flooding . . . I lost my phone on the subway on the way to the flood crisis center . . . Lying was a better option than silence, but still I did not reply. Reactions among my friends were . . . mixed.

"So, you're ghosting this white girl?" asked a good female friend, while we were in line at the movies.

"I'm ghosting her. But her being white had nothing to do with it." (It really didn't.)

"That's really disappointing coming from you, Ben."

When I asked why, she explained that I was not the typical ghoster. Not a "fuckboy," nor Felipe. No picture of my penis had ever been sent to an unsolicited party, which I'm told is the litmus test of fuckboy-ery. The argument that this person and I had never met held little weight in her eyes. In fact, it made things worse. I was supposed to be a good guy.

"That poor girl is going crazy, thinking there's something wrong with her."

In my nonaction, my friend saw the same dismissal she had herself experienced with some other good guy who had made a nice first impression, sometimes over the course of several dates, only to suddenly fall off the face of the earth. The streets are apparently filled with ghosts and wounded parties waiting for an explanation. She dealt with these ghostings by imagining each ghoster to be an asshole who was doing her a favor by showing their true colors early and bright.

Another friend of mine, Dave (not really Dave), shrugged it all off. "Ghosting's not a thing," Dave argued. "You're letting someone know you don't want to interact with them by not interacting with them! It's not your problem if they feel entitled to more."

To be fair, Not-Dave is a bartender and a renowned fuckboy in his own right. He mostly avoids apps, and his ghosting takes the form of incredibly light steps as he vanishes in the morning and adds one more entry to his list of bars across the city to avoid. His dick snapshots fly fast and furious. Heck, your last text notification might be a picture of Dave's dick. I do not have the looks, eight-pack, or self-confidence to date like Dave, but didn't Dave have a valid point? What exactly is owed here?

Dating apps and websites are the Wild West of interpersonal connections. It is not virtual speed-dating; it is virtual spam-folder cleaning with people you might want to meet instead of emails. Yes, you might upgrade someone to your regular inbox if you find their content appealing, but you are mostly browsing through bulk advertisement that either does not speak to you or is packaged in a way that feels too good to be true.

To be fair, you are likewise being callously sorted in return, which almost democratizes the process. We're all just huddled at the back of the school during recess trading Pokémon cards of ourselves. Racial preferences aren't problematic yet. Statistically, Black women and Asian men are at the bottom of the pile. The interactions in my inbox back up those numbers.

"I don't like Black guys, sorry!"

"Goofy but cute!"
"That's my entire brand. Hi!"

"Too bad ur definitely one of those niggas that only dates white women"
"No, I'm not"
(No reply ever comes to that one.)

The next time I found myself listlessly browsing OkCupid, I received a message from OneMilkTwoSugars, as my continued existence greatly displeased her:

"I see you on here so I know you're alive. I don't know what the deal is but this is beyond rude. Disgusting."

That green dot marking me as being online confirmed that I had not fallen prey to a falling AC unit while walking one day; I was not in a huddle of crying family members, living through some tragic and sudden loss; I was not suddenly asexual, having turned my back on dating altogether. Nothing was preventing me from playing a lackadaisical round of Quickmatch at 11:52 p.m., and this was "disgusting."

Someone out there hated me specifically because they hadn't met me—which, unless you take a firm ideological stance against Canadians, should be the minimum requirement for hating someone. Worse still, indifference was all I could muster. There was no guilt on my end.

I read over our past two weeks or so of correspondence, and in pixel form, my enthusiasm to meet matched hers. We'd had good banter along with some fairly intimate exchanges. It had also never really stopped; I had simply opted out of keeping it going. The prospect of coordinating schedules and finally meeting had grown more wearisome, and our first date was weighed by all this pre-intimacy we'd established. The simple answer was that we had waited too long to meet, so why was the prospect of writing about it more appealing than just telling her that in 160 characters? Was I a functioning sociopath for not wanting to be bothered?

What if I had met OneMilkTwoSugars? What if we'd gone for drinks, dates, and had sex before this unflappable indifference of mine had set in? Would that be preferable? Ending things at that point would be an entirely different process, but would it not eventually lead to a series of excuses in the hopes of achieving this same result? ("My phone died," "Didn't get your text," "I forgot to hit send," "I fell asleep, lol.")

I realized I could text her that—these exact words—and absolve myself of any further responsibility. But Not-Dave's words kept echoing: I did not know this person. We could ride the same subway train, sit right next to each other, and probably not recognize each other. There was admittedly a bit of egotistical curiosity there, too: How long could this person I had never met remain upset at the prospect of not meeting me?

"She likes you more than she ever would if she'd met you."

My roommate laughed. In a parallel universe, OneMilkTwoSugars and I had been dating for three weeks already.

To ghost someone is to put them in a no-win scenario: if they seek closure, they are crazy. The more closure they seek, the more annoying they come off. It is a Chinese finger trap right there on your phone where applying pressure only makes it worse. Eventually, both the ghoster and the ghosted convince themselves that they've dodged a bullet. That's the protocol, at least.

Fourteen unanswered texts/messages later, we'd both dug our heels into this pattern. She would not fade away under fear of being seen as the crazy chick; I would not block her number or provide a reply. Clearly, neither of us was an expert in ghosting protocols.

"Why do I owe you a breakup if we've never met?" I once considered asking, when I got a new text from her in the midst of a busy workday, before thinking better of it. OneMilkTwoSugars was attractive, smart, educated, photogenic, and hadn't listed "oxygen" among the six things she couldn't live without: surely, I was not her only prospect. I pictured all the guys she ignored in favor of spending so much effort on me, this would-be fuckboy. Was the sting of rejection that bad for the uninitiated? From dating sites to apps, every facet of dating has been streamlined via new technology; why couldn't the rejection be as well?

A few days later, after a few more prompts, I received my last text from her. The preview of her full text was enough:

Hey!! Niiiiiiiiiiiiiiiiiiggg—

For years, I will go on to tell this story with the altered fact that what OneMilkTwoSugars wrote to me was "Fuuuuuuuuuuu" or "Shiiiiiiiiiitbag." A harmless punch line that leaves half the dinner table on her side and keeps the conversation on the ethics of dating in the digital age lively and fun. I've found that *nigger* taints the story; makes it ugly in all the wrong ways.

Even with the twin layers of removal of being told by me and having been delivered to me in written form—on a dating site, no less—people shut down around it. My Black friends want to burn the world, and forget that cow. "They all think that secretly, man," one says.

If he's right, I don't want to believe it. Meanwhile, my white friends wince uncomfortably and bemoan the hopeless state of the world. Sometimes, I think this is simply a performance for my sake. They feel like it's what I need to hear. I don't fully buy the person who plugs his ears and winces. I want to get him drunk, sleep with his wife, sell drugs to his child, devalue his property, and emasculate him in a sauna and see what happens then.

Anyway, I now choose to always tell the full story. I drop the nigger bowling ball in the middle of the cake and watch what happens.

And maybe, that's all that the referendum of that word needs: I cannot use it without the hope that my doing so, in some minuscule way, takes power away from it, and you, white friend, cannot use it without the certainty that it is adding power to it. It's as simple as that.

New York City is one of the most densely populated areas and one of the loneliest places on earth. (See: every other song about New York.) You can swipe until your thumb is sore and not run out of singles in your age range. As a result, amazing people who would leave you with butterflies in a social setting are assessed and dismissed like weather app pop-ups.

I'm still no closer to a better insight for OneMilkTwoSugars, other than maybe the half-real person she had become through all of our texting was less appealing than the blank entry in the spinning wheel of online dating she had been when we first started interacting. The pressure of being rejected by that person was more tangible than the rejection of a hot stranger who amounted to nothing more than a few photos and lines of texts.

The effort of writing this essay is much, much longer than the three-sentence message and slight awkwardness I could have sent. But, I didn't owe OneMilkTwoSugars anything, right? That's the low expectation of "low-expectation dating." It was a chain of picking and choosing we all opted into with our first swipe, nudge, poke. Dating apps don't traffic in people; they traffic in distractions existing somewhere between a listicle and an unenthused game of Candy Crush. Was that something worth hearing, something I was obligated to point out so as to manage her expectations, her entitlement, her inexplicable sense of ownership over my person? Screw that. True as it might be, she wasn't owed this insight. She should know this already. We all should. "The ghoster" was an established role I could easily navigate and again, one that required nothing. There was no uncertainty in performing it. In this new reality, she was the creep for expecting more. It was all safe and familiar ground.

Ultimately, the main lesson of online dating might be a harsh one for everyone involved, from the dick pic–sending fuckboy to the person with whom you felt meaningful contact: that stranger you find attractive does not owe you anything. Check the contracts you accepted when you registered for your site or app of choice: "satisfactory resolutions" are never guaranteed.

TWENTY-FIVE

SURE, I'LL BE YOUR BLACK SIDEKICK

I'm the ripe-ish age of TWENTY-SIX and I experienced my first "bro" breakup. My (now former) roommate and (equally former) close friend and I parted ways permanently and acrimoniously. Cops were involved. This happened to coincide with my father's reemergence into my sphere of concern with rumors of a heart attack. Only one of these two events leaves me still reeling.

Neither I nor my former roommate—let's call him Mark—looks like the story that follows. We're soft-bodied plaid wearers and both known to be affable guys, one Black, one Jewish. At our best, we traded offensive jokes that could launch a thousand think pieces. Mark enjoys trivia nights with his other friends; I'm a karaoke guy with mine. We regularly made pots of lentil soup or pasta together, content to be Netflix homebodies in the city that never sleeps. For a while, our biggest argument was debating the awfulness of *Girls* characters: Marnie vs. Mimi-Rose.

"I don't know what I would have done if you hadn't moved in, Ben," he once said during a *Game of Thrones* marathon.

"You'd have been fine," I answered with a shrug.

"No," he said, eyes uncomfortably fixed on the TV, "I really wouldn't have been."

Our roommateship began when Mark's fiancée ended their engagement, leaving him an emotional mess halfway through his last semester of graduate school with an empty second bedroom. The result of his heartbreak was an incredibly fast and open friendship. An hour into my moving in with him, he was crying on my shoulder about the trauma.

Male friendships are typically forged on an anvil of casualness. Laughter, beer, fist bump, repeat. In trying times, a "Dude, that's rough" may be extended and past instances of vulnerability shared, but rarely more. Real-time vulnerability is an altogether different matter. I've lived by this unspoken code and, at times, even inched away from male acquaintances who went against it by wanting to share too much, too quickly. And yet, despite being born out of Manhattan rental necessity, this friendship was different.

"I miss her so much . . ." "Hey, is this a sore inside my butt crack?" "My family is poor, and I don't think I'll be the one to pull them out of it, even with two degrees . . ." ". . . Dude, why is there a sore inside your butt crack?"

There was no posturing, living with Mark. Codependent, precarious, whatever you might call it; there was something to be said for a space in which the XY chromosomes did not keep these topics at bay, even when at full sobriety.

"I think I need to pay you," he says one day after I come back from a quick evening walk with his dog. "For the dog walks. I feel bad that you're always walking my dog for me."

I'm the better looking of the two parties, I'm told. "You are,"

Mark insists. "You have that smile from across the room, man. It's like a freaking Hyper Beam." His references match mine, which I like.

"The smile is fake." I tell him the story from the Michener Center, lying head to toe on his bed with dimmed lights, a dog between us. I tell him how I practiced smiling again and again in the mirror until my face was Play-Doh that could be summoned the way a chameleon turns into a rock.

"It's tiring," I say and then backtrack, ever so slightly. "My face gets tired doing it, I mean."

"Well, it makes my day every morning, man," he insists. "The end result is dy-no-mite." He says the word like an old sitcom I recognize from the references but that I've never actually watched. I hate these types of jokes from most people but Mark is an absolute nerd, which is one of the things I like about him. These racially charged jokes would raise an eyebrow if I didn't hear him pantomime dialogue with his dog, giving the poor thing a Tony Soprano accent, and watch him drowning his sushi pieces with a long, agonizing damsel-in-distress wail as he dunks them in soy sauce. The Blackness in *dy-no-mite* isn't the punch line.

The problem with learning to smile a lot is that people imagine a dark threatening cloud over you whenever your face returns to normal. Mine is a Resting Black Face; allegedly intense eyes and sharp cheekbones.

But I don't push to explain any of this to Mark. I'm tired, and my mind is elsewhere. Plus, a tiny part of me is very happy to make Mark happy every morning. I'm already broke from moving back to the city. The kind of broke that makes you write essays online for people applying to graduate school who don't have the time or words to write essays. In my mind, this makes me a working writer. I miss my stipend.

I refresh Craigslist's Gigs section and pounce on them when they post, copy-pasting my email and attaching my résumé. I present myself as a TA making ends meet while pursuing a PhD, which is less sad somehow, though I don't quite remember the logic of *how* it's less sad. My bank account grows comfortable in the high two digits. The email notice announcing the critical balance no longer fazes me. I apply for a credit card that's denied. The Visa representative seems apologetic and cites my lack of income potential until I have a full-time job. A master's in creative writing and screenwriting isn't it. After all, I practice in make-believe.

He gets enough of a gist of the phone call I had that night while I'm accompanying him on a dog walk; he offers to pay me for the times when I walk the dog while he's at work. I say no: I love the dog already. Money makes things weird. "C'mon, dude. Let me. I feel bad."

I'm told it keeps things simpler and come to agree. Friendship over here; canine life assistance over there. The friendship is invaluable in that it has no assigned monetary value. Friendships shouldn't. *The employment amounts to $3 per walk.*

"Oh?" he says, with a frown. "Really? All right, let's talk about it later, okay?" I nod and grab the leash, heading for a walk with the dog while he prepares an assignment for school.

It's no longer an instance, but a haggle. "I'm broke too, y'know," he explains. His, I point out, is the kind of "broke" that gets $4,000 in the mail from his father in Massachusetts. That's nothing in Manhattan, he explains. "I'm also trying to get savings up and meet someone. Dates get expensive. Girls expect you to pay every time."

We settle on the $3 per walk. Online, dog-walking apps advertise $36–44 per walk or doggy daycare around the Upper West Side of Manhattan. I anonymously ask for feedback on the offer on a Reddit thread—the dog is extremely easy to take care of, after all—and then delete the thread when people say I'm being taken advantage of. They don't know anything. They are jaded aspiring actors and students being chewed up by the city. This is friendship: the pillar of my new adult life in New York City.

I take the $27 per week for nine walks and he generously rounds it up to $40 with a shrug. He doesn't like to talk about money except when he needs to talk about money. Now, it's him who occasionally accompanies me on my dog walks. He no longer feels guilty, telling me the dog looks bored while turning on the TV.

He pays me my second week by covering my half of the sushi he's ordering and the expensive roasted almonds from a specialty store nearby that he stockpiles before an announced snowstorm across New York City—the kind of meteorological event that gets a cute hashtag name trending and that homebodies look forward to—stocking up the fridge, lining up the Netflix and *Game of Thrones* episodes, and basking in coziness. My cell phone payment doesn't go through, I think, rewatching season 4 of *Game of Thrones*, looking ahead to the season 5 premiere in a few weeks.

"You know Arya is going to wreck shit up in Essos," he says, gleefully, around a mouthful of sesame-oil nuts. We both approve of the young traumatized girl acquiring faceless ninja assassin skills.

However exhausting it could occasionally get—to walk his dog every day, to cancel plans with other former friends still in the city when he was feeling lonely, and to write his essays for him when the juggling act of school and heartbreak got to be too much for him—being openly needed fulfilled its own need for me. At Christmas, I received a text from him: *You don't have to say it back but I want u to know ur my best friend.*

This guy would be a fixture in my life, I thought. My future children would call him "uncle" one day. This would last. And then, naturally, it failed: spectacularly as these things tend to. Mark and I will never speak to each other again. "I don't owe you anything," he wrote in one of his last communications to me. Mark might have been right. The point of male friendships might be that you never actually owe each other anything. This very essay might be too much analysis by virtue of us both being guys.

The "bro"-keup was as sudden as it was vicious.

The night I learned my father, somewhere in Cote-Des-Neiges, had stroked out (dads "have heart attacks"; absentee fathers you don't particularly like "stroke out") was the night of a prescheduled man-date with Mark for which I had cleared my calendar. *Good*, I thought. On the couch with my best friend was a safe space to process the news about my dad. Mark was someone I could speak to without the judgment of relatives or less intimate acquaintances who might expect waterworks for a man I loved but did not particularly like and hadn't spoken to in years.

I sipped my beer carefully, waiting for the right lull to broach the topic while a distracted Mark kept checking OkCupid on his phone. He was dating more aggressively now, on the hunt for his next girlfriend.

A woman had given him a gold star and was up for drinks nearby. "Can I go?" he asked.

"No," I snapped, before immediately backtracking to "Sure,"

as forcing someone to stay and care about your feelings is unappealing. Mark seemed to consider his options: pushing me to share what was on my mind vs. spending the evening with what I imagined was a brunette holding a mustache on a stick, flanked by two carbon-copy besties. "Well, if you're upset, I'm going to go," Mark eventually said.

"Fine. Go." A minute later, he was in the bathroom and the smell of nice, expensive cologne filled the apartment as he got ready. Being on the other end of the equation—needing him—was new and overwhelming. I was raised as an only child, and I'm a Sagittarius, which I will assume means something independent and horsemanlike.

Later that night, I wrote Mark an email. A good platform for open feelings as well as a few jabs. "You're thoughtless," it read. "I have to step back a bit. Let's just be roommates for a while. I have to expect less, dude."

"I can't live like that, Ben," he wrote back the next day, hurt. His date had been a bust; I existed again. The gist of his reply was a choice: stay and work on the friendship or leave. I was a subletter, and my name wasn't on the lease; such ultimatums could be made fairly.

I don't like being put in corners. What might have otherwise been solved with a tub of ice cream and two spoons was now a "thing." I replied that I could be out by the end of the month: a manipulative bluff to call his. The bluff, as it turns out, was a mistake.

An hour later, 1 a.m. or so, he was pounding on my door, evicting me immediately for "abandoning him." An abusive parent growing up, three serious breakups, and still this was the nastiest fight of my life. "I don't give a shit that you're so fucking poor," he screamed.

"You're going to die alone," I replied, nonchalantly enough to be vicious, hands shaking as I texted a friend, asking to crash on his couch. These were emotional nut shots and we knew it, based on the vulnerabilities we both knew well.

Something that had come up during our many late-night chitchats and at the peak of the Black Lives Matter movement was my deep-seated fear of cops. It was a relatively new addition—a harsh reality that had eluded me at Columbia—to the set of anxieties that came with being a foreigner in America on a temporary visa. Mark knew about my Canadian passport, which I always carried in case an officer stopped me on the subway. He knew about my airport TSA voice, and the fact that I used to read lengthy Reddit posts by people describing what a bullet feels like ripping through your insides, trying to imagine it after every gruesome news story.

Claiming I wasn't packing fast enough that night, Mark suddenly announced that he'd called the cops on me. Race—my Blackness—which had been a nonissue in all other facets of our friendship—was now being weaponized against me. Years later, I would realize that Mark is actually my first Karen. A few more years of viral videos of white men and women calling, or threatening to call, the police on Black people and I might have been able to recognize this as what it is.

This prompted me to call the police myself to explain the situation only to find out that Mark hadn't contacted them. This, in turn, led him to defiantly call them to save face. Neither of us realized we were playing Russian roulette with the NYPD—it's a schoolyard game of chicken. I'm young enough to think that two roommates, one Black, one white, same height and body type, calling the police will result in a fair doorstep trial that, who knows, might work out in my favor. (What can I say? I read For Dummies books in high school for a reason.) Fun fact, New Yorkers: if two people call the cops for the same address, a lot of cops show up. You expect two; you get seven. Neither of us, flabby beta males that we were, quite knew what to do when we opened the door. Accusations had to be made up on the fly. "The neighbors must love this," one unimpressed cop muttered. After hearing the story, half the squadron stayed with Mark at the door and the other half escorted me out of the building, offering me a ride to my friend's place.

The escalation was as surreal as it was out of sync with the memory of Mark and me on the couch, with his head on his dog's stomach and its snout resting on my lap, watching television. "The boys of apartment 4-G," I remember him saying, mid-yawn.

The next morning, as New York's latest snowstorm was underway, I returned to the apartment. Mark was at work. I hastily packed my things, leaving my keys behind. As I rode the bus back to Montreal, Quebec, I knew I might not have a home to get back to when I returned to New York. *Good*, I thought.

Prick.

The anger faded quickly, soon replaced by a well of regret as I returned to the city. Montreal had been numbing and exhausting and before I had realized, roughly seven weeks had passed. Luckily, the stroked-out estranged father card will earn you some leeway, and my support system of lingering college friends came through. I never had a shortage of couches to crash on while looking for a new place . . . Still, a few blocks away, my best friend would not answer my texts or emails begging him for a phone call. The handwritten offer to grab a beer at the bar next to our apartment left at his door was declined. The thought of having hurt him that badly was a vise closing on my neck. I needed to tell him about my father's rapidly declining health—a fact he still did not know—and to apologize for channeling my not-quite-grief into those unfair emails. My furniture was still there, after all. There was still time.

Fancying herself a master of "friendship drama," one of my oldest friends took it upon herself to pursue the crusade by contacting Mark behind my back. "This is what happens when men deal with their feelings," Morgan said with a sigh. I was a "Charlotte," Mark was a "Miranda"; there was protocol in play. I do not know what their interaction consisted of, but she eventually forwarded me Mark's final word on the matter of my father's health, which she had disclosed. "I'm indifferent," he wrote. "Frankly," he added, "I'm weirded out that Ben has been treating this like a relationship or something."

I could not quite process this. Maybe something had been lost in translation. I was the one kicked out under a snowstorm for giving notice; if "victim" and "bully" had to be established, my line ought to be "I forgive you," not "I'm sorry." Where was my friend? The guy who'd shared his darkest thoughts with me? The one I was planning on moving to Brooklyn with next year so I could get my own dog, of which he already claimed himself the uncle? The one whom I'd forgiven the hole punched in my door when he was upset? Wasn't it my turn to get a pass?

To say that I went "emotionally apeshit" is to underestimate the amount of primate defecation littering America's great zoos. I had an Eduardo-Saverin-learning-he'd-been-0.03-percented breakdown. A Paris-Geller-getting-rejected-from-Harvard breakdown. An Alexandra-Forrest-is-making-a-stew breakdown. An ex once wrote me an eight-hundred-word email in college. I remember being put off by this and deleting it halfway through the read. Over the following month, I wrote Mark close to fifty emails/texts. *I'm sorry, bro. I miss you, bud. Forgive me, dude.* Ending these raw pleas with *bro, bud, dude, broseph, brosephine* made them easier to write.

No new apartment was good enough. No new roommate, no matter how friendly or compatible, was the right fit. My just-right bowl of porridge was still the closet-size room in Morningside Heights on Amsterdam where my furniture still was and where I could hang with my best friend once this hurdle was crossed. It wasn't too late; I had to try. I emailed a friend of his, his brother, his mother, all of whom I superficially knew. (Yes, this is the point at which you turn from your screen and wince, with "Oh, honey.") "We were shitheads to each other; let him know I'm sorry. I'm here." His roundabout reply eventually came, again impossibly detached. "I'm over what happened that nite. Your hyper-emotionality is stressing me out, it has not made me want to be around you," now emailed the same guy who came into my room shirtless and teary-eyed at 6 a.m., rattled by a nightmare about his ex-fiancée he needed to talk out. "My dad had a heart attack, dude," was still all I could think to reply, so I said nothing.

My friend Nora, listening to me rant about the situation, sympathetically said, "You sound like me after my first breakup. I was catatonic for like, three months." Nora was right. I am a little heartbroken. The rejection, anger, and sadness were almost identical to those I had felt as a brokenhearted fourteen-year-old, only now sans the Evanescence soundtrack. Were Mark and I both one point further right on the Kinsey scale, this might have been an impasse with an easy, passionate resolution. Sadly, we weren't. These were the much murkier waters of two straight males, both emotionally unequipped for the journey back to where we were and only one of us apparently willing.

Unlike women's friendships, which allow for some tumultuousness and are subsequently made stronger by strife, men's are defined by blunt simplicity. It's either easy or it doesn't exist. We ride and die; apologizing and healing is not an option. "This is what happens when men deal with their feelings."

A few weeks later, one of my two new roommates was now a pasta enthusiast who smiled eagerly at me when I collected snacks at the fridge and returned to my room with my headphones on and a nod. The other worked nights at a nearby hospital. The three of us will eventually go on to occasionally share a drink and even watch the *Entourage* movie together, collectively trying to buy into the illusion of Adrian Grenier playing an employed actor. When the first of us moves out, it is with a thirty-day notice and a fist bump. The overall experience simple, friendly, and polite—everything I had been looking for when I first crashed into Mark.

"What's done is done," read one of Mark's last communiqués to me. That was the closure, I now realize. My shell is back, reinforced, and I'm grateful for it. In time, Mark will turn into a New York City Roommate Horror Story. I'll only remember him as the guy who kicked me out at 1 a.m. and was indifferent to my father's health. To be fair, so was I, to a degree. I edit that part out of the story and focus on the one that paints me best. "What a selfish asshole!" people say. I'm sure other gatherings, two subway stops away, are hearing the "What a stalker!" version. Eventually, we will both believe our own tales. But tonight, I miss my former best friend. Laughter, beer, fist bumps, repeat. Move on. "Besties" are for children in pigtails and Pokémon backpacks.

TWENTY-SIX

SURE, I'LL BE YOUR 2016 SHITHOLE RESCAPEE

My Blackness started elsewhere, somewhere in the Antilles, and comes threefold. Being Black in Haiti means "happy." Haitians are loud, gregarious. The entire country is a table of jocks laughing, telling stories while slamming their hands over and over again. "We're Black Italians," my Floridian cousin once said.

Being Black in Canada, on the other hand, meant "polite," "grateful." We were first-generation immigrants. The subtext there was: Don't make waves. Don't make us regret letting you in. Find your tribe and stick to it. This country never belonged to you. Fair enough. You really are grateful, after all.

Being Black in America, like most things today, means something else entirely. Haven't you heard? There's a quiet referendum on your value as a human being going on. It's in the red hats wanting to make the country great again, back to a halcyon time "they" had more and you had less.

Fun game: find a stack of calendars going back to 1776, take a marker, and circle when America was equally great for white people and people of color alike. Half the country has said "Nah" to ever building a better future. In my opinion, the only difference between "racist" and "white nationalist" is that white nationalists still inexplicably feel a bit of shame at their own views and don't like to look their bigotry in the eye. They will dismiss accusations of racism out of hand and elevate their hatred into what they believe to be a clear and coherent sociopolitical platform, lest they are considered yokels. It's not that they hate Black people, see? They just "respect the Western canon," whatever that means. White nationalism requires more reading, frankly. The reading of nonsense, yes, but reading nonetheless. They've done their due 4chan reading in coming to the choice to rationally champion the dehumanizing of others. They are historians, not bigots. Your run-of-the-mill racist has no time for that. You won't grab their attention with a pamphlet. No, you need another way to validate all the ugly little thoughts they carry sometimes loudly, sometimes under their breath, and sometimes in a corner of their mind that they prefer not to look at or wrestle with. These people keep their lives ordered and Caucasian and would prefer you to do the same on your side of the street, school system, dating app, mall, neighborhood, TV channel, so everyone can be happy.

However it chooses to self-identify, that hate is still there and always so very willing to be heard, marketed to, and granted plausible deniability. And what better, more fetching attire than to dress it in a desire to make America great again? What's wrong with that? A noble endeavor on the back of an eagle. That hate smiles at itself in the mirror while making pouty lips when it is rocking that little number.

No Black person was surprised by Donald J. Trump's November 2016 victory. Disappointed, yes, maybe, but not surprised. The first people I heard predict his win in 2016 were the older Black

Americans in my life; those cynics who had been waiting for that Obama pendulum to swing back.

"You ruffle waters, you stir up the crap at the bottom," my uncle's girlfriend Carmen says with a hand at her chin, discussing the prospect during the summer of 2016 and mixing a basket of metaphors to capture the sentiment. She hoped he would at least be a good businessman. She wouldn't vote. In Florida, her district was only ever red. Voting takes hours out in the hot sun and she has diabetes and a bad knee. I've never voted in this country, so what would I know?

The second people to predict Trump's win were young dis-affected white people—of which my life was full. I remember an old roommate, Chris, chewing his early afternoon cereal wishing Trump would be elected.

"Screw it! Let's blow this joint." He laughed, rolling an actual joint as we broached the matter. He was a bartender and Columbia MFA graduate who staunchly would not vote, but claimed that Donald Trump was the shock to the system the world needed. His parents had a house in Connecticut, he liked expensive plants; he was societally foolproof in a way that the societally foolproof were never quite aware of.

The Trump era—because that's what we're in at the time of this writing, an era, not an administration—was the beginning of a new unprecedented level of Black anger on my part. I began to make more jokes about white people, those foolproof daywalkers, and feel somehow sated by it. Truth to power, yada yada yada. It's pointless and unfocused, but for two years "race" was constantly at the foreground of my brain in a way it had never been before.

Being Black in America, like most things today, means "angry."

A particular spike of that anger came the week of January 11, 2018, a week during which America's racial-targeting mechanism moved from my nebulous Blackness to my specific Haitianness.

The orange-hued septuagenarian asshole at the center of this uptick in negative attention was, of course, the inescapable trending topic of the world. During a meeting with a bipartisan group of senators at the White House, Trump referred to Haiti and African nations as "shithole" countries.

It was not the first time reports of the most powerful politician in the world singling out Haitians for his outspoken racism had circulated the web. The comment, first reported in the *Washington Post* by a Democratic aide, came two weeks after Trump said Haitian immigrants "all have AIDS"[1] during a summer 2017 meeting about immigration.

The president later conceded to having "been tough" on Haiti but denied having ever used such crude language, just as the White House denied his AIDS comment two weeks prior. Both denials had that ring of *Nananananana, prove it!* to them.

It's still fair to say that the man known for Scotch-Taping his ties to his shirt, staring directly into the sun during an eclipse, and mismatching the red and blue when coloring in an American flag around a table of toddlers—instances all captured on camera—does not hold my country of birth in high regard. Yes, shocking, I know.

As I write this, I can already read the one-star reviews on this part of the book.

"Stay away from politics."—Sunglassed selfie in a truck

"This book was mildly entertaining until he got all pseudopolitical."—Pixilated photo of grandchildren in front of a cropped-out landmark

"Typical liberal making broad statements."—Stock photo of lilacs

Let me be clear: I have no goddamn choice here! I would much rather chronicle my poor dating choices or go on a worldwide expedition to meet all my lost half-siblings than talk about race. Do not doubt for a second that I would much prefer spending these remaining pages ranking Rory Gilmore's boyfriends in excruciating detail. (In summary, it goes: Jess, Early Dean, Late Dean, and then Logan at the absolute bottom.)

Not to get schoolyard about the whole thing but your boy started it. Apologies if your politics align with the clown du jour but that sheet of basketball rubber thrown over a lumpy Honda Civic repeatedly made his racism personal.

Blackness, your race, the skin you walk in, was always political in this country. Until Trumpism kicked into high gear, I had simply made a lifetime of pretending apolitical was an option when it was simply one more privilege many do not have access to.

DID YOU KNOW?

The 1791 revolution that freed the island of Haiti from French Colonial rule was and remains the only self-liberated slave uprising that led to the founding of a state ruled by nonwhite former captives.

I won't lie to you and say that Haiti is not indeed a very poor country. One of the poorest in the hemisphere. Those statistics quickly became the refuge of those desperate to defend or at least attribute some form of logic to the president's gratuitously racist comment.

This is primarily achieved by downplaying the fact that Haiti and Africa were called "shithole" in direct contrast to Norwegian immigrants; a better, milky-skinned class of immigrants that America should be aggressively recruiting.

When my mother, a Haitian immigrant, now naturalized tax-paying Canadian, heard the news, her only response was a heavy sigh and the question "But why Haiti?" (As someone who has been living in America since college, I'm now often expected to provide some form of insight into this man and his mouth.)

The country was already heavy on her mind at the time, on what was the eve of the eighth anniversary of the earthquake that claimed 100,000 to 316,000 Haitian lives in 2010. Siblings, cousins, neighbors, friends who all live in cluttered frames in her living room. Now, she wanted to know exactly what her homeland had done to Donald Trump to be on his lips so very often.

Why Haiti?

It was a good question. What had this poor, little country with a population roughly one-fourth the size of California's done to our commander in chief?

After all, there were no geopolitical reasons as to why the country is suddenly at the center of the president's border collie vocabulary. Trump's focus on Haiti felt much more specific than the continental "Africa" with which it is often paired; at once personal and completely random: a point on a map for which he harbors an open revulsion.

NO, REALLY, THOUGH: DID YOU KNOW?

The 1791 revolution that freed the island of Haiti from French Colonial rule was and remains the only self-liberated slave uprising that led to the founding of a state ruled by nonwhite former captives.

What I wanted to tell my mother was that it really couldn't be any other country *but* Haiti.

Our homeland sits only a short flight away from the tail end of Florida. There are also many of us around. Like Mexico, one of Haiti's primary sins in Trump's eyes is its proximity to America.

Haiti's crime of the moment seemed to be that the country was home to a suspicious number of Haitians, and two things are clear: with some Omarosaean exceptions, Black people generally aren't the best people (for those, seek Norwegians or your blonder Russians), and Haitians constitute the very worst of Black people that the globe has to offer. On his lips, the name "Haiti" is the placeholder for bad, gross, and icky: the hole from which shit pours.

The man sitting on top of the world these days is the worst sort of bully: the unimaginative kind. The one desperate to give labels that he hopes others will parrot; to brand those he dislikes with something that can't be shaken off. "Crooked." "Sloppy." "Pocahontas." "Little Rocket Man." In our case, "Haiti" itself is the pithy moniker. We, Haitians, are the Black people who, through a series of events, have become Donald J. Trump's go-to example for all the gross foreign Black people he does not want in his version of this country. All Haitians are unwanted Black foreigners, and all unwanted Black foreigners are Haitians. A logical progression from the Mexican rapists and Muslim terrorists.

You might never visit Haiti, and I don't blame you for that. It's not the prized touristic destination that it once was. I myself can't describe the blue vistas of Haitian beaches since my last clear memory of Haiti was of two maids wishing us Godspeed, concerned about their next meals. Try as I might, I can't remember the airport or even the flight into Quebec. I remember how cold and tingly the air was, and the Christmas lights at every streetlight of Montreal, which felt like a decadent dream.

But as I age and my memory fades, I know that Haiti will continue to be conjured up in similarly unflattering lights. A crater. A crime-ridden cesspool, the mecca of the loud, bad, Black people.

My disgust, anger, all-around beef with Trump isn't as a Haitian. It comes from the part of myself that now identifies as American; the one that America taught better. The country I call my borrowed home these days and whose greatness was assembled and built by immigrants from all corners of the globe.

But you will, in your daily life, run into Haitians and their children; fellow Americans whose country of origin the president adamantly only sees as the embodiment of an ill-defined foreign Black grossness. And when you do, you'll hopefully remember that Haitians are not faceless AIDS carriers, as the president of the United States once said without consequences.

You'll at least know one thing about Haiti:

That the 1791 revolution that freed the island of Haiti from French Colonial rule was and remains the only self-liberated slave uprising that led to the founding of a state ruled by nonwhite former captives.

That's objectively pretty cool, right? I've repeated it three times so that it sticks. It will not balance out the scales of everything you will keep hearing about Haiti, but if you take one thing from all my nonsense, let it be that. Imagine the fear and joy in that moment, all the way back in 1791, when a bunch of people who look similar turned to one another and realized that what they were seeing were people, and not tools as they'd been told their entire lives. That their scars were unnatural cysts inflicted upon them by other people no weaker or stronger than them. People who also could be made to feel pain. Imagine that first room full of hands realizing that their broken bodies discarded into piles upon expiration could lift barrels and toil the earth, yes, but also make fists and decide which way to aim them.

It's taken years for me to come close to accepting that my Blackness means something; that I wasn't simply born Black the same way I was born right-handed or able to curl my tongue. I was born into Blackness. That false simplicity is something you convince yourself of in order to fit in and avoid drawing the eye.

(And if you are distantly wondering what about the unfair inability to feel pride for being born into your whiteness right now, you and I are no longer friends. Every corner of the world, from museums to history, from Cartoon Network to CNN, from Westeros to Hogwarts, already cheers for your whiteness. I've been reading it since before I spoke a word of English.)

This Blackness of mine is both the same as the Blackness of some wailing Black infant born that exact same minute as I was in some hospital of Springfield, Any State, USA, and also something else entirely.

And while that child and I might have grown up rolling our eyes or screaming at the world with the exact same distrust and anger, my Blackness is specific. It's Haitian.

TWENTY-SEVEN

SMILE THROUGH IT

I'M TWENTY-FOUR again and sitting in a classroom of the UT-Austin campus, a good thirty-eight minutes before the fiction workshop is set to start. I like to give myself time to hike across campus and recover from desiccating from exposure to the Austin sun. James Magnuson, our professor and everyone's favorite would-be granddad, isn't there yet. Jane Williams walks in early, too. She is a third-year southerner and a department powerhouse in the sense that she has already published a novel, which is a climbed Everest to those of us who haven't been published yet. We rarely talk, but today I say something or other and she laughs, so a conversation tumbles.

"You're actually not standoffish at all, are you?" she notes with that hint of a polished southern twang.

"What do you mean?"

She shrugs.

"You have a fight face on but then you talk and it's like 'Oh, hi, Ben!'"

She mimics unexpectedly bumping into someone and looking

delighted at the surprise. The conversation stays with me. That night, I stand in front of the mirror, practicing my face. I stretch my neck, studying its angles. I put tinfoil over my teeth to make them look like grills while I frown and grimace until my gums start to bleed. I try on a T-shirt and then a dress shirt to see if there is a notable difference in approachability. There is. Jane is right; my face on neutral is, could be perceived as, mean. I want to say "defiant," but perhaps just unlikable. Dynamite cheekbones, though. Credit where credit is due, old man.

This isn't a Black thing, it's a Ben thing. A part of me wonders if this was what Jolene had first spotted across that party. A dangerous, mean-faced Black thug.

I practice smiling more often. Not simply raising the corners of my face, but a goofier, even more harmless smile. One that wrinkles my forehead upward like a Saint Bernard. I train myself to default to this smile, even at rest. It's my personal sphincter-tightening Kegel exercise.

Distantly, I wonder if all this face stretching will age me faster but ultimately decide, after coming up with a satisfied expression, that it may save my life. Being Black and looking mean in this country could kill you—or at the very least keep you lonely. I seek to avoid both. Smile, boy. After all, "Black don't crack."

That bit of Black-skin mythos is, unfortunately, tragically, not true; our skin might stay youthful a bit longer, sure, but when it cracks, boy, does it crack. See: my uncle Arnold's forehead. Cracked. Broken. Shattered. Shards all over—under the fridge, everywhere—and not enough glue or Retinol to pull it all back together. The man will look seventy through his fifties and beyond. (Sorry, Uncle.)

I'M TWENTY-EIGHT and it's becoming harder to keep smiling in America. I'm angry. I wake up angry, and my face naturally slips into what is, at its best, a weird rage rictus. The fight face is back.

As much as I would like to, I cannot put all my rage on that microwaved Troll doll currently serving as president. Little by little, the world is growing more comfortable saying the quiet part out loud. Young YouTubers I expect to break down the latest episode of *Game of Thrones* instead speak of a Zionist agenda, and the likes are adding up. The news cycle now makes a distinction between "racist," "white nationalist," and "nationalist."

I walked around angry. Angry at the bright-smiled folks who still proudly claim "No Blacks or Asians, just a preference" when swiping through dating profiles, at the friends who tell tales of their grandmothers spewing racism at Thanksgiving like it's a fun anecdote. I argue in my Twitter mentions (the practice of the deranged), and blame Obama for galvanizing the MAGA folks with his audacity. I also blame Oprah for not doing enough and Beyoncé for not holding a hunger strike, and myself for doing nothing about it beyond tweets. I delete all my tweets after every rant.

But that's still not enough anger. I'm equally angry at people joking about leaving America for Canada, rolling my eyes at their presumption that my adoptive motherland is a wide field of snow and simpletons, begging to be infected by this nonsense.

"I'm serious," a woman I don't know says a few seats down the dinner table of a dinner party. "Toronto is lovely. I'm going to look into it."

No, you're not, I think and then say, quieting down our corner of the dinner party. "Why lie? You're not moving anywhere. You're going to make sourdough bread in your apartment and tweet about Trump while secretly hoping he wins again because you like the sense of community it gives you to dump on him or whatever."

Yes, I'm occasionally mean. I am immediately downgraded from *friendly* to *unstable acquaintance* by the party host. I will not be invited to another dinner again. It's at times intoxicating, this new anger. My snark and witty banter have metastasized into a weird new anger I don't quite know what to do with.

"When did you get so political?" my coworker Crystal asks, walking back to work one day that year.

"What do you mean?"

"Your social media," she says. "It's like, angry as hell, these days."

"Aren't you mad?"

"Of course I am! But that's not productive. All this negativity."

"Apologies," I say. "I'll retweet one of your cactus plant shelves to make up for it tonight."

"I didn't vote for Trump, dude!" she snaps, after a beat.

No, but Nassau County, New York, hasn't been declared a universal shithole. You can find him disgusting from the sidelines, knowing these nerds in khakis and tiki torches marching for whiteness are not headed toward your house or the houses of people who look like you. You're still thriving under him.

Crystal purses her lips as if to signal she won't be adding any more gas to this fire I'm so invested in starting. I wait for the easy retort that doesn't come: *You're thriving too, Ben.*

"I think we shouldn't talk about this," I manage after being unable to tap into my go-to defuser smile. The one I reserve for tense situations. "I'm not, y'know, sleeping well."

"It's okay." Crystal smiles without believing me. "This is hard on everyone."

Every flare-up like this comes with a mention of my not sleeping well, or of me drinking too much coffee, or my considering adopting a "screenless bedroom" to center myself. It's all lies. I sleep instantly and dreamlessly; I don't own a coffee machine; and I nod off around 11 p.m. on most nights.

This anger is untethered to any outside stimulus. This country and its shiny lights have bamboozled me. It's illogical, but I realize that being a Black boy in Canada had not prepared me for the task of being a Black man in America. It's a boss level that I don't have the right weapons for. I'm using a slingshot and boomerang when what I need are arrows and magic spells.

I also know that I will run out of people soon, if I keep this going. I'll be the mercurial friend kept at a distance because people don't want to think of themselves as actively unfriending a Black guy for being too angry about the world. I don't want to be alone again, so my politics make way for a polite and functioning sort of social hypocrisy.

"How about a rule?" I preempt, setting the three large bags of Chinese food delivered at my door down on the counter of my kitchen and reaching for the plates. "No politics tonight. No Trump, none of that."

My three guests all but audibly sigh in relief, like some dread has left them and they no longer regret RSVP'ing to my invite. Four others couldn't make it that night and were pretty busy for the foreseeable future. It's okay: I like leftovers.

TWENTY-EIGHT

HOW TO LIVE STRICTLY ON COMMON GROUNDS

No one is apolitical. Not a single person. The few people I've met who proudly consider themselves as such tend to assume that not paying attention, not voting, isn't in itself a privilege. That it is not in itself proof that their day-to-day existence won't be affected by choosing to stay on the sidelines, tending to literal gardens. The fact of the matter is that if you have a life that leaves you foolproof to politics, your politics approximate to "privileged." Saying this out loud, however, isn't always conducive to post-2016 friendships. I never mind a political disagreement; I just pick them wisely these days. Self-care and what have you.

Johnny, for instance, is a friend I met during my sixteen-months-and-three-weeks stint working at a performing arts venue on the Upper West Side, teaching on the side and writing young adult manuscripts at night. He is Irish Catholic with a better work ethic than me, big blue eyes, and occasional attempts at a full vivid-red beard that he will grow for a few weeks and then shave off, unwilling to power through the awkward stages of patchiness.

I love Johnny, and post-2016 elections, I find myself reminding myself of that fact more often than before. Somehow, we find ourselves discussing affirmative action, of all things. We are both usually more careful but today, the topic slips through.

"Do you know how much student debt I have?" he says, always honest and steadfastly himself even while inhaling a burrito during our lunch hour. "Some people—who aren't even citizens, by the way—end college without owing a single cent, and I'm going to be paying this off until I'm like fifty. How is that fair? I'm not some banker. I work in the performing arts! For kids!"

I'm one of the said people who ended college without owing a cent, and Johnny and I both know it. I acknowledge this privilege without feeling bad about it. In fact, it floods my stomach with relief and gratitude whenever I walk by the gates of Columbia.

"You had a two-something GPA in high school!" I exclaim in return. "What's unfair about kids with good grades getting scholarships?"

Sure, I've made it personal because why shouldn't it be personal for both of us?

"Two-point-four, dick. Both my parents worked all day," he continues. "I had a kid brother to look after and part-time jobs since I was fourteen."

"I'm not saying you didn't have a full plate, dude," I say. "But those kids with perfect GPAs did, too. And maybe a language barrier! And, oh yeah, the legacy of slavery, too, for Black ones. That little nugget."

He rolls his eyes, and the buckets of bright red paint start stacking up in my mind.

"Irish people were slaves, too, you know."

"Here we go!" I scoff, pushing my plate forward and leaning back to cross my arms, somehow knowing this was coming.

"White people love to say that Irish people were slaves, too. I swear you cum to that crap."

I start using bigger words, for no reason other than the fact that I can. Slavery belongs to African American history, so of course white people would try to co-opt it and make it fashion.

"It's a myth, by the way," I say, biting into three stacked nachos. "Irish slavery? Yeah, that's just conflated history that confounds seventeenth- and eighteenth-century facts about Irish servitude with Africa's chattel slavery. Propagated by white nationalists for two centuries now."

"T-they were slaves! Black people don't have a monopoly on slavery!" he says, getting loud, though not red, because Johnny doesn't redden. "Slaves have existed throughout history."

"Are you kidding?" I ask, Haitian and louder, wondering how we got there so fast. "Irish colonial labor is not the same as American fucking slavery that built the bones of an entire country that still treats them like fractions."

"That's— You're Canadian!" he says with an angry laugh, half-nervous. "Haitian Canadian, whatever!"

"Still Black, thank you very much."

He rolls his eyes. "Like you'd ever let anyone forget?"

A better Ben—see also: taller Ben, sexier Ben—would be able to calmly and detachedly explain to Johnny that no ethnic kid took his spot at Harvard; that his privilege isn't about the gates that are opened for you but the bags of sand he doesn't have to go through the world carrying. This would all end in a hug. This Ben, unfortunately, does not exist.

It's Mean Ben who has something to say here. Something witty and intellectually unimpeachable that leaves Johnny feeling outmatched while highlighting the hypocrisy of his entire belief system.

Johnny is upset and I could match his red with mine and leave the walls of this at-capacity Mexican restaurant bloody. In truth, part of me wants to. *My mother went to high school with fifteen-year-olds at forty, you privileged little twat.*

Instead, I answer, "I get why you're mad."

I stop myself there and we chew in silence for a while, separately defusing in the corners of our own brains.

"I'm just saying," Johnny then says, almost apologetic but not quite after another burrito bite, "like, the system is unfair for everyone, all over."

"The system is bullshit, dude." I nod.

It's a universal platitude we can both take comfort in, and move into the blue again. If I can vent my anger over a president who just happens to share Johnny's skin color, I can also listen to his rant about some tilted system that, in his mind, prioritizes people who look like me over people who look like him.

If that anecdote outburst paints a problematic picture of Johnny or myself, well, you're entirely not wrong. People are problematic. It has been my experience that they're puzzle pieces that only "mostly" fit and never quite seamlessly. Only if you commit and give two pieces a good pounding, they might.

I know that Johnny also loves the show *It's Always Sunny in Philadelphia* in a borderline unhinged way, like you do. Johnny will likewise text you thoughtful memes and reaction GIFs curated to your specific interests, even if he has to Google five pages deep to find the correct one. Johnny will show up on a Sunday, having trekked to Harlem from Long Island to help you with a work assignment that leaves you completely out of your depth.

There are, as I've come to find out, a lot of Johnnys out in the world. Some I've vanquished without ever looking back, but others

I can make work. Johnny is a great person, and my life would be impossibly lessened by his absence. You are what you stand for, and I stand for this occasional friction.

One day we might both hit that red zone and tumble into a topic that's too sensitive to dance past or compartmentalize. He'll go to his Roman Catholic roots, and I'll meet him with my arrogant, Angry Black Man fight face. I already know that in the grand scheme of things, I'll probably have the moral high ground. But I do not wish for that moment to happen.

The older I get, the more of these conditional friendships manifest and the more value I see in at least trying to keep them. It may simply be cowardice for me. The opposite, after all, is to sit friendless, at the back of the class of life, while desks are eagerly being brought together around you. It is not worth it. Black or white, life gets lonely when lived in red.

TWENTY-NINE

SURE, I'LL BE YOUR BL– RACE WARS!!!

It's spring 2020. I'M THIRTY-ONE and I'm in the middle of drafting a book on the quirks and maybe light trauma of having been the Black friend in white spaces all my life. It's supposed to be a light, conversational read, and I'm on my Carrie Bradshaw bullshit. I spend weeks excavating my mind and old emails for microaggressions and tiny emotional scars as I write. I lie upside down on the edge of my bed and stare at the ceiling like a cheerleader gossiping on the phone, remembering slights. And then suddenly, as if the year's global pandemic wasn't quite enough, the world is on fire.

Black people are dying across America, which is nothing new, but the pattern stands out to the world this time. It happens in quick succession. First, Ahmaud Arbery is shot in Georgia and footage of his murder emerges online. His killer is reported as having called him a "fucking nigger" after the shooting. In Kentucky, three plainclothes Louisville Metro Police Department officers burst into Breonna Taylor's apartment, and she dies with eight bullets shredding through her body. None of her ex-boyfriend's drugs, the suspicious packages supposedly being delivered to her address and the cause of this no-knock search warrant, were found in the apartment. Finally, in Minnesota, George Floyd is filmed dying with a cop's full weight pressed on his neck while nearby people exclaim that this is unnecessary and excessive force. "He's not resisting!" can be heard in the background. He will be the spark.

From their phones and social media feeds, the world watches the eight minutes and forty-six seconds that he, George, spends with a knee on his neck. "I can't breathe," he says before simply crying out, "Mama! Mama . . . I'm through!" His mother had been dead for two years when George Floyd calls out for her as he is lynched. A lynching is defined as a killing committed by a mob; four police officers amount to a mob. Hours too late, the world hears George's choked whisper of "I can't breathe."

Rapper Megan Thee Stallion's eponymous song "Hot Girl Summer" appeared on every chart in 2019. But the summer of 2020 is known as the summer of Black Lives Matter. All it took for America to wrestle with itself was for a string of undeniable murders to be caught on camera. The country is outraged but does not appear to realize that the hands around its throat are its own.

Other nonfatal matches contribute to the flames as well. The Karens of America have also had a rough summer of mandatory social distancing, and their roots are now showing. The plural form of Karens is a Privilege of Karens. In the Ramble area of Central Park, a white woman named Amy Cooper is caught on video threatening to call the cops on a Black man, Christian Cooper—no relation, just one of those ugly little American overlaps. (White and Black people sharing the same last name often means ancestral ownership as some former slaves adopted—or were cursed with—the names of their former owners.) In this particular instance, Christian Cooper has made the mistake of telling Amy that she should have her dog on a leash in this particular area of the park.

"I'm taking a picture and calling the cops," Amy Cooper is heard saying in the video, with panic and outrage in her voice. "I'm going to tell them there's an African American man threatening my life." Social media has grown vicious after nearly four years of Trump, and Amy Cooper is swiftly torn apart across all platforms. She releases a generic apology after losing her job, and the expected sympathy begins. The media can't help but highlight her humanity as they admonish her. *Who among us hasn't had a bad day?* It's an argument that usually works on me but for the first time, a pound of flesh isn't enough. I find myself wishing we'd get down to the bones of this woman I do not know.

More Karens like Amy Cooper emerge from the woods. The fake viral meme of a Karen archetype gracing the *Time* Person of the Year cover becomes entirely too believable considering the year we're having. They've always been around, these inconvenienced and outraged manager-summoning white women playing with Black lives that displease them. The only difference is that people are now filming them. Society is taking it upon itself to shame their ilk into thinking twice before doing what they've been doing since I was a kid in Sherbrooke. Really, it's the year of the camera more than anything else.

It's clear that America doesn't quite know what to do with itself to address the moment. *Gone with the Wind*, which premiered on December 15, 1939, is taken off streaming channels and then re-added, after a backlash to the backlash. Closer to home and eighteen months after its release, my young adult novel is momentarily a top seller on Amazon's chart. White people are buying books written by Black authors in droves. For a few days, I can barely go three hours without my book being tagged on a list of Black authors "for the moment." I make no royalties on any of this, but the photos are nice. The gorgeous paperback cover by Steffi Walthall is colorful and harmless; it's an easy choice for a parent looking for Black books by Black authors that aren't too political for their kids' shelves. I'm categorized under "Black Joy." (If you've read this far into this book, you might get the irony.)

Brief talks of "defunding the police"—really, just of rethinking police departments' paramilitary budgets across the country—quickly turn to a focus on the removal of monuments and statues aggrandizing the slave owners who built America instead. The world is desperate to fist bump us into being cool again. What will look like a contrite-enough sacrifice to the riled-up hordes of Negroes? From my vantage point, America's hand-wringing looks exhaustingly performative; little dabs of a wet washcloth around a gaping wound of racism.

"Marches" turn into "protests" and "protests" lead to "riots" with bursts of "lootings" in between. Which word is given primacy in your mind depends on which narrative comes most naturally to you: "Black people are dying, as always," "Black people are hurting, again," or "Black people are stealing, like usual."

In the midst of it all—two months into the United States COVID-19 quarantine and over 100,000 American deaths deep—President Donald J. Trump tweets, because he is very attached to that presidential requirement.

. . . These THUGS are dishonoring the memory of George Floyd, and I won't let that happen.

Lines are drawn and sides are taken. *Blue Lives Matter. All Lives Matter. AnythingButBlack Lives Matter.* I see "Anti-Antifa" T-shirts, which is just grammatically redundant. There's an easier word there. Footage of armored policemen shoving white people with a strength typically reserved for a criminal do-ragged element joins the media feeds. I've stopped writing entirely. A software update is being added to my Blackness in real time; it's a good time to step away from the laptop and grab a snack.

I eat nachos in bed, balancing my phone on my stomach, watching with dead eyes the accounts of tearful anguished white protestors sitting on sidewalks watering their pepper-sprayed eyes, not understanding how a cop would do this to them. It genuinely confuses them. Surely, they can't all just be noticing *now*? You're supposed to throw the rope down; not jump in with us, I think. I want them to take me to the safe and shiny world they were in until a few days ago, not for them to be beaten and abused in mine.

I change my crumbs-ridden bedsheets multiple times a week. I wonder if these white protestors would still have gotten out of bed that day if they knew the cost of chanting "Black lives matter" would be bodily harm, return to a freshly made bed with a bag of Sour Patch Kids, and keep scrolling through it all. "Let's see how it turns out" is all I contribute to the few group texts I'm on, all discussing the important moment that this summer could be for the movement. Texting them my real thoughts, this Black foreigner's strange apathy, would probably cost me friends. Everyone wants me to be, assumes me to get, angry about Black lives, having no idea what that would actually look like.

Do you hate cops, Ben?

Nope. I also do not hate nurses. Or firefighters. Or EMT

workers. Not to mention that there are plenty of Black, Asian, Latinx, and other minority cops in these streets, right? So, no. I don't
hate cops.

I do not naturally *trust* cops. I'm not meant to. The societal
contract they have with white people is different from the one they
have with Black people. My polite conversations with white officers occur with their hands resting on their gun handles, trying
to assess if my eyes are glazed. The system isn't "broken": it was
improperly designed for your safety and my dread. It's a shelf that
starts to wobble the moment you put a single book on it.

If you're a minority in America, I suspect you already know
this. And if you're a white person, you won't fully believe me until
you're at the end of the baton so I won't belabor the point. I get
your apprehension: White parents instruct their children to "find
a cop" if they're ever in danger. Black parents instruct us to "find
a nice adult."

Late spring turns into summer. "Blackface" is upgraded to a
cardinal sin, and old sitcom episodes that feature it are stricken
from the record. On weekly comedy podcasts, I cringe through
hours of comedians awkwardly trying to side with the right side
of history, without thinking about it too hard and losing nothing. My phone's battery empties faster than usual as I consume
it all. I throw out the nachos and candy and begin to eat bright,
chemically orange carrot sticks instead after gaining five pounds in
quarantine. (Okay, fine: it was eleven pounds. Stop berating me. It
was a sensitive political climate.)

Across the web, MAGA morons swear that there is no way on
God's unvaccinated flat earth that this isn't some liberal "Antifa"
coup on this country. Some of my white friends share a single Black
square on their Instagrams. Others become tireless activists of the

moment and march every weekend while I stay at home scrolling my phone. I convince myself to feel no guilt in doing so. It's their time to do the work. I'll still be Black once they choose to move on to America's next Moment. For the first few days, I retweet the rioters while keeping safe from danger. I pretend it's because I am at a higher risk of retribution by angry policemen, but really, I'm a coward who prioritizes his safety over civil righteousness or morality. Or, I'm a foreigner here on a visa who will not risk an arrest on the Brooklyn Bridge. Or, I'm a cynic who does not believe in change when it's happening in the background of selfies with cardboard that reads CHANGE. All these things are true all at once: I've made my peace with that, so should you.

I Google the others who came before, trying to stir up something cogent and coherent for myself. I have draconically strict opinions about who should have been on the Iron Throne at the end of *Game of Thrones*; I should have something new and important to say about this, too, no? Now, of all times.

There's Eric, the giant unarmed bear of a man, begging for his life, repeating the words "I can't breathe" while lying facedown on the sidewalk. There's also Philando; the one with the daughter in the back seat. I find no photos of her but wonder what it's like to be a four-year-old already aware enough to shout, "*Mom, please stop cussing and screaming 'cause I don't want you to get shooted!*" at your agitated mother from the back seat and then watch your father get shot at point-blank, inches away, by a man who will later be acquitted of all charges because he was just doing his job.

Trayvon was by far the most photogenic of us. The kid was right out of a Nickelodeon sitcom casting call. You wanted to give him a head rub after giving him a speech on recycling. History still went to George Zimmerman, the Florida man who took an interest in Trayvon for the crime of "hoodie" and decided to kill him. Zimmerman will apparently sign your gun if you find him today, and sell you a painting, too.

I read the comments section of YouTube clips in which people never fail to bring up that racism is not a thing, that whiteness is not prioritized in America, that Black people amount to less than 15 percent of the population, so why do they want 100 percent of the oxygen in the room. These anonymous, typo-riddled thoughts feel "honest" somehow. The underbelly that I'm convinced makes up the majority of this country.

I can understand having been raised to believe that cops are the good guys, that racism lives in the uneven icing and not the flour and milk of the great American cake, but how can some Americans hear all these stories, line up all these body bags, and somehow still think we're all lying? That lightning struck all these Black men randomly and without malice or systemic ease?

Eventually, after days of delaying answering texts, I pick up the cardboard, too, and agree to join my friends. I've marched with women in pink hats, I've marched against kids in cages, and there's still cardboard and markers in the hallway closet from both. I can do this, too. If something should pierce through my growing certainty that all you can do is survive or escape in the end, it should be Black lives, no? I can at least be as hopeful as the earnest white folks outside.

I head for the Brooklyn Museum's plaza, like so many others that day. I have no map pulled up on my phone. For once, there's no wit or commentary to my signage. It's not a tweet. I go simple

with black, even block letters on three lines: BLACK LIVES MATTER.
Three words; no subtext.

After exiting the subway, I simply follow the signage and bodies, all dressed in symbolic colors. Today, the color to wear is crisp,
pure white. Enough people got the memo for the streets of masked
people in stylish white outfits to feel unsettling. Even up close,
sweaty, inspired, with signage cutting into my armpit and bodies
of all shapes and colors all wearing masks around me, I'm still as
unmoved as if I was on my bed with a phone on my stomach.

Why do I have to be here? I think as I move through the crowd
trying to keep a safe distance, in a white T-shirt and black jeans.
Why are these three words so hard to get across down here in
America of all places? The place that taught me flawless, happy,
and upbeat English through *Kenan & Kel*, *The Proud Family*, *The
Boondocks*, *That's So Raven*, *Key & Peele*, *Everybody Hates Chris*,
The Bernie Mac Show, *The Fresh Prince of Bel-Air*, *Girlfriends*, and
all the others? Why didn't any of them cut to black and say, "It's
all imagined, it's all fake, you know that, right?" at the end. Over
a decade later, I want a store credit or something.

I join my friends and their friends who introduce themselves
with head nods and solemn headshakes at passing images of
George Floyd. We're all appropriately diverse, in masks and cargo
shorts. None of us are taking selfies, which I'm grateful for. The
chants are loud and filled with genuine emotion. Everything is
Powerful and Hollow all at once. We move in circles as if waiting
for someone to come onstage at a dour music festival. Maybe the
point is simply to be seen right here, right now. To have witnessed.

The fireworks that have been going off nonstop thorough the
summer, and sparking conspiracy theories of coordinated unrest,

feel appropriate for this important summer that I fear we won't remember next year.

Why do I have to tell you that my life matters?

Why does the absolute bare minimum require thousands of sweaty bodies to amass and walk together in the middle of a viral pandemic?

Why haven't Breonna's killers been hanged from high branches yet?

"Are you okay?" my friend Francesca asks. She's from Israel, passes for white most of the year, and is constantly mistaken for Latinx when she tans in the summer. She is woke—the real A-side Woke, not the slur reserved for Millennials munching on avocado toast points. She recycles, donates, volunteers, and educates. Her arms are filled with elegant and meaningful tattoos. She works in a nonprofit and has advanced plant lives all over her apartment.

"Yeah, why?" I smile.

"Your eyes are like, dead. I have water if you're dehydrated."

Her tote bag is full of human empathy, good intentions, and healthy snacks from local small businesses. For a moment, I'm in awe of her. How wonderful it must be to go through life seeing others first.

"I'm good, it's just . . . a lot, y'know?" I lie, smiling at her from under my mask.

"I know." She nods. "It's so overwhelming. It's okay to be angry, Ben."

She moves to touch my shoulder before stopping herself. We can't hug. Pandemic: six feet apart at all times. That excuse is a very good thing right now.

"This might be it," one of her friends nearby says, having heard us. His red beard curls under his mask, and he has kind gray eyes, made striking by the red of his face right now.

"What do you mean?"

"The real change," he adds. "Reform, not just retweets. This can't go on."

Francesca nods meaningfully, inspired. I imitate Francesca. *This only ever goes on*, I think but don't say.

We keep marching. I'm barely here and then it's over.

On the train that evening, I count down the visible marchers and protestors as they file out at various stops and return home satisfied and sated at having touched no one, done nothing. I've left my sign at the scene after parting ways with Francesca and the others. She has already forwarded me details of the next march in three days' time. I suppose I feel better. Like, having gone through the hassle of going to the dentist for a teeth cleaning only maybe without the clean feeling that leaves you licking your teeth the whole ride home. The train stalls due to a combination of reduced COVID services, delays, and construction, and I spend seventy minutes on the local with my thoughts and 17 percent battery life on my phone. I Google a new name that I only learned because of someone else's signage.

Elijah. Age twenty-three.

In the photo results, he is softness personified—complete with thick-rimmed glasses and a toothy smile. Elijah wore face masks due to his anemia and the Colorado weather, and he looks like the type of lanky nerd I might share a lunch table with. On August 24, 2019, someone called 911 on him for spotting his erratic behavior. The police held him down, beat him, and injected him with ketamine. He went into cardiac arrest and died. The arm flailing in question was later attributed to an introvert dancing to his music. I buy it, too. That guy looks like a dancer with curated playlists.

Elijah, by all accounts, had none of the weird anger that I do. This isn't supposition or narrative like the bit of trivia that he "liked to play the violin to calm down stray cats"; I know this because, while restrained, Elijah is on record as having vomited several times, for which he apologized, saying, "I'm sorry, I wasn't trying to do that, I can't breathe correctly." What was his favorite color, I wonder? What was his first heartbreak? How did he lose his virginity? Where was he born? Was he a momma's boy, too? Breonna Taylor will later appear on the covers of *O, The Oprah Magazine* and *Vanity Fair*, less human and more angelic each time. Her flesh pierced by hot metal, blood splattered over her own home; her phone will never be unlocked again, but she looks stunning. One of us has to be the final straw, right? Please, let one of us be the final straw, a tipping point of some kind as opposed to this neverending accumulation of murdered bodies. It won't be this summer. I already know that.

A large bald white man in a V-neck that's almost translucent with sweat enters the train at Times Square. He looks around at the stray protestors and their signage and scoffs loud enough to be heard before finding his seat by the train doors, directly across from me. He wears no mask, and his wrinkles are profound. Black people were probably packed at the end of public transport when he was a young man. He shakes his head, visibly displeased with where all these young people have been today.

"This whole thing," he eventually says, loudly and to no one in particular, "this ends in a race war if you ask me. No two ways about it."

He notices me and adds, "I don't want trouble: I'm just saying."

The "I don't want trouble" is strictly for my benefit; to temper down the strange Black man smiling at him from under his mask.

I return to my phone, headphones on, containing the smile the rest of the way back up to Harlem.

I smile because, as ridiculous as the concept of a race war is, the fear of the concept lingering in people's minds pleases me. It brings a sudden manic joy to my heart. I don't want kinship and brotherhood. I don't want to jeer depictions of Donald Trump in diapers and a Ku Klux Klan hood. More and more, I want people to throw bricks and for those bricks to hit skulls. No more tiny parking lot fireworks of outrage; I want a forest fire to start and then never stop until it hits the other coast. Daenerys Targaryen at the head of a fleet of fire-breathing dragons; 3.797 million square miles of forest fires.

Making a few of us exceptional was your first mistake. We began to inspire each other more than we fear you. Oprah and Kaepernick are huddled up over maps and strategizing as we speak. Barack is hearing them out with a hand at his chin and his sleeves rolled up, considering all the eventualities, all at once. Kanye is our Joker; a wild card even to us. At some point soon, we'll get the signal, sharpen our "Excellence in Diversity" medals into jagged shards, and stab you in the eye with them before collecting your keys, wallets, and phones and convening to the nearest meeting spot to await the next set of instructions. You'll wake up in the middle of the night and run to your front yard barefoot and panicked, hearing us in the wind.

You miscounted the men, you dummy. Yes, we're only forty-something million here in the United States, but there are legions of us all over the world these days. A diaspora of tiny cells across the globe waiting for the breaking point. French Canadian northerners, Brazilians of African ancestry, and all the warlords and kids with distended bellies in Africa. There are hidden warehouses of weapons and shields all over. We're building ships and amassing wealth as we speak. Our laughs are louder and our kitchens were hotter and smelled spicier than yours when we were growing up: I promise you we will win. Our parents let us touch the stovetop to learn from the burn to keep away from it. Unlike your imagined slights and grievances—the lyrics you can't sing, the dreads you wish you were allowed to wear—we know what's at stake. We will march the Edmund Pettus Bridge in Selma, Alabama, again, only with blades in hand in this time.

And even that won't be "overwhelming," as Francesca says. It will be just enough.

And to be clear, it's not up to us, Black people, people of color, to fix this. We could all stay home eating nachos all day and be entirely in the right to do so. How come? Because this is not a shared burden. Black people built this country. That is a fact as simple and tedious as you having built your Ikea TV console. The agriculture, the textile, the toil, the soil, we did it all. We simply had no say in how it would all be put to use; only the certainty that it wouldn't be for our benefit. So, no: we do not share the blame, nor do we share the power to enact this change "we" now all want.

And if you can't fix this—really fix it—then the old asshole on the train was right: the minister's dream, that beautiful dream I grew up thinking was a given and that I now realize was just another bit of social media content created around a Black man's executed corpse, well, that dream will end. You don't have a lot of time before it does, either. People are chugging melatonin and scrolling through their phones all night. It's harder and harder to fall asleep, let alone to dream these days. And the moment it does end, the inevitable climax to this story will indeed become war.

And I won't march alongside you then. Sorry, Francesca,

Marty, Kevin, Johnny, Jane, Georgie, Will, and all the other white people I love so much. Sorry, Mia. Sorry, reader. Doubting this, thinking I'm an Oreo—white on the inside and more like you than not—well, it might be your undoing then, friends. When this race war hits its crescendo, I'll gather you all into a beautifully decorated room under the pretense of unity. I'll give a speech to civility and all the good times we've shared. I'll smile as we raise our glasses to your good white health while the detonator blinks under the table, knowing the exits are locked and the air vents filled with gas. Movements need martyrs with anger to spare—and my side was decided at birth.

THIRTY

ONE OF THE GOOD ONES

One thing that might have fallen through the cracks of all these stories is that I am, at heart, a Black man who likes himself enough to have developed a *vested* interest in not dying. No, really: terrorism imagery aside, I actually do love it here among the living. As small as it may be, I love my life on this dying rock of a planet, zip code: America.

My "Black joy" isn't a single monolithic thing. It's a series of small and ordinary pleasures you might call basic. Candy and desserts. A good from-the-gut laugh you didn't see coming. Winning over a classroom of teenage students with the right pop culture reference. A hockey game turning out exactly like I want. Watching someone smile while they're reading a book I've read on the train. Leaning in for a kiss with closed eyes, sensing the other person is leaning forward, too. My dog's cold nose on my foot when I've overslept. Nailing a new recipe and the satisfaction of clean kitchen counters.

And in order to go on enjoying my neat and ordered little life, I need my joy to be cataloged as something other than the counterpoint to another Black person's suffering. I, shall we say, bristle at the idea that it only comes into focus when Black blood is splattered across the pavement or once asphyxiation has occurred.

"I can't breathe. I can't breathe. I can't breathe. I can't breathe. I can't breathe. I can't breathe. I can't breathe I can't breathe. I can't breathe. I can't breathe. I can't breathe."—Eric Garner

"I'm sorry, I wasn't trying to do that, I can't breathe correctly."—Elijah McClain

"I can't breathe! Mama! Mama . . . I'm through!"—George Floyd

It's not a slogan or a hashtag coming to these men who look like me at the hour of their deaths. They aren't quoting one another. These are terrified people dying and hoping while dying that someone, for a brief moment, will remember that they are human beings with airways that require oxygen. They are hoping, praying, begging for their *killers* to remember that they're actually killing someone. They're tapping out. You win. Just spare us.

How many others have there been that you and I will never hear about? How many Black hearts were violently stopped between Emmett Till and George Floyd? Away from crowds and before cell phone cameras?

Being a Black man in America has been an entirely different experience from being Black everywhere before. Blackness is just different here. Here, it comes with a community and a history but also with an immediate fear and a proportional rage at having to be so afraid all the time. And, make no mistake, white friends: I truly am afraid all the time. There is nothing I can do to remove the need for oxygen from my lungs. I can drown right here on solid ground in this country and—I promise you—no one thinks about my death more than me. I've been watching variations of it since

my first horror movie. Freddy, Chucky, and Jason have all gleefully driven sharp metal into a body like mine in the basement as
the pretty white people upstairs suspected something sinister was
afoot. It is always a little gorier than it needs to be; a close-up shot
on the beautiful contrast of black skin and glistening red pouring
out. I'm so rarely mourned. The last chapter of the young and
Black is familiar, no? Another shame, another blow to some amor-
phous community.

I promised myself when I started this book that it would, if
nothing else, be honest. So, let's do just that right now, shall we?

I know I'm "one of the good ones."

There, I said it. As much as I abhor that toxic description that
gauges human life on a messed-up internalized scale of white ap-
proval, I also won't kid myself and pretend I haven't always been
aware of it. Whatever the exact test is, I know I pass it. It wasn't
equality that I was looking for; it was privilege and maybe the
safety that comes with the word.

I've done everything right since crossing that first border on a
Greyhound bus with an Ivy League acceptance letter in my hoodie
sleeve and my mother's hand on my knee. Every last thing. I got
the first fancy degree, and then the next. I pay my bills on time
and don't spit on the ground. I have no hint of a criminal record.
I've also been a good immigrant, never outlasting any of my visas.

I cross the street coming out of the subway at night because
that little old lady in front of me is visibly terrified of the Black
man behind her and she shouldn't be scared but she is literally
shaking, so why not do her that unfair kindness?

I start every email with "I hope all is well." And sign them off
with a friendly "Cheers." It's a framework meant to make every-

thing I say friendly and approachable; written with a smile. When requested, I present my ID to officers with a smile and my headphones off. By even the harshest assessment, I might amount to "moody, insecure, underwhelming human being with trust issues, but still a good Black." The one you're not talking about when you talk about *them*.

I've done everything that would make me respectable and safe in this country. It wasn't conscious but it also didn't happen without my notice. I was told that if I did then I might just be in the shorter line of the ones you begrudgingly let into your gated community when some have to be let in.

And even still, after a decade of this never-ending, backbreaking game of hopscotch, no one will tell me that I, or my future kids, or my grandkids, won't die exactly like George and the others—at the hands of people we were taught to trust and obey if we wanted to be safe. No one can.

So, what status quo is there to be attached to if maintaining it doesn't lessen that possible outcome? Why wouldn't I feel some curiosity for that all-encompassing fire that burns it all to a crisp?

"It's okay to be angry, Ben."

No, it's not. God bless your heart, Francesca, really, but the absolute well-meaning caucasity of thinking that letting myself get angry about the treatment of Black lives in this country simply ends at a march and a cardboard sign . . . Of thinking that you'd all be safe if we, even the good ones, allowed ourselves to express the anger that this world deserves.

So, no: I cannot let myself get that angry. I can express measured frustration. I can march and protest. Be snarky on Twitter or try to pen an essay for *The Atlantic*. I can make white friends, pick my battles, and slowly change their minds about a few specific things, hoping it spreads . . . I can compartmentalize and smile through it. I can flirt with the anger, allow myself a stray comment here and there, making a dinner party awkward, but I cannot let it take the reins.

Angry with a capital A? Nah, that's not allowed. Robert's son is smarter than to gamble it all away quite yet. That anger extinguishes the goodwill I've lived my life accumulating, and like I said: I like my life. I want to see it through to a satisfyingly boring conclusion. My final Pokémon evolution is old Haitian man with thick-ass leather sandals in the summer, walking around the neighborhood with his two old English sheepdogs, Melvin and Gilmore. It's going to be great.

So, no: I, Ben, still do not want to die in this country. I don't consent to the cost of admission into this country being my potential lynching if I have a bad day and displease you. I don't want to be a T-shirt, poster, chant, or statistic. Like every other Black body roaming this land, I want to be safe here and I want to be safe here now. I'm a coward and I don't want to die.

And before you ask, no, I'm not leaving either now that I'm here. Womp womp. Too much of my Black joy is tethered to this place, sorry. Besides, this whole continent is about people claiming land that isn't theirs and chasing occupants out, isn't it? I have no problem ripping your homeland from your clutches now that I've found my tribe. You leave if you have a problem with my continued presence here. *You* go back to Canada, *you* go back to Haiti.

To quote Kimberly Latrice Jones, a Black Lives Matter activist whose viral video will come to define the summer of 2020 for me: "They are lucky that what Black people are looking for is equality and not revenge."

You really are, friend. Goddamn blessed. Because some of us? Some of those with the bright smiles, cute dogs, soy milk in the fridge, and *Gilmore Girls* reruns in the background . . . Some of us do want payback for all of this.

> *Negroes,*
> *Sweet and docile,*
> *Meek, humble, and kind:*
> *Beware the day*
> *They change their minds!*

—LANGSTON HUGHES

THIRTY-ONE

CONCLUSION:
HOW TO THRIVE IN A BLACK BODY AT ANY AGE

You're four or five years old, it's hard to remember which. Your world is Creole and you're completely naked.

You love the power of your newly discovered nakedness. It freaking thrills you to run through gardens, dick out, butt high, shriek-laughing while everyone at your parents' fancy garden party stares at you. Anyone who makes eye contact with your dick is a pedophile! You don't even know what that word means, but you know they're the ones doing something wrong, not you. You stop by the clothed table of food and strike a pose. Twenty Haitian socialite pedophiles, coming up! You won't know what shame is for another few hours.

Claudine, a family friend, laughs and claps for you as you lap circles around the maids and your dad. "He's darker-skinned than you would expect from you and Robert," you hear her tell your mom who is also laughing, and you note that *Black* comes in ranked shades. You either carry light or darkness in your skin.

Your dad sees no humor in your objectively hilarious wiener

flopping around on a Sunday. You might have stood on a chair at some point? You don't remember it. He is furious, embarrassed, and humiliated all at once. And scary, so overwhelmingly scary. His five-feet-nine looks like a skyscraper crumbling over you. Once the guests are gone, you're made to kneel in the solarium for forty minutes while he rages, and then you get your first belt-whipping. The one that draws blood. You really should never be naked.

You're five or six, and your world is not Creole anymore. It's the second time. He didn't draw blood this time.

"You can't keep doing this to him once we're in Canada!" Mom says, dressed in her white nursing uniform, getting home from work late to find you kneeling in the corner of Dad's office. The maids are just outside, peering in with their hands on their mouths at all the screaming. There's no one to call in Haiti.

"Kids need structure," he says. "He's not the angel you think."

You want to say, *But I didn't unstructure anything! I was just playing with it*, but it comes out as a shriek of pain. You can't poop after you get the belt. Your butt is numb for days until it isn't.

Mom is crying now and kissing all over your head, and she doesn't have to say anything; you already know you're the most important thing in the world to her. You want to tell her you're okay and that you barely felt this one compared to the first one, that your skin is hard and Robert-proof now, but it's all coming out in wails and blubber and tears.

"I'm a nurse. I have syringes and I have drugs," she says. "If you ever touch him again, I'll kill you. I know how to."

You hold on to her and let yourself be carried out on her wet shoulder. Your mom is not a violent woman; your dad just requires a reconsideration of what she thinks herself capable of doing. This is the part where she ices your butt with tears in her eyes. There's safety in her violence. No one else will ever love you this much. You will never not remember these moments.

You decide you don't like this person anymore. You can't see if he's staring back at you because of the light reflecting in his glasses, but the thought is sharp in the back of your mind as you watch his desk shrink away: *Someday when I'm big, I'll get you back for this. For her crying, me crying. For all of it.*

You're seven or eight, and your world is not Creole anymore. "Do you know what tomorrow is?" Mrs. Germaine asks you on October 30, apart from the other students. "Do you have Halloween in Haiti?"

You don't want to go to school the next day. You have clothes that adapt to the changing weather. No immigrant family allocates money for a day of make-believe when budgeting for this strange country. *Please, God, don't make me go to school. Ship me back to Haiti, I don't care! They're all going to be ninjas, and Batman, and princesses, and I won't be anything!*

"He's going to school," Dad scoffs from the kitchen, watching TV and eating without looking at you or your mom. You wish he wasn't here.

"Mom," you plead again. You know she would be happy to let you stay at home if it was just her.

"I'm thinking," she says.

We're poor here and are still settling in. We don't have money for things like costumes you only wear for one day. She ties one of her big scarves around your neck and puts you in one of her paisley blouses with a belt around your waist. She inexplicably puts a line of lipstick on both of your cheeks and rubs them in with both thumbs.

"There! You're a pirate now." She smiles. "It'll be fine. There will be candy."

"That's not a costume," Simon, a tiny robot whose chest plate lights up, says during math hour later that day. George snickers with him in agreement. Simon licks his thumb and wipes it across my cheek. "You're just Black like usual."

Maude, a nice girl with fun erasers, raises her hand as soon as she sees and proceeds to reach for the ceiling until Mrs. Germaine finally calls on her.

"Rubeintz is crying." She's a well-meaning little narc.

"No, I'm not," you say, sticking your head inside your school desk, a metal box with a wooden top where you keep your notebooks inside. "I'm just looking for my ruler!" It makes no sense, but it doesn't have to.

"Kevin, George, Rubeintz," Mrs. Germaine snaps from the board. "Stop playing around back there or no candy later!"

You're fourteen, and your world is French. You're walking home from school to your condo with Mom on the South Shore of Montreal and have your new iPod headphones in.

An angry, white man with a gray mustache and no hair pulls his blue sedan right next to you at the bus stop. "Hey, *le noir*!" ("Hey, blackie!") You remove your headphones, and he repeats himself. "I said, pull up your damn pants here!"

They're not loose, you bald bitch. That's the whole point! "They used to fashionably sag a little, but my ass is expanding, sir!" you wish you'd screamed back as he drives away, but you didn't. You almost recognize him. He lives around here. His neighborhood is changing and he's afraid, you tell yourself. You never scream. Dad's lessons run deep:

Fe Respow. Fait Ton Respect. Earn your respect.

Years later, famous sociologist Shamus Khan will define "respectability politics" at the board of his sociology lecture in the bowels of Knox Hall, clicking something into place.

You're fifteen, and your world is French. You get into the habit of pressing your hands into your chest whenever your stretch or yawn, trying to push the nascent man-tits back in.

"You're fat now," Alex Yi notes flatly while you're waiting to file into geography class. "All Black people are either super fit or just fat as hell. You're the fat-as-hell kind."

He's big, too; the big-and-tall kind. He'll be big all his life and thus carries it better. Your fat wobbles and weaves, expands and contracts. You adopt a new uniform under your school uniform; an undershirt a size too small, tucked in, followed by two polo shirts on top of it. You pop both collars like Chuck Bass on *Gossip Girl*. This slims down your man-tits. Scratch that: this elegantly contours your man-tits. You know a real man wouldn't care about that, but you do.

You're eighteen, and your world is English. You have to fulfill three science requirements to graduate and you're—

Fucked. Wow, you are just so fucked. The Science of Psychology exam is around the corner, and you've done too much creative writing and essay vomiting to train your brain in analytics again. You're a literary hipster now. Case in point: you have chosen to study in a bar in the middle of the afternoon because two hours ago, it was quiet. You never think ahead. More importantly, you're fucked, fuckity, fucked—

"Can I sit with you?" someone says.

"What?"

She's already sitting down across from you when you look up.

"This guy is being creepy," she repeats, looking over her shoulder. "Can I sit with you for a bit?"

You look over at the bar and a guy with a bubble vest over a plaid shirt is shaking his head at you, pretending to smirk, but clearly annoyed. His prey has made it into the force field.

"Um, yeah, of course," you say, moving your books aside to make room for her purse. You know why she picked your booth.

"Thanks." She smiles and then starts browsing her phone. She doesn't want to give you the wrong idea either. You exist as a threat of violence trying to memorize a paper on Positive Reinterpretation of Negative Emotional Images. You end that class with a C minus because science is nonsense.

You're twenty-five, and your world is English. Texan English. With a touch of *y'all*s and *Howdoyoudo*s.

You get home at 8:42 a.m. with a headache, still smelling like a stranger's Axe Chocolate. The air-conditioning in your apartment is already low, and you kick it into the tundra and give yourself an AC cold. You still can't fall asleep, and it's only after taking a shower that you realize you're wearing the wrong underwear. These are a lighter gray than your gray boxer briefs and a different brand than the bundle you buy. The sexiness of an anonymous Craigslist hookup is instantly vanquished by the fact that you sat in a cab with the aggressively skidmarked underwear of another man.

Two days later, you get an email from that Craigslist address you never expected to hear from again. It reads: "He found your underwear! You ruined my life!!!"

You're on the outside of dramatic betrayal and hurled plates. You imagine your very own version of the poster of 1975's *Mandingo*, with a cucked boyfriend in tears against a blood-orange painted backdrop with a tag that reads:

"Expect the savage. The sensual. The shocking. The sad. The powerful. The shameful . . . Now you are ready for Mandingo 2012, *starring Ben Philippe."*

You can't think of a reply so you don't send one. Maybe that's the easiest story for anyone to write in the end; collide into other people's lives and leave them slightly wrecked around the edges? You'll take it. It's a good story but you have no friends to tell it to in this entire state. You're lonely here, you realize. Maybe you've been lonely everywhere.

In training yourself to be less eager and to push people away, you've untrained yourself to doing the reverse motion. You wish you could move the furniture around, lie flat on the living room floor, and practice the motion of pulling them back in again without the danger of drowning. Somewhere along the way, you've made yourself into an outside dog of a human being. The type that should only be let in with careful supervision and the good carpet rolled up.

You're twenty-six, and your world is English. You're back in New York City at last, and Mark wants to start running together. As a lifestyle choice.

You say yes but then when the time comes to start jogging, you plop down on the couch, making yourself go limp, lazy, and barefoot in your basketball shorts. Your personal mascot is now Garfield, an aged cat who will never trim down like that asshole in the hat.

"No, dude," Mark whines, sweatband on and ready. "You promised."

"I'm a liar, Mark," you say, dragging yourself counterclockwise around the couch until he's upside down and you're the Cheshire Cat. "You'll learn that about me."

"Ben!"

"I can't afford running shoes right now, you butt," you sigh, embarrassed. You wiggle your toes near his head, hoping to gross him out of the entire endeavor.

He stares at your bare no-longer-ashy toes. "Really?"

"Really."

You're an Ivy League cautionary tale with seventy dollars in the bank account. You still have boxes in Texan storage, no money to get them back, and you'll snap your shins right there in Riverside Park if you try running with your all-season pair of Timbs. There's no grace, as it turns out, in being a starving artist. When you attempt to split a late $52 charge over three cards and two are denied, a T-Mobile operator with a loud keyboard tells you, "Never mind, hun. You've got another month. Just go for a walk, okay?"

"Okay, wait," Mark says before disappearing into his room and then yours, and coming back with a box with a swoosh and a pair of socks from the laundry basket on your bed.

He grabs your bare feet, joins them, and flips you around the couch.

"Let go of me!" you protest with the enthusiasm of a cat letting itself move around inside a sunbeam. "This is a violation of my autonomy and of—"

"Shut up," he commands with a laugh. "God, you talk so much!"

His dog watches as curious as you are as Mark plops on his coffee table and places your foot between his thighs, unrolling a sock around it with a dedicated frown.

"You want me to sweat into your new shoes?"

"My mom mailed me two pairs and we're both size tens." They're very good shoes. Flyknit with untouched white soles. You suspect he was saving these white ones for special occasions until a few moments ago.

"These are yours now."

"What? No way, dude. I'm not—"

"Look, I'll run barefoot right next to you if I have to," he says, now lacing with a smile. "I'd just rather not."

"I can do the other one myself," you say, something now in your throat.

"Shh," Mark says, still focusing on the lacing, leaving you with nothing to do but watch him. A friend is someone you're a little in love with around the edges.

"There!" He grins, moving both your feet to the ground and squeezing them once.

"I hated that," you grumble, getting to your feet.

"You just said you're a liar," he says. "Now hurry up!"

We will run three times a week for the next month until we are no longer roommates.

You're twenty-six, and someone calls you a nigger.

It wasn't a song lyric, or an accidental slip, or a broad slur to all African Americans. Nor was it a passing car. It was said to you and for you. "You nigger." The specifics aren't important. You won't give the universe the satisfaction of writing it all out. You walk home missing your mom. You'll call her, but later, not right now.

Racism is tiring in the most boring and unoriginal of ways. Sometimes, there is simply nothing to extract from it. You throw your apartment keys into the bowl and rest your head against the wall of your hallway for a second. A flamboyant man could have been called a faggot. A woman might have been called a cunt. An Asian person a chink. This world will never run out of ways of shrinking those on the margins to a pit they'll then have to carry in their own stomach.

When you look up, it's been half an hour, but you're not quite ready again. You've never been a crier. The opening ten minutes of Pixar's *Up* leaves your eyes completely dry. Don't you cry now. Your parents were both born in villages 1,500 miles away, one of your grandmothers used to strap infants to her back and hike over a mountain to get them vaccinated and bring them back; you've never had a rope around your neck—how dare you cry because of a word, lost to the wind the moment it was spoken. Not one tear, you punk. *Fe Respow.*

You're twenty-six, and your world is English. You're in Los Angeles and taking general meetings. There's a whole strand of your life that takes place over on the West Coast. It's equal servings victories and humiliations but does not belong in this book.

Your Airbnb rental is a couch in Studio City meant to in turn minimize the cost of all your car rides around the city over the next four days, taking meetings that won't lead to anything but a face sore from smiling in the end.

You hiss at an Uber driver gifting—not even selling, *gifting*—you a crystal. She's a chatty part-time doula and one of no less than three part-time doulas you will bump into during that trip. Los

Angeles is bright and prioritizes ease while everything about you screams effort and artifice. It's not a match.

Your new manager Derek waits outside the restaurant for you, in sunglasses and a polo shirt, which is the Los Feliz equivalent of a business suit. In Los Angeles, your actual business suit might as well be a *Downton Abbey* tuxedo, complete with top hat and vintage monocle.

"Are you wearing a freaking tie right now?" Derek asks in a cackle. He's accompanying you to the first few meetings.

"She's from CBS!" you try. "That's CBS sitting in there."

"Nah, dude," Derek says, putting his phone away. "They're meeting a wunderkind Haitian writer from Harlem with an Ivy degree who grew up in French projects. No ties!"

He undoubles the Windsor knot around your neck with one hand, undoing the three replays of a YouTube tutorial you had to study to perfect, and rips it away from your neck leaving a rope burn, as cheap fabric tends to.

"You're a New York Black guy, man." He laughs. "Jesus! No jacket tomorrow, okay?"

"You got it." You smile. Derek means well, keeps your nerves at bay, and signed you when he didn't have to. What good is there in saying anything?

To this day, your books still are not TV shows, and you're now too old to be a wunderkind.

You're twenty-eight, and your world is English. Harlem English, with bursts of Spanish and Russian depending on the street. You love living in Harlem and taking your dog around St. Nicholas dog run twice a day. It's peaceful and—

The finger snaps, less than a foot from your face, are what

bring you out of whatever bit of prose or dialogue you were typing in your phone's notes.

"Pay more attention," the woman casually instructs.

You remove your headphones and smile, raising your eyebrows. Mode: friendly.

"Excuse me?"

She's short, with dry blond hair that's brown at the roots, and her dog-park style might qualify as military-inspired athleisure. Kickboxing, not yoga. You wouldn't be surprised to learn that she won a middling season of *Survivor* a decade ago.

"You've been on your phone since you got here," she says. "Isn't the point to come here and play with the dogs?"

Now, your dog is both well behaved and adorable. No, really: that thing leapt right out of a Purina commercial. And this woman's problem appears to be that Blue is currently too calm, scratching at and sniffing patches of dirt nearby.

"Are you . . . explaining what a dog park is to me?"

People start glancing your way, but you've recently decided that you were done keeping your voice low not to embarrass them. It's small, so very small, but it's a start.

The benevolent dog lover points to Blue, your fifty-five-pound white lab mix, happily chewing a stick in the sun and at a distance from the other dogs. She's a loner, too. There are exactly four dogs she likes and will chase around this dog run, otherwise, only a chew stick from her favorite tree will hold her interest.

"He could choke on that."

"She is not going to choke on that," you say.

"Are you a vet?" she scoffs.

"I am, actually!" You grin. "Why? Are you a vet, too?"

She's less certain now, but unfortunately for Karen/Sharron/

Cheryll/Cheyenne/Kate/Marie, you've decided that Harlem is your neighborhood now. It was waiting for you since James Baldwin called it home a century ago. And now your neighborhood is changing and you're the angry one. Who knows, she might have actually lived here longer than your four chronological years, but twenty-four years ago, she would not have been here, and fourteen years ago she wouldn't have made eye contact with you, let alone snapped her fingers in your face.

"Do we know each other? Have we maybe run into each other at a vet conference?"

She's exasperated with pretending to humor you, and your smiling annoys her, which now makes it genuine.

It's a new combination: fake smile plus real endless pit of anger. Real because, actually, fuck you.

"I know you think this is very funny," she says, "but I'm sure this dog's owner is not paying you to be on your phone. You should play with her. She is so cute and bored."

Let the record show, whatever else you may take away from this book, that my dog was not goddamn bored. This, I promise you.

"That's my dog, lady!" You snap, you're suddenly exhausted. "Black guys own dogs, too! We don't just walk them."

How dare she? Do people like that really exist outside of viral videos? Have they strayed this far north, to Harlem, of all places?

She rolls her eyes. "That's obviously not what I was saying."

"That's exactly what you're saying."

"Look, calm down, I was just saying—" Uncertainty slips into her voice.

"No," you say calmly but firm for once in your life, now having the collected confidence of an adjunct professor when addressing a room. "You started talking to me, so explain it to me. Why would you assume I'm the dog walker?"

She seems aware that you're in public, that people are watching, and seems to regret her decision to enage. She gives you a once-over, looking for an easy one-word answer but not finding one.

"Your attire. It's an honest mistake. I did not mean—"

Attire. Screw you, lady.

"I'm wearing a hoodie and sweatpants," you interrupt. "Which is perfectly fine dog park *attire.* Your problem isn't with my clothes. It might be clothing in general? Because you're dressed for the geriatric *Hunger Games.*"

Someone chortles nearby, which is all you need. Bitch mode: activate.

"Instead of minding me, maybe use this time to bond with your dog, who clearly hates you, by the way."

"My dog does not hate me!"

"Your dog absolutely hates you. That thing darted away from you the second it was off the leash. Does it hide under the table when you want to cuddle at home, too?"

You've always had zingers. After all, you learned English from sitcoms, thinking there was an invisible audience that could be made to laugh at any point.

The people looking from a safe distance are not laughing, but entertained, though uncomfortable. The bearded guy nearby keeps throwing you glances like the mall cop he was born to be. The threatening "Is everything okay there?" is ready on his lips. You've somehow never been in a fight. Not a real one. This guy, you'll fight. You'll use your teeth if you have to and strictly target his nuts.

You realize you're still ranting and whatever you're saying must be stinging. Something about the levels of sadness of her life. You didn't write it down. Maybe Mark had a point; maybe you do talk too much. But part of you wants to see if you could make her cry.

"You shouldn't talk to people that way!" she sputters, embarrassed and bright red, pretending to pay attention to her dog and not the conversation she started. They change colors so easily, don't they?

I should, actually. More often, I should talk to people exactly like this.

"And I shouldn't be able to pick up your body odor inside a dog park but here we are."

"That is so rude! This is a friendly park! Your dog seemed bored! I was trying to help and you're getting very agitated." It's an attempt to flip the narrative, to turn me into the unstable Black guy making everything about race. She's playing to the audience, too. *Racist* is the last thing I want to call her; I haven't even commented on her hair or noticeably yellow teeth yet.

You transition the building aneurysm into an exhale. You're a polite Canadian but also half social butterfly like your mom and half child whipper like your dad. It's a volatile combo. What would Belzie do? What would Robert do? What do you want to do right now in front of a perfectly nice audience of casual park nodders and chitchatters who until now probably considered you one of the polite good ones?

"Go fist yourself, lady," you enunciate clearly, standing up and no longer smiling. If they won't see you as a person, why should you? Leave the infinite patience and grace to Michelle Obama; I was always more of a Muhammad Ali guy: when they go low, you duck and counter with an uppercut.

"I'm not your friend. I'm the Black guy you thought was walking someone else's dog. Put on some deodorant."

You whistle, and Blue startles from her stick to follow you toward the exit. She's a very good dog like that, provided there are no distractions around. One squirrel, and your dramatic exit would have been vanquished.

It's the first time you've cursed out an adult, someone who was already an adult when you were a child in Haiti, and it feels good.

You return to the park every weekday evening at the exact time and claim your space, even when it's inconvenient to your schedule. One day, you see her walking toward the park. She makes eye contact with you and then turns around with her two mutts, chin high. A weird part of you wants to hop on a bench and start howling in victory.

After that, you stop paying attention to her entirely. You don't know if you're a dog park bully or a dog park hero, and in truth, you don't care. You simply wish life didn't involve making so many first impressions without realizing it. What it must be like to be a blank slate to the world, a racial blank slate that can wear a hoodie and walk his dog without enduring petty microaggressions from iron-haired dog park Karens that never heard of Emmett Till.

You're twenty-eight, and then twenty-nine, and then thirty, and your world is English. You're a bona fide New Yorker now. It's Mother's Day. Three Mother's Days in a row, in fact.

You've sent Belzie a bouquet of gigantic flowers, or a box of gigantic chocolates, or both, and later, you'll video chat together. You always remember all the important dates and holidays. You're a good son that way even though you're not as close as you once were. Maybe it's because you're an adult now and that's how it's supposed to be.

The first time it happens you're appropriately on social media. Of course you were: cataloging and ranking one another's memories and lives was a system designed to trigger panic attacks. The dry heaving is built into its code.

You find a nice photo of her, from the Sherbrooke era. You're a cute kid posing right next to her without a scar to show. You write a nice caption that doesn't take itself too seriously. It will get a lot of likes and you'll move on with your day, but only one of those things happens.

Because all you can think about is the fact that one day she won't be there. There will be black shoes and folding chairs at a reception. You see it so clearly that you already want to throw up. She'll die and you'll be all alone, across three countries all at once.

You start to tear up, and then cry, and then wail quietly to catch your breath until it hurts your chest. No glass of water or open window helps. You're so alone that it hurts. Sit with it in the bathroom and lock the door, even though you live alone, crying into your dog until she no longer knows what to do and starts to whimper, too.

Every year you want to call her, more than anything, but you know you can't call. She'll get sad that you're sad. No, she'll be devastated that you're sad. She'll think she wasn't a good mom. She won't understand that what this overwhelming sadness means is actually that you owe her everything and that everything good about you comes from her. *Please don't think I was trying to leave you behind, too. I promise I wasn't. It just maybe happened. Please, God, don't die. Please never die, Mom. There's no one else. I'll be too alone.*

A few hours later, you will wake up, groggy, with a barking

dog and ceramic tile imprinted on your cheek. Three years in a row, the bathroom floor is always where it stops. You hate Mother's Day. It only makes you think of pain ahead.

You're thirty years old, and your world is English. You've settled in at 165 pounds and go on dates wearing nice jackets and expensive jeans, perfecting the art of dressing like a Black man who gets called "sir" at restaurants.

You're a published author, which makes you both accomplished and interesting when advertised in a format that requires swiping. You try to meet people right away if only to pretend at growth.

Nicole is a Black law student from Washington, DC, who does not see what the big fuss about hiking is, which puts her above 90 percent of the population. You're not spiritual and, thank God, neither is she. Rather, she's blunt, straightforward, and has the confidence of someone who has seen a lot of bullshit but tries not to let it sour her.

You meet her after work at a dimly lit bar with expensive cocktails in a hotel lobby where she has perfect posture and her freshly ironed hair catches the light when she takes a sip of wine. You might call her bougie in the same way you'd call me an Oreo.

The conversation is fun but challenging, which you like. It's your third date together, but there won't be a fourth.

"So, you don't want kids?" she asks, twirling her glass with two fingers, watching me. "Never?"

It's something I had mentioned on our last date and that I suspected would come back up again. It usually does.

"Never," I repeat, without any bite. "I take it you do?"

"At least two." She nods. I get the logic. Only children grow up lonely and crooked.

"And you're sure?" she asks again at the end of the night, as I walk her to the Chambers Street station. I nod. I'm as sure as she is. I suspect we both made our decision at an early age, and neither of us is looking to be convinced. Leaving a legacy is profoundly overrated.

"Fair enough." She smiles, and we kiss one last time. "I'll look for your next book, even if I don't read it. Supporting Black authors and all that."

I laugh and take a car home. It's a little sad to never see her again, but we're busy grownups and maybe both a little jaded these days. Who isn't?

LEXICON TO A BLACK EXPERIENCE NARRATIVE

Affirmative Action:
Education, employment, and housing policies that support members of disadvantaged groups that have suffered past systemic discrimination. Also, a filter through which every Black person's accomplishment can be lessened and dismissed as a participation ribbon.

Afro-Punk:
The participation of Black people in punk music and other alternative and predominantly white subcultures. Or, the feeling you might get wearing a trilby hat and black nail polish on two nails at a Montreal Vans Warped Tour concert in 2008. See your Dead Kennedys, your Wesley Willis Fiasco, your Suffrajett. (Regular early '00s punk is also very good but—and I cannot stress this enough—extremely white.)

African American Vernacular English (AAVE):
AKA Black vernacular, AKA Ebonics. (Don't call it Ebonics.) A vernacular primarily associated with middle- and lower-class Black people, at the casual end of the sociolinguistic continuum and at the front end of a lot of online communities.

Basically, all those terms you Google after stumbling across them on Twitter. See also: *bae, basic, ratchet, lit, shade*, and all those podcast names taken from Black culture by two white roommates in Williamsburg, Brooklyn, for the name of their podcast.

An "Am I Racist?" Moment:

A moment of self-reflection in which a Person of Non-Color catches themselves expressing a racist thought, feeling, or, in some cases, shouting some slurs. See Michael Richards, circa 2006. Level-10 Racists don't tend to experience this syndrome because their racism simply isn't jarring to them. To them, calling a Black person the N-word is the same as referring to a mug as a cup: a distinction without a difference. These are much messier moments, baked in at the intersection of you being a generally good person while also being aware that we exist in a world in which race can be weaponized and sometimes involuntarily flexing your grasp on that weapon.

Ashy:

Ashiness occurs when Black skin goes unlotioned. At a glance, it might look like you've stepped in a pile of ashes. Now, it's no dryer than white skin—it's just more visually striking. Moisturize and it goes away. Socially, however, it is more than a temporary condition; it denotes a lack of self-awareness and self-love, frankly. People will be rude about it.

Example:

"Why are you wearing flip-flops, Ben?"

"Morgan, the movie literally starts in twenty minutes!"

"We're not going anywhere until you go back up to your room and either put on some shoes or moisturize those ashy-ass toes."

Beyoncé:

The alleged Queen Mother. I'd personally say (oh boy . . . safe space, Ben, safe space) that I like Beyoncé a solid 8/10. It's an unsafe state of existence in a world where nothing short of 10/10 is acceptable for many. Confession: I've opted out of seeing her in concert. Twice. Once for work and another time simply because I was terrified that I would find her underwhelming in person and be unable to hide this "eh" reaction from my friends. Like, then what? That's the last shot of a *Twilight Zone* episode I do not want to live in.

Black people are mostly cool about it. They sum it up to my lifestyle of bad taste. Like so many things in life, it's young white women you have to look out for. They love Beyoncé. They'll dig their nails into your arm while telling you how much they love Beyoncé. Your cries of anguish will go unanswered as they start to sing the lyrics to "Single Ladies." If they could, they would storm Beyoncé's castle, hold her by the throat, and inhale her essence, leaving her a skeleton. This would not altogether satisfy them, mind you. Their glare would turn to Lizzo next.

Black Illuminati:

The internet gets bored and comes up with nonsense. There's nothing to this. Don't worry about it. Where would we even get the resources to meet every three months at 405 specific locations around this country? You sound unhinged right now . . . Are you okay? I worry, as your Black friend.

Black Twitter:

That secret club I'm not a part of even though I'm verified on Twitter. Whatever. Lame. I don't even care. Nor would I even have the time to be let into the inner sanctum of that secret garden of dank memes and content curated by self-actualized twenty-four-year-olds with impeccable joke delivery. "Hi, I'm Jaboukie Young-White! I'm woke, dashing, and have been on *The Daily Show* since early pubescence!" Stupid Millennials and their phones.

Black Women's Hair:

See also: *edges*. See also: *braids*. Black women's hair takes effort, some measure of science, and sometimes just plain old buckets of money. Admire, but keep your hands to yourself. I bear no responsibility if you're caught reaching for a feel of the texture of the Black woman in line ahead of us. I'll take a step back and pretend to be a stranger texting while you're eviscerated. (Kidding: I'll obviously be filming the whole thing.)

"Is this your boy?" she might ask me while your eyes plead with me for assistance.

"I don't know this fool!" will be the only reply.

Bootstraps:

A hollow life philosophy that your white dad gave you the summer he made you get a paper route and that you might have internalized into thinking that you've earned every good thing that's happened to you while the people who do not have those things have simply chosen not to work as hard as you. What a steaming pile of poop, that one. To quote Martin Luther King Jr.: "It's a cruel jest to say to a bootless man that he ought to lift himself by his own bootstraps." Everything you've earned or built was the result of gifts from the world and opportunities to thrive that others are systemically denied. (This is not an indictment of your character; I'm sure you still wake up super early.) And while we're at it: there is no such thing as a self-made billionaire. The numbers simply do not add up.

Bougie:

Short for *bourgeoisie*. Elements of Blackness perceived as upscale from a blue-collar point of view. It can be an insult for someone putting on airs or a simple descriptor. Or even a bit of both . . . For example, I'm currently taking sips from a very bougie bottle of imported beer while writing. Bougie sips. Yummies.

Caucasity:

An effortless second-nature audacity restricted to white people.

Ever been in line behind a white person berating a minimum-wage minority employee? Has the aggrieved customer ever then turned to you and scoffed in an *I mean, really!* way meant to signal that you're both on the same team against this minimum-wage employee's incompetence? That, my friend, is a caucacious look. Little Smithie gets arrested drunk outside his gated community, goes, *"Oink, oink!"* in the back of the cop car the whole way, and is still safely dropped at his parents' doorstep? The absolute caucasity of that boy.

Colorism:

The discrimination and self-hate that occur around the wildly erroneous notion that the lighter the skin tone of a Black person, the better they are in one way or another. Lighter-skinned Black people are often openly or subconsciously believed to be smarter, more educated, and more beautiful than darker-skinned Black people. It comes down to the idea that not only has your Blackness been diluted but that your whiteness has been increased. It's incredibly screwed up and somewhat normalized across all cultures. See all the languages of all the whitening and skin bleaching lotions and serums across the various beauty stores in a place like New York City.

Women suffer disproportionately from it, as they tend to do in all appearance-related matters in the world. (As they tend to do in all matters in the world.) Imagine looking in the mirror and considering yourself ugly because your Black skin is too Black? What barriers can you place around that thought to keep it from spreading? Especially when the content pouring into your phone seems to say that you're not wrong.

Nicole: "Boo-hoo, Ben! Do you know how messed up it is to swipe right on a Black man and for your thought to be *Oooh, I hope he likes Black women*?"

Field Dreams:

I dream a lot about being a slave these days. It's very off-putting; like a weird set dressing over otherwise perfectly mundane, borderline-clichéd dreams.

I will find myself at the dentist's or back in high school, in an exam I did not study for—only the dentist will be dressed like the massa of the house, the classroom is a small wooden shack surrounded by scarred slaves in rough linen passing notes or cheating off one another in an exam. The contents of the dreams themselves never quite acknowledge this horrific setting. My dentist will ask if I saw Trump's latest tweetstorm and what an idiot that guy is, although Biden is also out of touch with the cultural moment. He'll transition into asking me for a recommendation letter for his daughter. The only other thing I can remember once I wake up is his whip that was leaning against the door behind him the whole time. (Thanks for that one, America.)

Fleek:

That thing you should stop saying. Like, now.

The Habitual *Be*:

Yeah, son: we're getting grammatical up in here! The habitual *be* refers to the use of *be* in conjunction with a present-tense verb or adjective, often within the African American Vernacular English. This is done to indicate a perpetual (or habitual) action or state.

See, it's a common misconception that AAVE speakers simply replace "is" with "be" across all tenses, with no added complexity. That is patently false. To be reading means to habitually read, not presently. Right now you're reading. When your friends go out without you and wonder what you do with your evening, they might suppose you always be reading. In that context, *be* becomes synonymous with "is always" or "am always."

The takeaway for you here is that, AAVE? Yeah, it's a real language. With its own grammatical rules. It's not slang or a lack of education. Black kids who speak it fluently are absolutely bilingual. How do I know this? Because I am a Black person who doesn't speak it. It's the awkward language I borrow and step around in. I'm grateful to understand it and envious of kids who rattle it off seamlessly. You don't have to teach it in your classroom (although, you totally could) but put some respect on it.

Example:

I be about dat ass.

Too crude? Okay, better example:

I be about white friends who can acknowledge systemic racism without shifting the emotional focus onto themselves with performative displays of guilt. But also occasionally that ass, though.

The Hard-"R" Clause:

You can't say it. You just can't. Well, that's not entirely true. You can say whatever you want. I, in return, have the right to boil your entire existence into you speaking these syllables near me and write off the whole thing. I'm vastly indifferent to your feelings or logic on when and how you ought to be allowed to use it. It's not unfair and it's not policing your language; it's awareness. Not using it shows you have the slightest awareness of the world we live in. It's a word, a single word, versus the entire history of the world stolen, pilfered, and remade into your image. You've made it this far into this book. We're friends. It shouldn't be that hard for you.

Hotep:

Oh, jeez. These clowns. What can I say? Men can be assholes across races. Hotep ideology (in the YouTube channels and Reddit sense of the word) is rooted in performative pro-Blackness that aims for nothing but to replace WHITE male patriarchy with

BLACK male patriarchy with a dash of Afrocentricism thrown into the mix.

There is no intersectionality to Hoteps. It does not account for nor does it champion Black women or Black queerness. It's just a font change on familiar nonsense. Not everything deserves a thumbs-up just because you slap a thin layer of pro-Black rhetoric onto it. Sexism, homophobia, transphobia . . . all that garbage is still garbage if you make it Black.

Misogynist creeps, but make it Black. A Hotep has more in common with the creepy bearded white guy running an Alabama commune of sheltered wives who are not allowed to go outside than they do with African revolutionaries.

They are also . . . really corny niggas. That guy calling Black women "brown-skinned Nubian goddesses" while demanding they worship him and pay his bills and cook his food and breed his Black children to replenish the soil of Blackness while also wanting Black women to recruit white concubines for him as nothing less than an active harem will quench the . . . You get it? Pass me with your copy of the Willie Lynch letter, nerds. (Their parking lot pamphlet.)

Your IBAS (Idealized Black Advocate Self):

The flawless, perfect, wokest Black self-advocate. That mythical Black person who takes just the right amount of a stance in every instance. They never over- or underreact. They know when to take out their phone and record, when to comply, when to pop off, when to thoughtfully explain something over coffee, when to storm off. Toni Morrison is always proud watching this person . . . They are in charge of their own emotions and navigate the world bettering race discourse in America at every turn. And if this person exists, I don't know them.

Karen:

The catchall for young-to-middle-aged women who demand to see the manager. Their discomfort or reticence in any situation means that the situation should not be happening—someone must be made aware of this. It's more than regular old caucasity. Broke people can be caucacious. No: Karens are the walking avatars of Yelp reviews that start with "I used to love this establishment but no longer." Their plight of receiving their salad with the dressing mixed in instead of being on the side—which they forgot to mention but that the waiter should have divined—is a story that simply must be told.

Karens have increasingly gotten more racist in popular culture. First, there were viral clips of them approaching Black families in parks, demanding to know if they had a license to be barbecuing, or listening to music. This lone finger on the chin then moved to little girls selling water bottles outside their buildings without a permit. They then began to notice Black people coming home from work and walking into their buildings. "Do you live here? You don't look like you live here. I know everyone who lives here."

Karen no longer petitions the entire street and knocks at your door at 7 a.m. on a Sunday to inform you that "Everyone wants you to trim your hedges." No: now Karens hiss at you for daring to tell them that their dog should be leashed. They have their phones in hand, have affected a white tremble to their overwhelmed voices, and have Death in their eyes, telling you that they are calling 911 and telling them that "there's an African American man threatening my life."

By the year 2020, Karens are no longer simply busybodies but outright racists. Naturally, Karens will not have this. (They were so chill about everything else.) They refer to the slur of their own first name as "the K-word." They are persecuted and depressed. Hatred is so ugly when you're not wielding it yourself.

If you're a good person named Karen, just realize we're not talking about you. I know a couple of Karens who can hang. They wear "This Karen Supports Black Trans Lives" T-shirts at marches and get high fives for it. If you can't realize that this isn't actually about you, even though it might share your name, I am sorry to inform you that you just might be a Karen.

"Mandingo":

The goulash of media narratives, pornography, slavery-era propaganda that amounts to a singular image of Black men as overpowering and hypersexual creatures and a fetish/kink/deviancy rather than people. Beyond how problematic it is, being your thug fantasy is, incidentally, also a lot of freaking pressure. (Not tonight, babe, I have a headache.) Sexual stereotyping—Asian women are submissive, Black men are dominant, etc.—and fetishization both reduce people to the most racialized aspects of their beings that you find attractive. It is way less flattering than you may think to be slotted into those cheesy roles.

Niggacity:

A type of Black audacity restricted to a Black twenty-one-year-old college student with a Yu-Gi-Oh T-shirt who absolutely thinks he'll be right at home at an open-mic roast battle at a Bronx comedy show. This was my first and last attempt at New York City standup. There are skinny Asian guys in baggy FedEx polos and shy smiles out there who will drag every cell in your body to absolute hell once handed a mic. I was a niggacious little thing thinking I could go toe-to-toe with them and not get burnt. (I told you this was a tell-some, not tell-all.)

Ofay:

A would-be derogatory term for white people. This one is more of a factoid than anything. I don't see a white family being driven out of a new home by having *ofay* burnt onto their lawn, y'know? There's a history behind it, sure, but it's not the white N-word. The same way "cracker" isn't a slur that comes anywhere close to nigger. It's not the C-word, now, is it? (Also, it's been suggested that white slave foremen were called "crackers" for their practice of cracking the little whip to drive slaves and cattle. I'm not feeling the dehumanization in that one.)

Oreo:

It me, according to many and for a long time.

According to Urban Dictionary: When a young Black man doesn't like to associate with other Black people and would never go out with a Black girl. He behaves like a white person, has white friends, always dates white women. For all intents and purposes is "Black on the outside, but white on the inside."

Example:

"Holden isn't going to go out with you. That bougie punk would never date a Black girl."

"Is he an Oreo?"

"Get your glass of milk, honey."

Race Card:

The rumored ability to benefit from your race by simply bringing up your race. This mythical card is misused by both Black and white people; for matters as small as my aunt noticing our bread basket isn't as full as the next Olive Garden's table, and as overwhelming as gerrymandering across Black districts. On an everyday basis, the fear of being accused of using "the race card" is as dreadful as being in a situation where your race is being used against you. It is useless to internalize this. As a writer, I can promise that it is the same as any old impostor syndrome.

Rachel Dolezal:

I don't know her, but she loves my hair. Google the name if you're one of the three people blessed not to know it by now. Honestly, the closest definition I can come to here is a deep forty-three-second sigh of exhaustion from the bottom of my very soul. (Just, please don't call her "sis.")

Sexual Racism:

Sexual racism is racism. A restaurant that proudly displays NO BLACKS ALLOWED is unacceptable in today's day and age. Even if you privately agree with the sentiment, you would pause seeing it so brazenly displayed. So, why accept it under the generic and interchangable hiking photos of dating apps?

It's not just a preference. Vanilla or chocolate is a preference. Aisle seat or window seat is a preference. Deciding—and then decreeing—that you are not sexually aroused by an entire ethnic group is a choice. Unlike preferences around gender, racial "preferences" in dating are usually the result of societal conditioning. Nothing innate or biological here. You did not sit down and read a book to learn it, but it was cultivated over time. Now, I am not telling you to unlearn it. (I mean, you probably should; I'm simply acknowledging my inability to carve that journey for you.) What I hope you will do is stop weaponizing it on these platforms that find most people at their most vulnerable. Taking the time and malice to write "No Blacks, no Asians; Whites Only" or anything of the kind under a photo of yourself at Macchu Picchu? (*Oh my god, fun!*) That's an ugly choice and an action you can very easily control.

ToDoG; or TODOG:

Noun. A "Tim or Dan or Grant." Your generic white guy of 8-or-above attractiveness. I sincerely believe that being a TODOG is the equivalent of wearing Thanos's glove with all the Infinity Stones but in the wrong order. All you need to do is figure out that blue goes before purple to unlock the powers of the universe.

Tried'it:

A person attempting to do something—or perhaps to get away with something—and failing. That person effectively tried'it. This one is pretty straightforward. For instance, remember when Sony Pictures decided to reboot *Spider-Man* by casting twenty-nine-year-old British man Andrew Garfield as angsty American teen Peter Parker? And then doubled down on a sequel? Oooh, they tried'it. God bless 'em, they tried'it. Thank God, Marvel webbed Tom Holland right into our freaking hearts, amirite?

Uppity:

Taking liberties or assuming airs beyond one's place in a social hierarchy. Assuming equality with someone higher up the social ladder.

Mr. Smith does not allow his subordinates to address him by his first name; it shows uppityness, and he will put you in your place with a good tongue-lashing.

Wakanda:

The corner of the Marvel Cinematic Universe where all the fashion designers live while the rest of the superheroes of this world are left to only wear hoodies at leisure when not in costume as punishment for their sins.

Yes, we know it's not real; we just acknowledge that it's great to see people who look like us celebrate a heightened, highly fashionable culture on-screen after so many decades in the bowels of Steven Spielberg's *Amistad*.

Weed:

Cannabis. Marijuana. That thing that no, I don't currently have on me at all times for your recreational usage . . . We're in the middle of a lecture on an Ivy League college campus, for Pete's sake! No, I don't have a loose spliff to sell.

"Well-spoken":

See also: *articulate*. Depending on the school, Black kids are mocked both for speaking poorly and for speaking well. As far as I can tell, we're supposed to speak "poorly" (which isn't poorly at all; see AAVE), but strictly within our own neighborhood, away from the well-spoken white kids and dutiful minorities who are allowed to thrive. It is not a compliment to be looked at as an exception to everyone who looks like you.

Delighted schoolteachers exclaiming, "You're so well-spoken! You must be foreign!" was never a keen worldly eye into my Haitian features. It was a dismissal of all the Black people you had met before me and whose voices and tones had displeased you. Nothing more. The equivalent would be my taking a stroll through your family albums and calling you a stunning beauty, compared to your crooked, droopy-eyed family of milk cartons.

White Nonsense:

According to Urban Dictionary: when white people do something clearly stupid without expecting any negative consequences.

Example:

"They built a replica of the Titanic! *Let's go on its maiden voyage!"*

"What kind of white nonsense is that?"

Actually, thank you, Carly Targaryen (September 20, 2016)

for the quotes above: that sums it up perfectly. When the world is made of padded, cushiony walls, throwing yourself against them can be kind of fun. We get the bricks.

Woke (The A Side):

This one is a bit harder by 2020 standards, as there is no unifying theory of Woke yet. There are, as far as I can see, two ongoing definitions, both used with equal fervor across the land.

According to Urban Dictionary: a word currently used to describe consciousness and being aware of the truth behind things "The Man" doesn't want you to know. (I.e., classism, racism, and any other social injustices.)

Example:

"Stay woke, nigga! Stay woke!"

Woke (The B Side):

Also according to Urban Dictionary: the act of being very pretentious about how much you care about a social issue. Yeah, most people don't care about parking spaces for families with disabled pets. "I wish they were woke like me. #Woke #SocialJusticeWarrior #hipster #progressive"

The distinction between Woke A and Woke B is that Woke B is often used to trivialize Woke A in an attempt to diminish its message and core truths. It's nothing new. ("The Queer movement" vs "Look at that queer over there!") and again highlights the power of words and ownership in these conversations.

The XYZ Of It All:

There's so much more I want to say to you but, um, yeah, I have to go now. I think it's time.

How do you end a book on Blackness as nothing more than one of 43,984,096 people (give or take a few thousands) currently living in a country you were not born in but still call home? How do you account for a full 13.4 percent of a population, having only lived the one uneven life?

Hell, how do you even end a book on the full scope of your Blackness at age thirty-one when you hope to at least make it to sixty-two . . . and will presumably still be Black then, too? (Although, who knows where this dystopia is headed: we might all be purple by 2034.)

What conclusion could I possibly rev up to? I'm not being cute here: I don't have an answer to any of these questions. (Cornel West! Be a brother and elegantly end this for me, will you?) Honestly, the most natural thing to do at this point is probably wet myself under the scrutiny and run off the stage crying for my mom.

If reflection must be had, I think I'm a slightly different person ending this book than I was when I started it . . . That's an arc, right? Close enough to personal growth. I wish I was a better son, a better person. Faster metabolism. Less petty, less mouthy, less angry, less lonely. A hundred beers/walks/subway rides later, what is your verdict? Was it whipped cream over a steel door or a steel door hiding fluff? You might have a better metaphor altogether.

As for you, friend, I wish you so many good things; I really do. I hope you're a nice person. I hope you'll be safe out there and that you'll pay it forward. Whatever your race, I hope you're not too lonely, too. There's no comfort in knowing others are alone out there; it doesn't fill your silence.

How do you befriend someone after monologuing your life at them for 81,000 words? Should we dance it out to a Tegan and Sara song like Meredith Grey and Christina Yang did when the latter left the show? (Yes, I still watch *Grey's Anatomy;* shut up. It's going to be me and you watching the world burn from a cliff at the end, Shonda Rhimes.)

Maybe I'm that bad friend who invites you to brunch, apologizes profusely for being twenty minutes late, speaks only about myself for three hours without asking you a single question about your life, takes a selfie leaning into you and throwing fingers up at the camera while you're left to sign the credit-card receipt. I'll give you a quick back pat, locking you in on a promise of doing it again soon before dashing off because I didn't walk my dog before meeting you and I have to go, like, now. It's a lie but, hey, every friendship carries a few, no? I've lied to you a total of four times in this book.

You know way too much about me for me to simply be your wacky Black friend moving forward. Sorry about that. Although, who knows, it might have been my plan all along. You still haven't walked a mile in my shoes, which were still pretty comfortable shoes given all the privilege I've been doused with my entire life.

It's not always easy being your friend either. In the grand scheme of things, I much prefer if you dislike me for being Ben than if you like me simply for being Black. Thanks for covering the bill, by the way. The next one is on me, swearsies!

Cheers,

Ben

ACKNOWLEDGMENTS

Honestly, all my books (fuck yeah, plural!) are acknowledgments to my mother. I owe everything soft and open about me to her, and these things are requirements to being a writer as far as I'm concerned . . . So, hi, Mom! All right, that's enough of that.

I will also use this space to shout out two other names: Amber Oliver and Sarah Ried, my editors. While I bear a striking, truly uncanny resemblance to both Michael B. Jordan and peak Denzel, I never thought I would be given free rein to just vomit my unremarkable life and thoughts into a book. But, against many odds, Amber saw something in my proposal. And when the Black Lives Matter moment of 2020 happened, she allowed—urged—me to lean into the angry soup of feelings I was navigating through.

And when Sarah came on board, she also highlighted the glaring omissions, the tangents that were too tangential, and the work I hadn't done, back when I thought that witticisms would be enough and that I could write a book like this while staying comfortable. That notion fell by the wayside very quickly, and looking back, I can only thank Amber and Sarah for that. This would not be a book without you. You were kind, incisive, and so very patient, and for that, you have my eternal gratitude.

Thanks, Amber and Sarah!

NOTES

Chapter Nineteen: Sure, I'll Be Your Black Guy—Emphasis on *Guy*

1. Valeri Wilson, Janelle Jones, Kayla Blado, and Elise Gould, "Black Women Have to Work 7 Months into 2017 to Be Paid the Same as White Men in 2016," Economic Policy Institute (blog), July 28, 2017, accessed October 2020, epi.org/blog /black-women-have-to-work-7-months-into-2017-to-be-paid -the-same-as-white-men-in-2016/.

2. Ariane Hegewisch. "The Gender Wage Gap: 2017; Earnings Differences by Gender, Race, and Ethnicity," Institute for Women's Policy Research, September 13, 2018, accessed October 2020, iwpr.org/iwpr-issues/employment-and-earnings /the-gender-wage-gap-2017-earnings-differences-by-gender -race-and-ethnicity/.

Chapter Twenty: How to Go Through Life Without Drowning, Part III

1. Jeff Wiltse, "Why So Many Black People in the U.S. Can't Swim," AJ+ (Al Jazeera Media Network), August 13, 2019, accessed October 2020, youtube.com/watch?v=zjC2Ucpr__E.

Chapter Twenty-Six: Sure, I'll be Your 2016 Shithole Rescapee

1. Michael D. Shear and Julie Hirschfeld Davis, "Stoking Fears, Trump Defied Bureaucracy to Advance Immigration Agenda," *New York Times*, December 23, 2017, accessed October 2020, nytimes.com/2017/12/23/us/politics/trump-immigration.html.

ABOUT THE AUTHOR

Ben Philippe is a New York–based writer and screenwriter, born in Haiti and raised in Montreal, Canada. He has a bachelor of arts from Columbia University and an MFA in fiction and screenwriting from the Michener Center for Writers. He is the author of the young adult novels *Charming as a Verb* and the William C. Morris Award–winning *The Field Guide to the North American Teenager*.

His membership into the Black Illuminati was turned down by a vote of 443 to 1, but he is grateful to Whoopi for the vote of confidence.

Find him online at www.benphilippe.com.

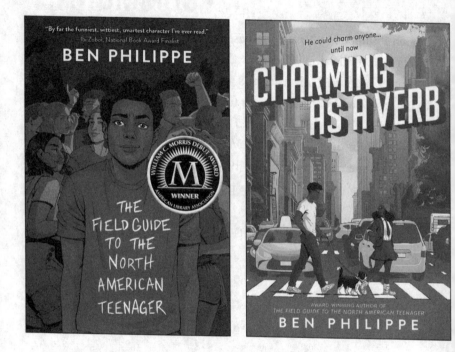

JOIN THE

Epic Reads
COMMUNITY

THE ULTIMATE YA DESTINATION

◀ **DISCOVER** ▶
your next favorite read

◀ **MEET** ▶
new authors to love

◀ **WIN** ▶
free books

◀ **SHARE** ▶
infographics, playlists, quizzes, and more

◀ **WATCH** ▶
the latest videos

www.epicreads.com